THE DESIGNS OF
WILLIAM E. POOLE

100 CLASSIC HOUSE PLANS

HOME PLANNERS

Published by Home Planners, LLC
Wholly owned by Hanley-Wood, LLC
3275 West Ina Road, Suite 220
Tucson, Arizona 85741

Distribution Center:
29333 Lorie Lane
Wixom, Michigan 48393

Jayne Fenton, President
Linda B. Bellamy, Executive Editor
Arlen Feldwick-Jones, Editorial Director
Vicki Frank, Managing Editor
Laura Brown, Associate Editor
Nick Nieskes, Plans Associate
Matthew S. Kauffman, Graphic Designer
Sara Lisa, Senior Production Manager
Brenda McClary, Production Manager

Front cover:
Plan HPT770004 page 14
Photograph courtesy of William E. Poole

Back cover:
Plan HPT770006 page 20
Photographs by Maura McEvoy

Title page:
Plan HPT770075 page 166
Photograph by Kenneth S. Collier, courtesy of
    Chadsworth's Columns

This page:
Plan HPT770075 page 166
Photograph courtesy of Hickory Chair Furiture

Book design by Matthew S. Kauffman

First printing, February 2003

10 9 8 7 6 5 4 3 2 1

Printed in the United States of America.

ISBN 1-931131-11-2 Softcover

Library of Congress Control Number:
2002112991

Contents

Welcome

Home is a reflection of who we are and all we love—the American Dream—a place for family, friends, laughter and tears. A mix of cultures past and cultures present speak a clearly American dialect—bold and simple, urbane and chic but relaxed enough for bare feet. This collection of my 100 best-selling designs blends the polish and formality of classic styles, the charm of authentic details and the convenience of twenty-first century technology. Here are plans with flexible spaces and lots of natural light, intimate facades and artful details, *tomorrow* designs that answer the call for beautiful homes everywhere today. Of course, a great place is about us—our individual character, our space and our connections. Personal attention to detail, composition and flow means the difference between being at home and *feeling* at home.

The William E. Poole collections of fine furniture and casual living will inspire you to create finished rooms and outdoor living spaces that are deeply satisfying. In fact, my signature line of licensed building products—from classical columns to gilded mirrors—raises the standard of excellence for completing a home.

Today's homes, with the timeless grace of yesterday, must keep in step with the familiar as well as move forward into the future. Evocative exteriors are asked to do much more, unquestionably, than draw you through the front door—they must introduce flowing, open and comfortable interiors that satisfy all the desires and needs of everyday life. This is what I do: design homes that capture the warmth and innocence of friendly, tree-lined streets, yet strike a fresh balance between the old and the new—classical homes that reflect an historic influence, yet link yesterday with today and on toward tomorrow.

Come home with William E. Poole...you'll be glad you did.

To view plans, see page 22.

DESIGN HPT770001

Photos by Islands of Beaufort, Beaufort South

Chesapeak Bay

Ahh...the "Chesapeake Bay." What memories...this private old home on Maryland's Eastern Shore, with gracious lawns spreading beyond the porches all the way to the water's edge, is the perfect place for gatherings, garden parties, weddings, afternoon teas, croquet, cookouts and the most tantalizing treat of all—local crabs boiled in spices and served up in buckets as (mallets in hand) one anticipates the noisy, tasty and fun-filled evening with friends and family.

This home, as shown in the photographs, may differ from the actual blueprints.
For more detailed information, please check the floor plans carefully.

Chesapeak Bay

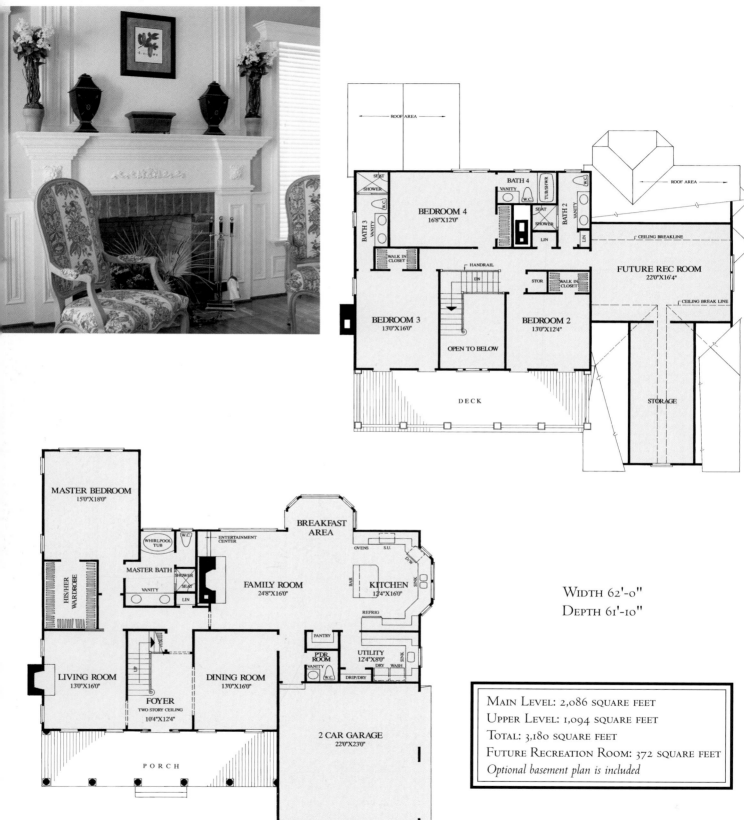

ROOF AREA

BEDROOM 4
16'8"X12'0"

BATH 4
VANITY
SEAT
TUB/SHWR
W.C.
SHOWER

BATH 2
VANITY
W.C.
LIN

SEAT
SHOWER
W.C.
BATH 3
VANITY

ROOF AREA

CEILING BREAKLINE

FUTURE REC ROOM
22'0"X16'4"

CEILING BREAK LINE

WALK IN
CLOSET

HANDRAIL

LIN

STOR

WALK IN
CLOSET

BEDROOM 3
13'0"X16'0"

OPEN TO BELOW

BEDROOM 2
13'0"X12'4"

STORAGE

DECK

MASTER BEDROOM
15'0"X18'0"

BREAKFAST
AREA

WHIRLPOOL
TUB
W.C.

ENTERTAINMENT
CENTER

OVENS   S.U.

D.W.

HIS/HER
WARDROBE

MASTER BATH

VANITY

SHOWER
SEAT
LIN

FAMILY ROOM
24'8"X16'0"

BAR

KITCHEN
12'4"X16'0"

SINK

REFRIG

LIVING ROOM
13'0"X16'0"

FOYER
TWO STORY CEILING
10'4"X12'4"

UP

DINING ROOM
13'0"X16'0"

PANTRY

P'DR.
ROOM

VANITY
W.C.

UTILITY
12'4"X8'0"

DRY   WASH

DRIP/DRY   SINK

2 CAR GARAGE
22'0"X23'0"

PORCH

WIDTH 62'-0"
DEPTH 61'-10"

MAIN LEVEL: 2,086 SQUARE FEET
UPPER LEVEL: 1,094 SQUARE FEET
TOTAL: 3,180 SQUARE FEET
FUTURE RECREATION ROOM: 372 SQUARE FEET
Optional basement plan is included

DESIGN HPT770002

The Beaufort II

In North Carolina there is a little seafaring town filled with the charm and antiquity of the 18th Century. One of the old homes of West Indies influence, The Beaufort II has been lovingly restored by a noted writer of fiction. Considered by some to be a mystery himself, he wanders about at night in the mists and delights in the eerie noises of ships echoing throughout the harbour. From these solitary musings comes the stuff that books are made of. We are left to wonder, what next...?

The Beaufort II

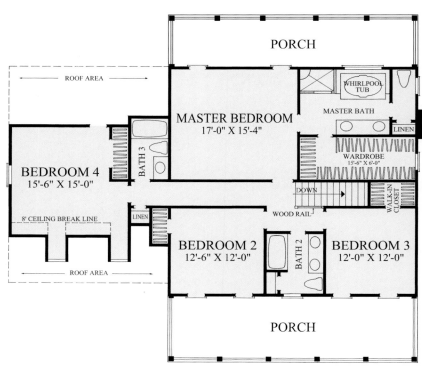

PORCH

ROOF AREA

MASTER BEDROOM
17'-0" X 15'-4"

WHIRLPOOL TUB

MASTER BATH

LINEN

BATH 3

BEDROOM 4
15'-6" X 15'-0"

WARDROBE
15'-6" X 6'-0"

DOWN

WALK-IN CLOSET

8' CEILING BREAK LINE

LINEN

WOOD RAIL

ROOF AREA

BEDROOM 2
12'-6" X 12'-0"

BATH 2

BEDROOM 3
12'-0" X 12'-0"

PORCH

MAIN LEVEL: 1,273 SQUARE FEET
UPPER LEVEL: 1,358 SQUARE FEET
TOTAL: 2,631 SQUARE FEET

WIDTH 54'-10"
DEPTH 48'-6"

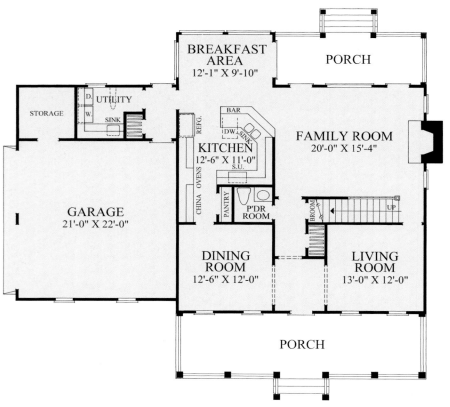

BREAKFAST AREA
12'-1" X 9'-10"

PORCH

STORAGE

D. UTILITY

DW. SINK

BAR

REFG.

DW. SINK

FAMILY ROOM
20'-0" X 15'-4"

KITCHEN
12'-6" X 11'-0"

S.U.

CHINA OVENS

PANTRY

P'DR ROOM

BROOM

UP

GARAGE
21'-0" X 22'-0"

DINING ROOM
12'-6" X 12'-0"

LIVING ROOM
13'-0" X 12'-0"

PORCH

This home, as shown in the photographs, may differ from the actual blueprints.
For more detailed information, please check the floor plans carefully.

DESIGN HPT770003

Photo courtesy of General Shale Brick, Photo by Peter Montanti

New Iberia

One balmy spring, eight of us, all with southern roots and a love of things worn-well-with-time, went south—both to enjoy the company and reconnect with our romantic past. And reconnect we did—Cajun music, crayfish gumbo and boat rides in the bayous were fun alright. However, the most inspiring moment occurred on the upper porch of a grand old home. From there we could hear footsteps on the heart pine floors within, we could see the rolling river beyond the fields below, we could remember the families whose lives made history before our time. This place (New Iberia), this moment—a reflection, a connection with then and now.

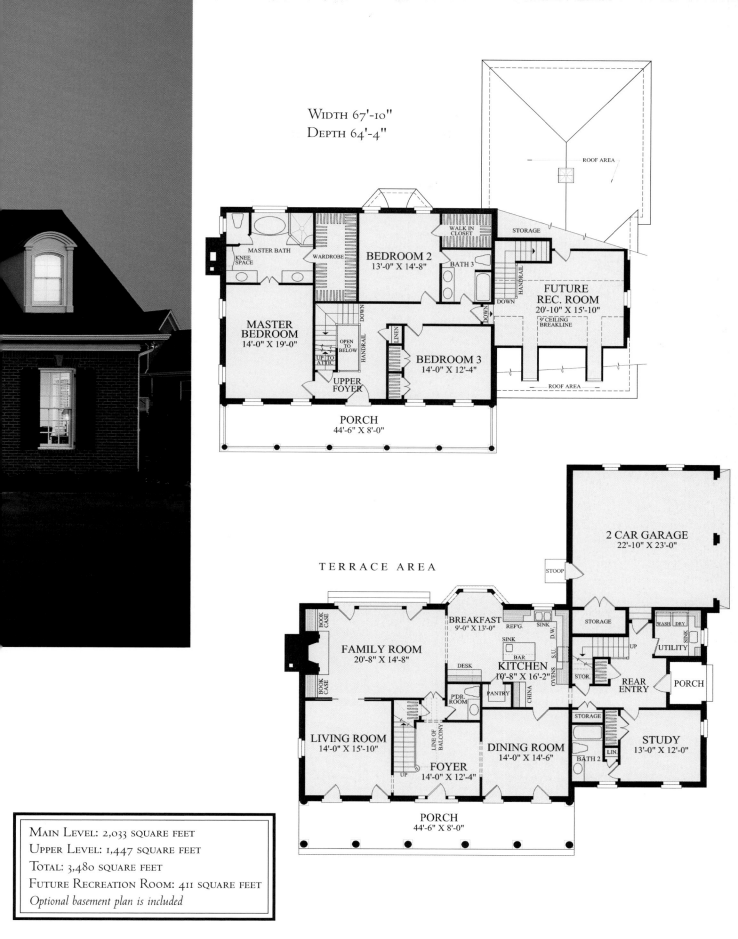

WIDTH 67'-10"
DEPTH 64'-4"

ROOF AREA

MASTER BATH

KNEE SPACE

WARDROBE

WALK IN CLOSET

STORAGE

BEDROOM 2
13'-0" X 14'-8"

BATH 3

HANDRAIL

DOWN

FUTURE REC. ROOM
20'-10" X 15'-10"

9' CEILING BREAKLINE

MASTER BEDROOM
14'-0" X 19'-0"

DOWN

OPEN TO BELOW

UP TO ATTIC

HANDRAIL

LINEN

BEDROOM 3
14'-0" X 12'-4"

DOWN

UPPER FOYER

ROOF AREA

PORCH
44'-6" X 8'-0"

TERRACE AREA

2 CAR GARAGE
22'-10" X 23'-0"

STOOP

BOOK CASE

FAMILY ROOM
20'-8" X 14'-8"

BREAKFAST
9'-0" X 13'-0"

REF'G.

SINK

STORAGE

WASH DRY

SINK

UTILITY

SINK

BAR

DESK

KITCHEN
10'-8" X 16'-2"

S.U.

UP

STOR.

OVENS

REAR ENTRY

PORCH

BOOK CASE

P'DR. ROOM

PANTRY

CHINA

LIVING ROOM
14'-0" X 15'-10"

LINE OF BALCONY

UP

FOYER
14'-0" X 12'-4"

DINING ROOM
14'-0" X 14'-6"

STORAGE

LIN

BATH 2

STUDY
13'-0" X 12'-0"

PORCH
44'-6" X 8'-0"

MAIN LEVEL: 2,033 SQUARE FEET
UPPER LEVEL: 1,447 SQUARE FEET
TOTAL: 3,480 SQUARE FEET
FUTURE RECREATION ROOM: 411 SQUARE FEET
Optional basement plan is included

This home, as shown in the photograph, may differ from the actual blueprints.
For more detailed information, please check the floor plans carefully.

Photos by Gross & Daley

Melrose Plantation

Take a step back in time to the old Mississippi plantation home. A place where the joy of life itself filled the house and grounds around it with all the bustling activity that comes from running so large a self-sustaining home place. Hands toil in the fields, staff runs the house, children run throughout delighting in the daily pleasures surrounding them at the Melrose Plantation—their home forever, no matter where their future paths shall lead.

This home, as shown in the photographs, may differ from the actual blueprints. For more detailed information, please check the floor plans carefully.

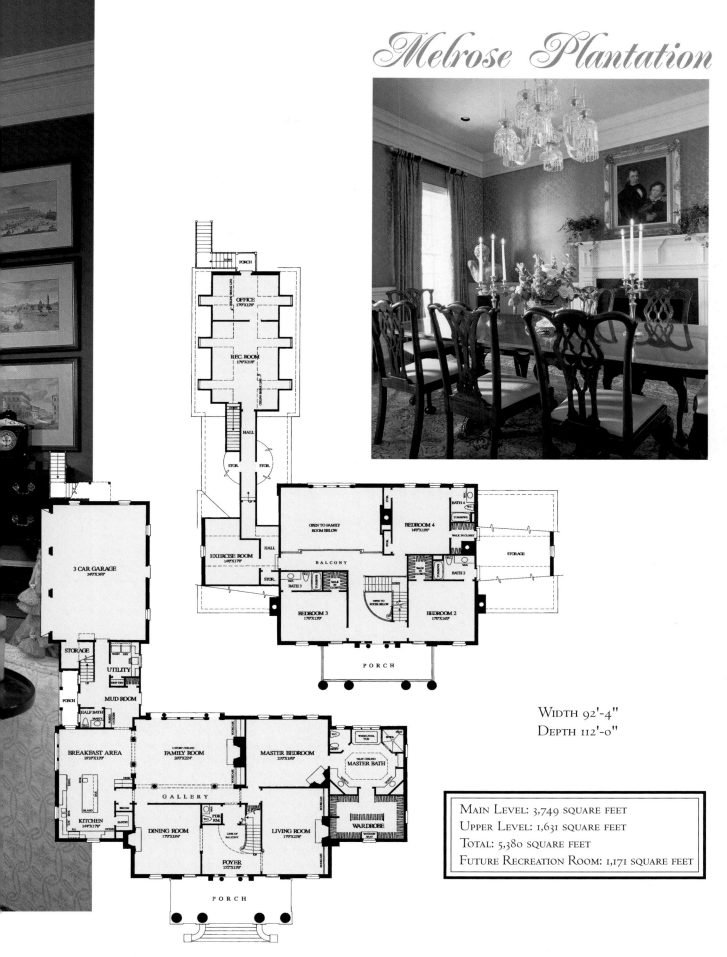

Melrose Plantation

3 CAR GARAGE
24'0"X36'0"

STORAGE

UTILITY

MUD ROOM

HALF BATH

PORCH

OFFICE
17'0"X12'0"

REC. ROOM
17'0"X21'0"

HALL

STOR. STOR.

EXERCISE ROOM
14'0"X17'8"

HALL

STOR.

OPEN TO FAMILY
ROOM BELOW

BALCONY

BATH 3

BEDROOM 3
17'0"X13'0"

BEDROOM 4
14'8"X18'0"

BATH 4
W.C.

STORAGE

BATH 2

OPEN TO
FOYER BELOW

BEDROOM 2
17'0"X16'0"

PORCH

BREAKFAST AREA
18'10"X12'0"

FAMILY ROOM
26'0"X22'4"

MASTER BEDROOM
21'0"X18'0"

MASTER BATH

WHIRLPOOL
TUB

GALLERY

KITCHEN
14'0"X17'0"

DINING ROOM
17'0"X18'4"

FOYER
15'2"X13'0"

LIVING ROOM
17'0"X22'8"

WARDROBE

PORCH

Width 92'-4"
Depth 112'-0"

Main Level: 3,749 square feet
Upper Level: 1,631 square feet
Total: 5,380 square feet
Future Recreation Room: 1,171 square feet

DESIGN HPT770005

The Ashley

The Ashley, a home of elegant Georgian architecture, is reminiscent of the grand homes in the battery section of Charleston, South Carolina. Horse-drawn carriages pass along the streets, seagulls circle overhead and lovers stroll hand-in-hand along the waterfront today, just as they did the day before and the day before that.

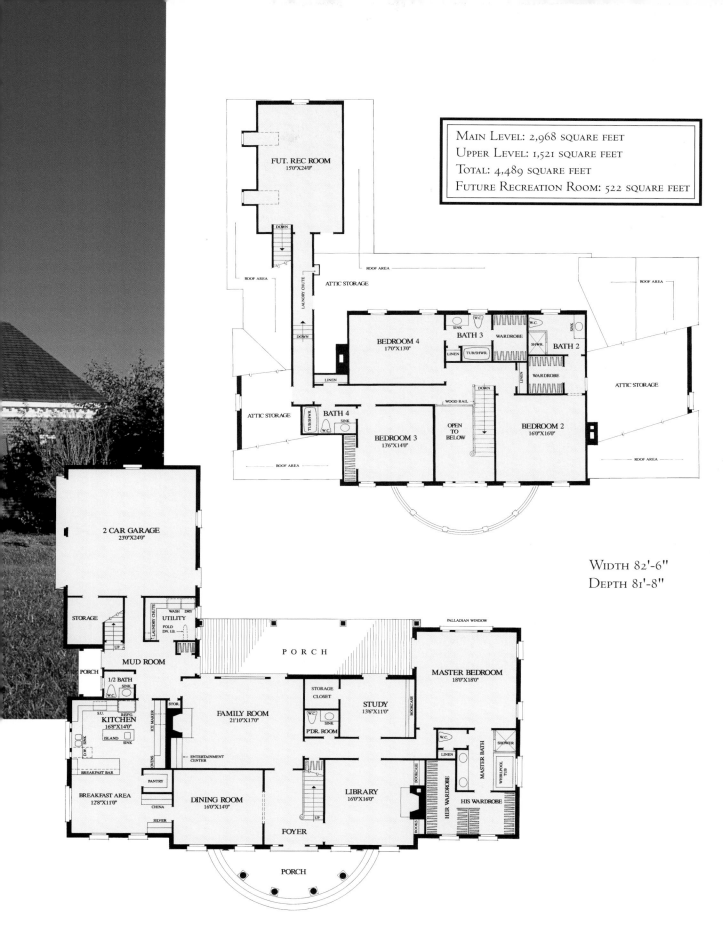

FUT. REC ROOM
15'0"X24'0"

MAIN LEVEL: 2,968 SQUARE FEET
UPPER LEVEL: 1,521 SQUARE FEET
TOTAL: 4,489 SQUARE FEET
FUTURE RECREATION ROOM: 522 SQUARE FEET

DOWN

ROOF AREA

ROOF AREA

ROOF AREA

ATTIC STORAGE

LAUNDRY CHUTE

DOWN

BEDROOM 4
17'0"X13'0"

BATH 3

SINK

W.C.

WARDROBE

W.C.

SINK

SHWR.

BATH 2

LINEN

TUB/SHWR.

LINEN

WARDROBE

ATTIC STORAGE

ATTIC STORAGE

BATH 4

WOOD RAIL

DOWN

TUB/SHWR.

SINK

W.C.

BEDROOM 3
13'6"X14'0"

OPEN
TO
BELOW

BEDROOM 2
16'0"X16'0"

ATTIC STORAGE

ROOF AREA

ROOF AREA

WIDTH 82'-6"
DEPTH 81'-8"

2 CAR GARAGE
23'0"X24'0"

STORAGE

WASH DRY

UTILITY

LAUNDRY CHUTE

FOLD
DN. I.B.

UP

MUD ROOM

PORCH

1/2 BATH

SINK

W.C.

PALLADIAN WINDOW

PORCH

MASTER BEDROOM
18'0"X18'0"

STORAGE
CLOSET

STOR.

KITCHEN
16'8"X14'0"

S.U.

REFG.

ICE MAKER

FAMILY ROOM
21'10"X17'0"

W.C.

SINK

STUDY
13'6"X11'0"

BOOKCASE

W.C.

SHOWER

MASTER BATH

SINK

ISLAND

SINK

OVENS

P'DR. ROOM

LINEN

DW

ENTERTAINMENT
CENTER

WHIRLPOOL
TUB

BREAKFAST BAR

PANTRY

BOOKCASE

BREAKFAST AREA
12'8"X11'0"

DINING ROOM
16'0"X14'0"

CHINA

LIBRARY
16'0"X16'0"

HER WARDROBE

HIS WARDROBE

BOOKS

SILVER

FOYER

UP

PORCH

This home, as shown in the photograph, may differ from the actual blueprints.
For more detailed information, please check the floor plans carefully.

DESIGN HPT770006

The Providence

Homes that I have enjoyed in my travels throughout Rhode Island and Connecticut were my inspiration for the Providence. The fine detail found in houses of the Federal (Adams) period such as Palladian windows, fluted pilasters and pedimented entries are all incorporated in this design. What better place to showcase The Providence than in Williamsburg, Virginia–built in the very center of our colonial heritage. The Providence is also available with a brick exterior and a total square footage of 4,360.

The Providence

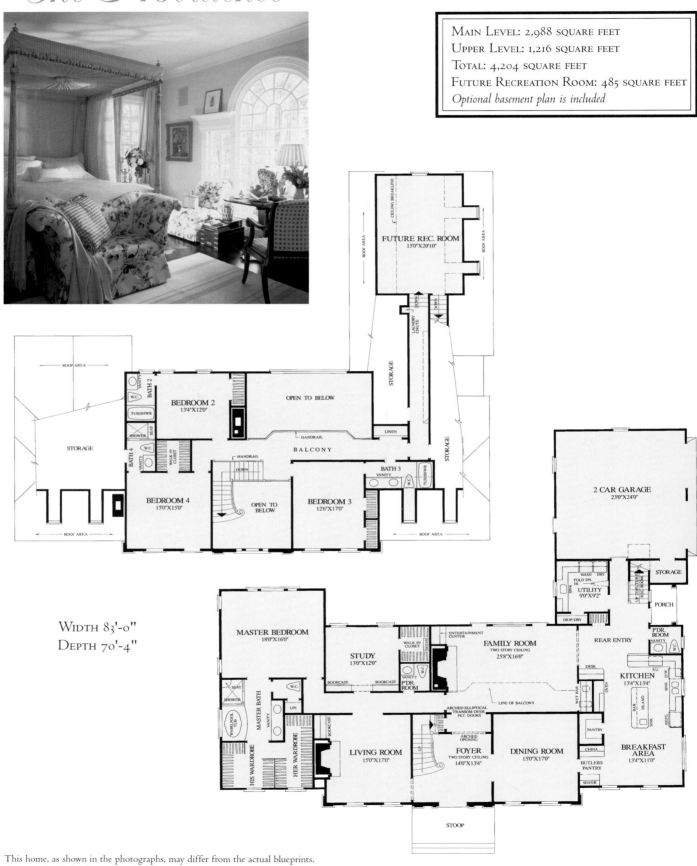

Main Level: 2,988 square feet
Upper Level: 1,216 square feet
Total: 4,204 square feet
Future Recreation Room: 485 square feet
Optional basement plan is included

FUTURE REC. ROOM
15'0"X20'10"

ROOF AREA

STORAGE

CEILING BREAKLINE

LAUNDRY CHUTE

DOWN

STORAGE

VANITY

W.C.

BEDROOM 2
13'4"X12'0"

BATH 2

TUB/SHWR

SHOWER   SEAT

W.C.

OPEN TO BELOW

HANDRAIL

LINEN

BALCONY

BATH 3
VANITY

W.C.

TUB/SHWR

STORAGE

ROOF AREA

BATH 4

WALK IN CLOSET

VANITY

HANDRAIL

DOWN

BEDROOM 4
15'0"X15'0"

OPEN TO BELOW

BEDROOM 3
12'6"X17'0"

ROOF AREA

ROOF AREA

2 CAR GARAGE
23'0"X24'0"

WASH   DRY

FOLD DN. IB.

SINK

UTILITY
9'0"X9'2"

STORAGE

REF.

PORCH

DRIP/DRY

Width 83'-0"

Depth 70'-4"

MASTER BEDROOM
18'0"X16'0"

STUDY
13'0"X12'0"

WALK IN CLOSET

ENTERTAINMENT CENTER

FAMILY ROOM
TWO STORY CEILING
25'8"X16'0"

REAR ENTRY

P'DR. ROOM
VANITY

W.C.

SEAT

SHOWER

MASTER BATH

W.C.

VANITY

LIN

BOOKCASE

BOOKCASE

VANITY

P'DR. ROOM

W.C.

DESK

OVEN

KITCHEN
13'4"X13'4"

S.U.

BAR   ISLAND

SINK

D/W

WHIRLPOOL TUB

HIS WARDROBE

HER WARDROBE

BOOKCASE

LIVING ROOM
15'0"X17'0"

UP

FOYER
TWO STORY CEILING
14'0"X13'4"

ARCHED ELLIPTICAL TRANSOM OVER PKT. DOORS

ARCHED OPENING

LINE OF BALCONY

WET BAR

DINING ROOM
15'0"X17'0"

PANTRY

CHINA

BUTLERS PANTRY

SILVER

BREAKFAST AREA
13'4"X11'0"

STOOP

This home, as shown in the photographs, may differ from the actual blueprints.
For more detailed information, please check the floor plans carefully.

DESIGN HPT770007

Photos by Taylor Lewis

The Natchez II

The Briars in Natchez, Mississippi is one of the most sophisticated examples of the planter's cottage architecture of the lower Mississippi valley, and from the Briars evolved the Natchez. Jefferson Davis married Varina Howell in the parlor of the Briars and one may still visit this beautifully preserved site today. Our Natchez, the most popular home design ever, has struck a universal chord...thereby inducing many to call it "home."

23

This home, as shown in the photographs, may differ from the actual blueprints. For more detailed information, please check the floor plans carefully.

The Natchez II

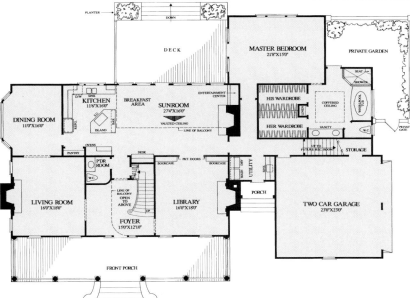

WIDTH 82'-0"
DEPTH 60'-4"

MAIN LEVEL: 2,648 SQUARE FEET
UPPER LEVEL: 1,253 SQUARE FEET
TOTAL: 3,901 SQUARE FEET
FUTURE RECREATION ROOM: 540 SQUARE FEET

DESIGN HPT770008

Edisto River Cottage

What if you could spend summers by the water, or better yet, live there year round? The Edisto River Cottage is designed to meet both these needs and meet them well. The front porch lends itself to rocking chairs and storytelling. This is especially enjoyable after playing a game of hide and seek with neighborhood friends and then—best of all—having a "sleepover" upstairs where whispers and laughter are not easily detected by the grownups all tucked safely into their beds below.

This home, as shown in the photographs, may differ from the actual blueprints.
For more detailed information, please check the floor plans carefully.

Edisto River Cottage

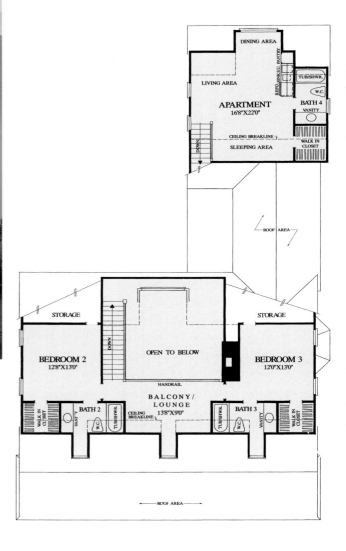

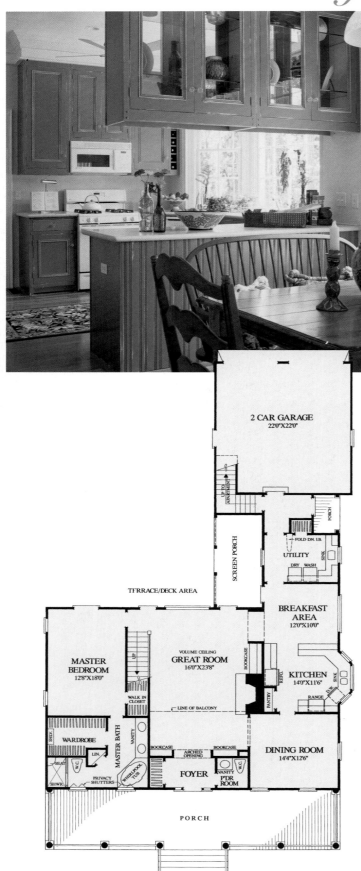

APARTMENT
16'8"X22'0"

DINING AREA

LIVING AREA

REFG. SINK S.U. PANTRY

TUB/SHWR.

W.C.

BATH 4

VANITY

CEILING BREAKLINE

DOWN

SLEEPING AREA

WALK IN CLOSET

ROOF AREA

STORAGE

STORAGE

BEDROOM 2
12'8"X13'0"

OPEN TO BELOW

BEDROOM 3
12'0"X13'0"

DOWN

HANDRAIL

WALK IN CLOSET

VANITY

BATH 2

W.C.

TUB/SHWR.

BALCONY/ LOUNGE
13'8"X9'0"

CEILING BREAKLINE

TUB/SHWR.

W.C.

BATH 3

VANITY

WALK IN CLOSET

ROOF AREA

2 CAR GARAGE
22'0"X22'0"

UP TO APARTMENT

PORCH

FOLD DN. LB.

UTILITY

SINK

DRY WASH

SCREEN PORCH

TERRACE/DECK AREA

BREAKFAST AREA
12'0"X10'0"

VOLUME CEILING
GREAT ROOM
16'0"X23'8"

UP

BOOKCASE

KITCHEN
14'0"X11'6"

REFG.

MASTER BEDROOM
12'8"X18'0"

WALK IN CLOSET

LINE OF BALCONY

PANTRY

DW

SINK

RANGE

SHLV.

WARDROBE

LIN.

MASTER BATH

VANITY

BOOKCASE

ARCHED OPENING

BOOKCASE

DINING ROOM
14'4"X12'6"

SEAT

W.C.

WHIRLPOOL TUB

VANITY

W.C.

SHWR.

PRIVACY SHUTTERS

FOYER

P'DR ROOM

PORCH

WIDTH 50'-0"

DEPTH 82'-6"

MAIN LEVEL: 1,704 SQUARE FEET
UPPER LEVEL: 734 SQUARE FEET
TOTAL: 2,438 SQUARE FEET
FUTURE RECREATION ROOM: 479 SQUARE FEET

DESIGN HPT770009

Photos courtesy of Islands of Beaufort, Beaufort, SC

Battery Creek Cottage

Where creeks converge and marsh grasses sway in gentle breezes, the Battery Creek Cottage is a classical low country home. Steep rooflines, high ceilings, front and back porches, plus long and low windows are typical details of these charming planters' cottages. Spanish moss, alligators and horseflies go with the local scenery too. However, this pleasant and cozy home illustrates a way of life that crosses regional boundaries and looks great anywhere. We just can't export the 'gators.

Battery Creek Cottage

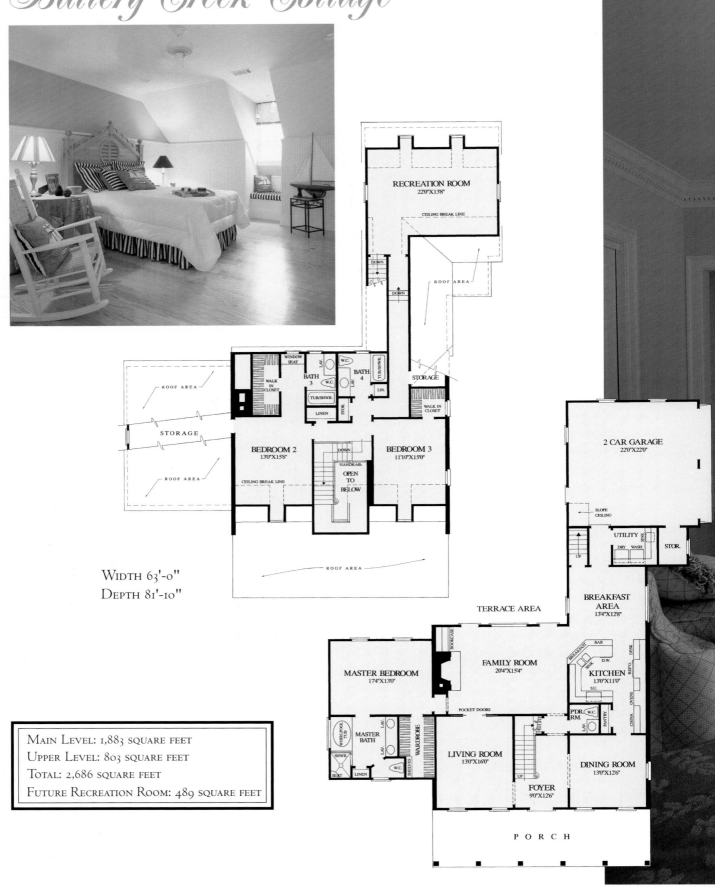

RECREATION ROOM
22'0"X13'8"

CEILING BREAK LINE

ROOF AREA

DOWN

DOWN

ROOF AREA

W.C.

BATH 3

BATH 4

TUB/SHWR.

STORAGE

WINDOW SEAT

LAV.

W.C.

LAV.

LIN.

WALK IN CLOSET

ROOF AREA

TUB/SHWR.

WALK IN CLOSET

STORAGE

LINEN

STOR.

ROOF AREA

BEDROOM 2
13'0"X15'8"

DOWN

BEDROOM 3
11'10"X15'0"

HANDRAIL

OPEN TO BELOW

CEILING BREAK LINE

WIDTH 63'-0"
DEPTH 81'-10"

ROOF AREA

2 CAR GARAGE
22'0"X22'0"

SLOPE CEILING

UTILITY

SINK

UP

DRY

WASH

STOR.

BREAKFAST AREA
13'4"X12'8"

TERRACE AREA

BAR

BREAKFAST

SINK

D.W.

DESK

REFG.

MASTER BEDROOM
17'4"X13'0"

FAMILY ROOM
20'4"X15'4"

KITCHEN
13'0"X11'0"

S.U.

OVENS

BOOKCASE

POCKET DOORS

P'DR. RM.

W.C.

PANTRY

CHINA

WHIRLPOOL TUB

MASTER BATH

LAV.

WARDROBE

LAV.

LIVING ROOM
13'0"X16'0"

UP

DINING ROOM
13'0"X12'6"

SHWR.

SEAT

LINEN

LAV.

W.C.

SHELVES

FOYER
9'0"X12'6"

PORCH

MAIN LEVEL: 1,883 SQUARE FEET
UPPER LEVEL: 803 SQUARE FEET
TOTAL: 2,686 SQUARE FEET
FUTURE RECREATION ROOM: 489 SQUARE FEET

This home, as shown in the photographs, may differ from the actual blueprints. For more detailed information, please check the floor plans carefully.

DESIGN HPT770010

Photo by Steve Diggs

Sulphur Springs

The planters' cottage architecture that is so appealing in The Natchez (my most popular home design ever) has now been translated into this smaller, yet perfect new version. There were so many requests for a home of this same character, but with less square footage while maintaining the charm and proportion that—lo and behold, the Sulphur Springs has arrived!

32

WIDTH 71'-0"
DEPTH 53'-0"

ROOF AREA

STORAGE

OPEN TO BELOW

STORAGE

CEILING BREAK LINE

CEILING BREAK LINE

HAND RAIL

BALCONY

LINEN

BEDROOM 4
12'6"X12'0"

DOWN

LAUNDRY CHUTE

STORAGE

DOWN

VANITY

W.C.

OPEN TO BELOW

VANITY

BATH 2

TUB/SHWR.

STORAGE

DN.

FUTURE REC. ROOM
17'4"X19'6"

BATH 3

W.C.

BEDROOM 3
11'4"X13'4"

BEDROOM 2
13'4"X12'8"

TUB/SHWR.

WARDROBE

CEILING BREAK LINE

WARDROBE

CEILING BREAK LINE

LINE OF HOUSE
ROOF LINE

DECK

DOWN

MASTER BEDROOM
17'4"X13'4"

W.C.

SEAT

SHOWER

BREAKFAST AREA
9'6"X13'4"
VAULTED CEILING

KITCHEN
10'2"X13'4"

SINK

D.W.

HER WARDROBE

MASTER BATH
13'0"X11'4"

WHIRLPOOL TUB

FAMILY ROOM
20'8"X15'4"

BAR

ISLAND

REFG.

HIS WARDROBE

LINEN

VANITY

LINE OF BALCONY

DESK

OVENS

PANTRY

WASH

FOLD DN. I.B.

UP

STORAGE

W.C.

DRY

UTILITY
9'8"X8'0"

LIVING ROOM
11'4"X15'0"

P'DR. ROOM

OPEN TO ABOVE

UP

DINING ROOM
13'4"X14'8"

SINK

2 CAR GARAGE
21'4"X21'6"

LINE OF BALCONY

PORCH

FOYER

PORCH

UP

P O R C H

MAIN LEVEL: 1,927 SQUARE FEET
UPPER LEVEL: 879 SQUARE FEET
TOTAL: 2,806 SQUARE FEET
FUTURE RECREATION ROOM: 459 SQUARE FEET

DESIGN HPT770011

Photos courtesy of Islands of Beaufort, Beaufort, SC

Bayou Cottage

Down in Louisiana where the jambalya, catfish stew and spicy Cajun food are so delightfully savored, the homes are equally unique and enjoyable. With the high foundation typical of a raised cottage, sweeping roof, covered porch and details influenced by the French, the Bayou Cottage is the perfect setting for festive occasions punctuated by zydeco music, laughter of friends and family and tantalizing aromas of simmering gumbo.

This home, as shown in the photographs, may differ from the actual blueprints. For more detailed information, please check the floor plans carefully.

Bayou Cottage

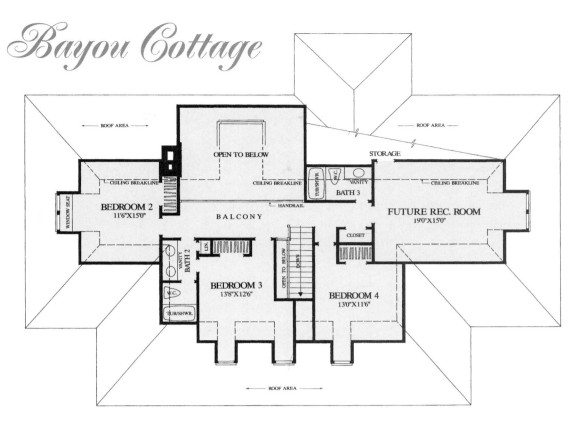

ROOF AREA   ROOF AREA

OPEN TO BELOW   STORAGE

CEILING BREAKLINE   CEILING BREAKLINE   CEILING BREAKLINE

TUB/SHWR.   W.C.   VANITY

BATH 3

WINDOW SEAT

BEDROOM 2
11'6"X15'0"

BALCONY

HANDRAIL

FUTURE REC. ROOM
19'0"X15'0"

VANITY BATH 2

LIN.

OPEN TO BELOW   DOWN

CLOSET

W.C.

BEDROOM 3
13'8"X12'6"

BEDROOM 4
13'0"X11'6"

TUB/SHWR.

ROOF AREA

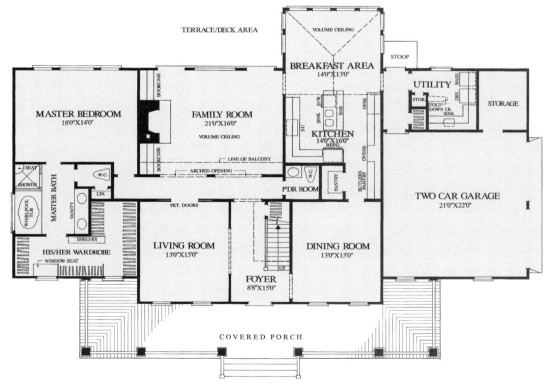

TERRACE/DECK AREA

VOLUME CEILING

BREAKFAST AREA
14'0"X13'0"

STOOP

BOOKCASE

D.W.   BAR

SINK   DESK

STU.

MASTER BEDROOM
18'0"X14'0"

FAMILY ROOM
21'0"X16'0"

UTILITY

WASH   DRY.

STOR.

FOLD DOWN IR.

SINK

STORAGE

VOLUME CEILING

KITCHEN
14'0"X16'0"

REFG.

OVENS

BOOKCASE

SEAT

W.C.

LINE OF BALCONY

SHOWER

ARCHED OPENING

W.C.

PANTRY

BUTLERS PANTRY

MASTER BATH

WHIRLPOOL TUB

VANITY

LIN.

PDR. ROOM

TWO CAR GARAGE
21'0"X22'0"

SHELVES

PKT. DOORS

UP

HIS/HER WARDROBE

WINDOW SEAT

LIVING ROOM
13'0"X15'0"

DINING ROOM
13'0"X15'0"

FOYER
8'8"X15'0"

COVERED PORCH

WIDTH 75'-8"

DEPTH 53'-0"

MAIN LEVEL: 2,142 SQUARE FEET

UPPER LEVEL: 960 SQUARE FEET

TOTAL: 3,102 SQUARE FEET

FUTURE RECREATION ROOM: 327 SQUARE FEET

DESIGN HPT770012

Rose Hill

Atop a knoll in the historic district of Lexington, Kentucky, sits a lovely southern home, the Rose Hill. The streets all meet and rise to greet this grand old house. Awe is instinctive, yet the closer one gets, the broader one smiles. Children tumble about the yard, pets frolic alongside and a lemonade stand is set up beside the drive. As one quickly observes, the formality of the home is a deceptive foil for the rollicking family who live within.

38

This home, as shown in the photographs, may differ from the actual blueprints. For more detailed information, please check the floor plans carefully.

Rose Hill

GARAGE
21'0"X23'0"

TERRACE

SQUARE FOOTAGE: 3,136

STORAGE

WASH DRY UTILITY

SINK

BEDROOM 4
11'0"X13'0"

BATH 3

W.C

TUB/SHWR

BROOM

PORCH

BREAKFAST
AREA
14'6"X12'0"

FAMILY ROOM
18'0"X19'0"
VAULTED TRAY
CEILING

BOOKCASE

DORIC COLUMNS

ENTERTAINMENT CENTER

MASTER BEDROOM
15'0"X19'0"

SHWR.

WHIRLPOOL
TUB

W.C

MASTER BATH

LINEN

WARDROBE

S.U. OVENS

KITCHEN
16'0"X13'0"

SINK

REFG.

SINK

PANTRY DESK

DINING ROOM
16'0"X14'0"

LIVING ROOM
18'6"X13'0"

POWDER
ROOM

W.C

FOYER

BEDROOM 3
15'6"X13'0"

BEDROOM 2
16'0"X13'8"

BATH 2

LINEN

W.C

TUB/SHWR

PORTICO

WIDTH 80'-6"
DEPTH 72'-4"

American Classics

Homes inspired by history excite people. Timeless places such as The Briars in Natchez–where Varina Howell and Jefferson Davis wed–still grab year-round crowds, who come not to explore 19 acres of rolling terrain but to experience the peaceful ambience of a well-crafted parlor.

American Classics features Georgian, Cape Cod and Charleston styles–a collection that successfully combines the architectural integrity of the past with today's luxurious amenities. Each time-honored design captures the spirit of our rich history, invigorated by inviting living spaces that will create a warm and welcoming place to call home.

Williamsburg
COLLECTION™

Included in this chapter is a collection of the most treasured homes at Colonial Williamsburg. William E. Poole, with the cooperation of the Colonial Williamsburg Foundation, has captured the very essence of Tidewater Virginia architecture in this extraordinary collection. Each plan has been created with exacting details lovingly gleaned from the original homes.

The central portion of the Lightfoot House (page 60) is an authentic replication of a Williamsburg home. Our plan features a screen porch–the perfect place to enjoy a steaming cup of strong coffee or fragrant tea, and your favorite periodical.

Mount Ellen

My grandmother wanted everything perfect. She wanted formality with graciousness, comfort with good taste and, most of all, livability with a sense of grandness; but, on a scale that would promote warmth and on a level that would enable her to avoid stairs. My grandmother found perfection with the Mount Ellen and created her own perfect world within.

3 CAR GARAGE
24'-0" X 35'-4"

STORAGE
6'-0" X 4'-8"

WALK-IN CLOSET

UTILITY

W. D.

SINK

DRIP-DRY

BEDROOM 4
12'-0" X 13'-0"

BATH 3

BREAKFAST
15'-0" X 12'-0"

STOR.

CATHEDRAL CEILING

FAMILY ROOM
25'-0" X 18'-0"

ENTERTAINMENT CENTER

SITTING

WHIRLPOOL TUB

MASTER BATH

LINEN

REFG.

S.U.

ISLAND

BAR

SINK

D.W.

KITCHEN
15'-0" X 14'-0"

OVENS

DESK

CATHEDRAL CEILING

MASTER BEDROOM
15'-0" X 18'-0"

BOOK CASE

WARDROBE
15'-0" X 11'-8"

PANTRY

P'DR ROOM

DOWN

UP

ARCHED CEILING

DINING ROOM
15'-0" X 14'-0"

LIVING ROOM
16'-2" X 14'-4"

FOYER
9'-0" X 12'-0"

BEDROOM 3
14'-0" X 12'-0"

BEDROOM 2
15'-0" X 13'-0"

LINEN

BATH 2

PORTICO
15'-0" X 8'-8"

SQUARE FOOTAGE: 3,600
Optional basement plan is included

WIDTH 76'-2"
DEPTH 100'-10"

Winnabow

A sudden glance...a quick intake of breath...the Winnabow to the right as we drove slowly by. This little cottage, simple yet warmly and charmingly detailed, stirred our hearts and we longed for it to be–home.

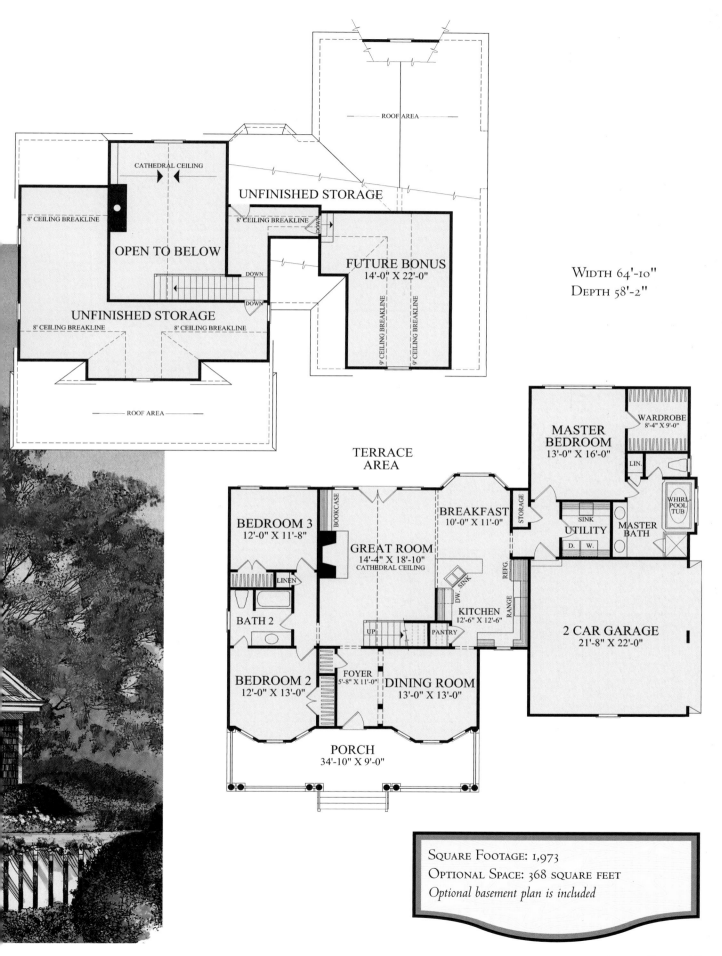

ROOF AREA

CATHEDRAL CEILING

8' CEILING BREAKLINE

OPEN TO BELOW

UNFINISHED STORAGE

8' CEILING BREAKLINE

DOWN

DOWN

UNFINISHED STORAGE

8' CEILING BREAKLINE   8' CEILING BREAKLINE

DOWN

FUTURE BONUS
14'-0" X 22'-0"

9' CEILING BREAKLINE

9' CEILING BREAKLINE

ROOF AREA

WIDTH 64'-10"
DEPTH 58'-2"

MASTER
BEDROOM
13'-0" X 16'-0"

WARDROBE
8'-4" X 9'-0"

LIN.

WHIRL-
POOL
TUB

TERRACE
AREA

BEDROOM 3
12'-0" X 11'-8"

BOOKCASE

BREAKFAST
10'-0" X 11'-0"

STORAGE

SINK

UTILITY

MASTER
BATH

GREAT ROOM
14'-4" X 18'-10"
CATHEDRAL CEILING

LINEN

DW. SINK

REFG.

D.   W.

BATH 2

KITCHEN
12'-6" X 12'-6"

2 CAR GARAGE
21'-8" X 22'-0"

UP

RANGE

PANTRY

BEDROOM 2
12'-0" X 13'-0"

FOYER
5'-8" X 11'-0"

DINING ROOM
13'-0" X 13'-0"

PORCH
34'-10" X 9'-0"

SQUARE FOOTAGE: 1,973
OPTIONAL SPACE: 368 SQUARE FEET
Optional basement plan is included

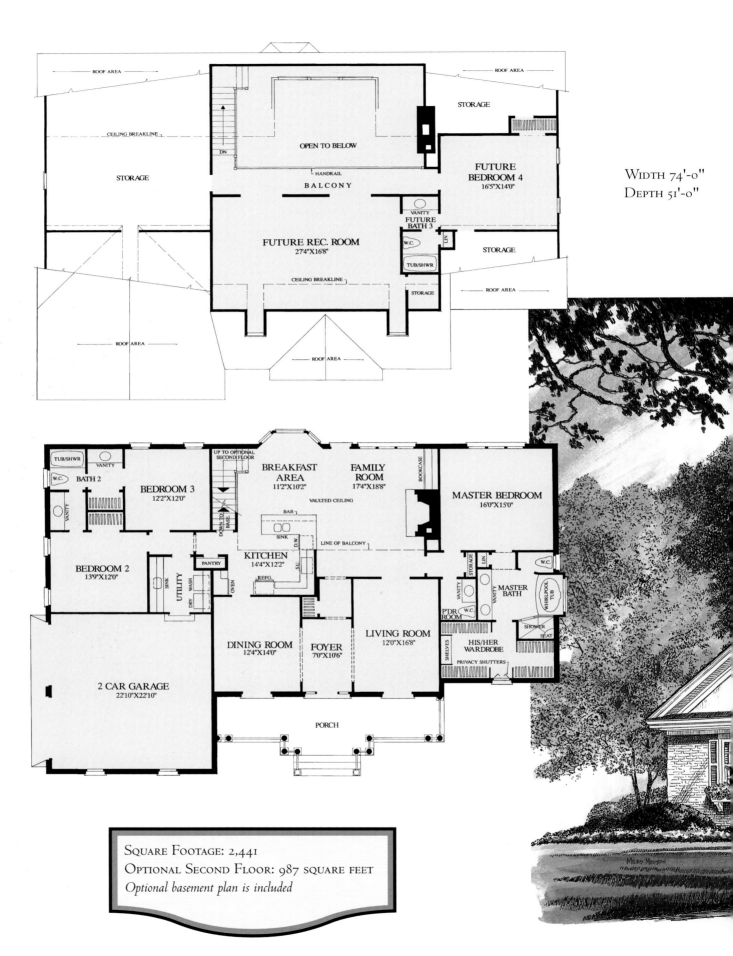

ROOF AREA

ROOF AREA

CEILING BREAKLINE

STORAGE

STORAGE

OPEN TO BELOW

HANDRAIL

DN

BALCONY

FUTURE
BEDROOM 4
16'5"X14'0"

VANITY

FUTURE
BATH 3

FUTURE REC. ROOM
27'4"X16'8"

W.C.

LIN

STORAGE

TUB/SHWR

CEILING BREAKLINE

STORAGE

ROOF AREA

ROOF AREA

ROOF AREA

WIDTH 74'-0"
DEPTH 51'-0"

TUB/SHWR

VANITY

W.C.

BATH 2

BEDROOM 3
12'2"X12'0"

UP TO OPTIONAL
SECOND FLOOR

BREAKFAST
AREA
11'2"X10'2"

FAMILY
ROOM
17'4"X18'8"

BOOKCASE

MASTER BEDROOM
16'0"X15'0"

VANITY

VAULTED CEILING

BAR

SINK

DOWN TO
BASE.

D.W.

LINE OF BALCONY

W.C.

BEDROOM 2
13'9"X12'0"

SINK

UTILITY

WASH

PANTRY

KITCHEN
14'4"X12'2"

SU.

STORAGE

LIN

MASTER
BATH

WHIRLPOOL
TUB

DRY

OVEN

REFG.

VANITY

VANITY

2 CAR GARAGE
22'10"X22'10"

DINING ROOM
12'4"X14'0"

FOYER
7'0"X10'6"

LIVING ROOM
12'0"X16'8"

P'DR
ROOM

W.C.

SHOWER
SEAT

SHELVES

HIS/HER
WARDROBE

PRIVACY SHUTTERS

PORCH

SQUARE FOOTAGE: 2,441
OPTIONAL SECOND FLOOR: 987 SQUARE FEET
Optional basement plan is included

Camden

The Camden is the home that everyone wants to possess–the one in the neighborhood that never needs to be advertised for sale. Why? Because all of your friends have said, "John, if you even think about selling your home, please call me first." And of course, you do. The Camden welcomes each new family to its hearth with the warmth and glow of home–that special place where the heart is.

Abbeville

She was an independent woman, a witty and caring woman, who had lived in the Abbeville for so long that she was thought of as "one" with her home. Stories abound, like the day she was in a hurry but needed to stop at the bank. Due to unavailable parking space, she left her car in the middle of the road. A new policeman—not knowing the "dos" and "don'ts" of a small town—was stopped in the nick of time from writing her a ticket. As the bank president stepped out front, he smiled, waved away the ticket and explained, "Miss Lottie lives in the Abbeville."

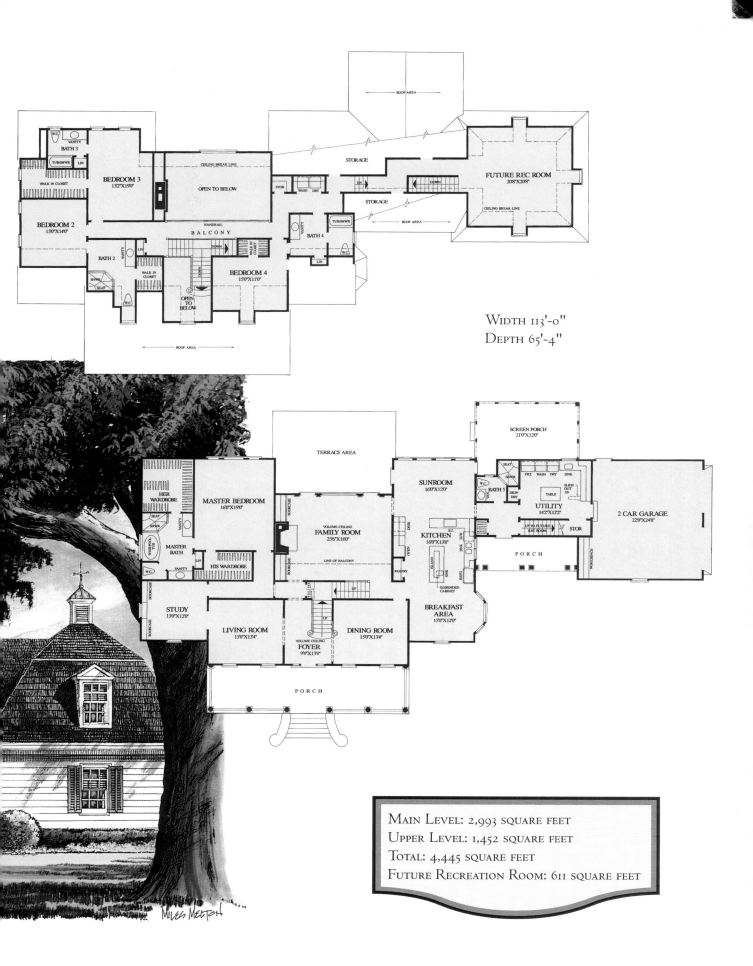

Upper Level Floor Plan:
- W.C.
- VANITY
- BATH 3
- TUB/SHWR
- LIN
- WALK IN CLOSET
- BEDROOM 3 13'2"X19'0"
- OPEN TO BELOW
- CEILING BREAK LINE
- STOR
- STORAGE
- WASH DRY
- LIN
- DOWN
- STORAGE
- ROOF AREA
- FUTURE REC ROOM 20'8"X20'8"
- CEILING BREAK LINE
- BEDROOM 2 13'0"X14'0"
- HANDRAIL
- BALCONY
- VANITY
- BATH 4
- LIN
- BATH 2
- VANITY
- LIN
- DOWN
- WALK IN CLOSET
- W.C.
- SHWR SEAT
- WALK IN CLOSET
- W.C.
- OPEN TO BELOW
- BEDROOM 4 15'0"X11'0"
- ROOF AREA

WIDTH 113'-0"
DEPTH 65'-4"

Main Level Floor Plan:
- TERRACE AREA
- SCREEN PORCH 21'0"X12'0"
- HER WARDROBE
- SEAT
- SHWR
- MASTER BEDROOM 16'0"X19'0"
- BOOKCASE
- VOLUME CEILING FAMILY ROOM 23'6"X18'0"
- SUNROOM 16'0"X12'0"
- SEAT SHWR
- W.C.
- BATH 5
- FRZ WASH DRY SINK
- DRIP DRY
- TABLE
- SLIDE OUT LR.
- UTILITY 14'2"X12'2"
- 2 CAR GARAGE 22'0"X24'8"
- MASTER BATH
- WHIRLPOOL TUB
- VANITY
- DESK
- OVEN
- S.U.
- KITCHEN 16'0"X13'8"
- SINK
- D/W
- UP TO FUTURE REC ROOM
- STOR
- PORCH
- W.C.
- LIN
- HIS WARDROBE
- BOOKCASE
- LINE OF BALCONY
- PANTRY
- ISLAND
- SINK
- REFRIG
- SUSPENDED CABINET
- BOOKCASE
- VANITY
- BOOKCASE
- STUDY 13'0"X12'0"
- LIVING ROOM 15'0"X13'4"
- UP
- VOLUME CEILING FOYER 9'4"X13'4"
- UP
- DINING ROOM 15'0"X13'4"
- BREAKFAST AREA 15'0"X12'0"
- PORCH

MILES MELTON

MAIN LEVEL: 2,993 SQUARE FEET
UPPER LEVEL: 1,452 SQUARE FEET
TOTAL: 4,445 SQUARE FEET
FUTURE RECREATION ROOM: 611 SQUARE FEET

George Pitt House

George Pitt House (c. 1717-19) Dating to the early 1700s, this attractive house was home to Dr. George Pitt in the mid 1700s. Pitt used the small shop adjoining the house to operate his apothecary business, the Sign of the Rhinoceros. At the same time, his wife Sarah, ran a millinery business from their home. Sarah was described as a most amiable wife and was referred to as "much marrying Sarah," due to her three previous husbands. Unfortunately, the original house was destroyed by fire in 1896. Some 40 years later, Colonial Williamsburg architects were able to reconstruct the house on its original foundations, using a photograph taken before the fire and written descriptions. This distinctive home, with its steeply pitched roof and weatherboard siding, is considered a premier example of early Virginia architecture.

Williamsburg

COLLECTION™

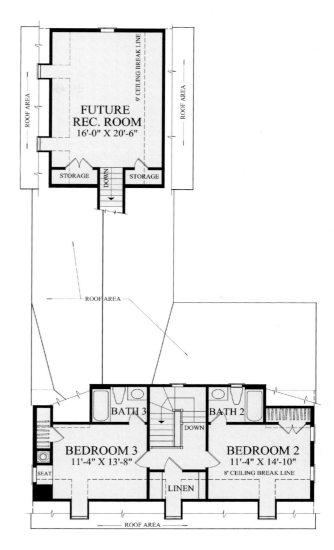

FUTURE REC. ROOM
16'-0" X 20'-6"

9' CEILING BREAK LINE

ROOF AREA

ROOF AREA

STORAGE   DOWN   STORAGE

ROOF AREA

BATH 3   BATH 2

BEDROOM 3
11'-4" X 13'-8"

DOWN

BEDROOM 2
11'-4" X 14'-10"

8' CEILING BREAK LINE

SEAT

LINEN

ROOF AREA

2 CAR GARAGE
22'-0" X 23'-2"

STORAGE

PORCH

UP

W. | D.

UTILITY
5'-8" X 8'-6"

SINK

P'DR. ROOM

PANTRY

PATIO AREA

REFG.

SINK   DW.

ISLAND

KITCHEN
12'-4" X 15'-6"

S.U. | OVENS

PASS THRU

DINING
15'-8" X 11'-8"

WHIRLPOOL TUB

LINEN

MASTER BATH

DOWN   STOR.

HER WARDROBE

GREAT ROOM
16'-0" X 21'-0"

UP

FOYER
8'-2" X 16'-4"

MASTER BEDROOM
14'-10" X 13'-0"

BRICK GUTTER

CELLAR BULKHEAD

WIDTH 41'-8"
DEPTH 74'-6"

MAIN LEVEL: 1,591 SQUARE FEET
UPPER LEVEL: 608 SQUARE FEET
TOTAL: 2,199 SQUARE FEET
FUTURE RECREATION ROOM: 414 SQUARE FEET
Optional basement plan is included

Greenhow Tenement

Williamsburg
COLLECTION™

FUTURE REC. ROOM
16'-2" X 23'-2"

ROOF AREA

DOWN

STORAGE

WIDTH 56'-11"
DEPTH 81'-5"

2 CAR GARAGE
23'-0" X 22'-0"

STORAGE

STORAGE   STOR.

UTILITY
7'-0" X 6'-4"

W.
D.

STORAGE

P'DR
RM.

UP

TERRACE AREA

BREAKFAST
AREA
14'-0" X 12'-0"

REFG.   BAR

KITCHEN
14'-0" X 13'-0"

DW·SINK

RANGE

DESK

PANTRY

GREAT ROOM
23'-8" X 17'-0"

BOOKS

LINE OF WALL ABOVE

BOOKS

WARDROBE
10'-0" X 6'-0"
8'-0" CLG. HGT.

MASTER
BATH

WHIRLPOOL
TUB

STOR.   DOWN

UP

MASTER
BEDROOM
12'-0" X 16'-2"

DINING
ROOM
12'-0" X 15'-0"

FOYER
7'-4" X 17'-0"

CELLAR BULKHEAD   PORCH   BRICK GUTTER

ROOF AREA

OPEN TO BELOW

ROOF AREA

BATH 3

BATH 2

STORAGE

BEDROOM 3
12'-0" X 13'-8"

DOWN

BEDROOM 2
12'-0" X 13'-8"

ROOF AREA

SEAT   LIN.   LIN.   SEAT

ROOF AREA

MAIN LEVEL: 1,814 SQUARE FEET
UPPER LEVEL: 627 SQUARE FEET
TOTAL: 2,441 SQUARE FEET
FUTURE RECREATION ROOM: 401 SQUARE FEET
Optional basement plan is included

Greenhow Tenement (c. 1730-50) In the 18th Century, tenement referred to both smaller rental dwellings and well-appointed townhouses rented to the genteel class. This pleasing cottage, situated next door to the shoemaker's shop, was owned by John Greenhow, an enterprising Williamsburg merchant. Greenhow owned an eight-ton schooner that often sailed to Philadelphia with agricultural products and returned assorted merchandise for his store on Duke of Gloucester Street. Architectural historians used insurance policies and verbal descriptions from long-time residents to reconstruct the house on its original foundations. Another town landmark, Greenhow Brick Office, is used as the architectural basis for a garage at the rear of the house. Local tradition holds that this structure once served as a debtors' prison. The exact date of the Greenhow Tenement and Office is uncertain; both structures appear in tax records during the mid-1700s.

Williamsburg
COLLECTION™

Main Level: 2,286 square feet

Upper Level: 1,148 square feet

Total: 3,434 square feet

Future Recreation Room: 559 square feet

Optional basement plan is included

FUTURE REC. ROOM
17'-8" X 22'-0"

9' CEILING BREAKLINE

ROOF AREA

DOWN

STORAGE

ROOF AREA

BEDROOM 4
14'-0" X 12'-0"

OPEN TO BELOW

BALCONY

BATH 2

LIN. CAB.

WALK IN CLOSET

BATH 4

WALK IN CLOSET

BEDROOM 3
14'-0" X 12'-0"

OPEN TO BELOW

DOWN

BEDROOM 2
16'-0" X 12'-8"

BATH 3

8' CEILING BREAKLINE

ROOF AREA

ROOF AREA

2 CAR GARAGE
25'-0" X 22'-0"

WIDTH 83'-0"

DEPTH 77'-4"

UP

STORAGE

STORAGE 7'-6" X 7'-0"

UTILITY 8'-8" X 7'-6"

W   D

SINK

STORAGE

PANTRY

DRIP-DRY

BREAKFAST
16'-0" X 10'-0"

HALF BATH

CELLAR BULKHEAD

WHIRLPOOL TUB

MASTER BATH

BOOK CASE

START LINE OF CURVE

GREAT ROOM
24'-9" X 17'-4"

LINE OF BALCONY ABOVE

KITCHEN
16'-0" X 11'-4"

REFG.

ISLAND

SINK   D.W.

SINK

PORCH

WARDROBE
8'-1" X 7'-6"

ENTERTAINMENT CENTER

DESK

RANGE

MASTER BEDROOM
16'-7" X 17'-4"

WARDROBE
6'-7" X 6'-4"

FOYER
15'-4" X 12'-2"

UP

DINING ROOM
16'-0" X 13'-0"

P'DR ROOM

PORCH
58'-7" X 9'-0"

BRICK GUTTER

Christiana Campbell's Tavern

DESIGN HPT770019

Christiana Campbell's Tavern (c. 1765) Tavern mistress Christiana Campbell considered this generous house with its gracious porch ideally suited for entertaining guests in the best of southern style. In 1771, she began advertising "genteel Accomodations, and the very best Entertainment" at her tavern located behind the Capitol. George Washington frequently ate at Campbell's Tavern while attending the House of Burgesses. Virginians gathered in candlelit rooms of the tavern or sought refreshment on its comfortable porch to talk of politics and horse racing. In 1954, Colonial Williamsburg architects began reconstruction of Campbell's Tavern and in 1956 opened the restaurant to the public. Today, the tavern house is filled with crackling fires, strolling minstrels and delighted guests who come year after year to sample delicious Virginia.

The Red Lion

DESIGN HPT770020

The Red Lion (c. 1737) Inns and taverns have been identified by trade signs bearing the rampant lion since the Middle Ages. Red Lion Inns were especially popular in England and America during the colonial period because of their association with the red lion of England, which appears in the royal coat of arms. The stately brick Red Lion Inn in Williamsburg was built by innkeeper Francis Sharp, in the early 1700s. Sharp sold the property to tavern keep Henry Wetherburn in 1742. The tavern was later acquired by wigmaker Walter Lenox who sold it to John Crump in 1789. By the early 1800s, court records had begun referring to the property as the Union Tavern. The Red Lion was reconstructed on its original foundations.

Williamsburg
C O L L E C T I O N™

FUTURE REC. ROOM
26'-6" X 18'-8"

9' CEILING BREAKLINE

DOWN

DOWN

STOR.

STORAGE

WALK IN CLOSET

BATH 4

ROOF AREA

BEDROOM 4
11'-8" X 14'-0"

ROOF AREA

9' CEILING BREAKLINE

LINEN

WALK IN CLOSET

DOWN

BEDROOM 3
18'-0" X 12'-8"

BEDROOM 2
15'-0" X 16'-2"

WALK IN CLOSET

BATH 2

BATH 3

2 CAR GARAGE
26'-0" X 25'-0"

W. D.

STORAGE

UP

UTILITY
7'-4" X 8'-6"

ENTERTAINMENT CENTER

GREAT ROOM
24'-0" X 18'-0"

WOOD BEAMS

SCREEN PORCH
20'-6" X 11'-8"

CELLAR BULKHEAD

BAR

DW SINK

S.U.

BREAKFAST AREA
10'-0" X 12'-8"

KITCHEN
10'-0" X 12'-8"

REF'G.

LINEN

MASTER BEDROOM
18'-0" X 14'-0"

DESK

OVENS

P'DR ROOM

PANTRY

DINING ROOM
16'-0" X 12'-0"

FOYER
6'-2" X 12'-0"

UP

WARDROBE

MASTER BATH

WHIRLPOOL TUB

BRICK GUTTER

WIDTH 55'-8"
DEPTH 81'-4"

MAIN LEVEL: 2,025 SQUARE FEET
UPPER LEVEL: 1,217 SQUARE FEET
TOTAL: 3,242 SQUARE FEET
FUTURE RECREATION ROOM: 774 SQUARE FEET
Optional basement plan is included

Guilford

DESIGN HPT770021

A New England Saltbox is solid, sturdy, handsome, of clean design and is equally at home on the rugged coast, in the pretty villages or amid the rolling countryside. The Guilford, with its eye-catching simplicity, is definitely understated; but, what is left unsaid is of far more importance.

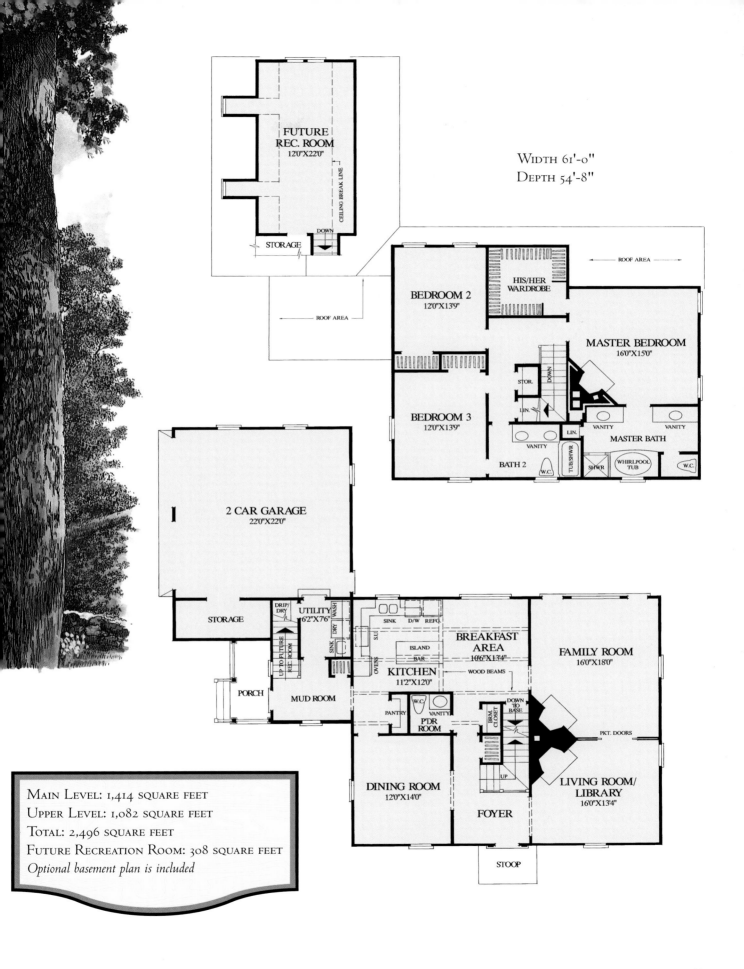

WIDTH 61'-0"
DEPTH 54'-8"

FUTURE REC. ROOM
12'0"X22'0"

STORAGE

DOWN

CEILING BREAK LINE

ROOF AREA

ROOF AREA

BEDROOM 2
12'0"X13'9"

HIS/HER WARDROBE

MASTER BEDROOM
16'0"X15'0"

DOWN

STOR.

LIN.

BEDROOM 3
12'0"X13'9"

LIN.

VANITY

VANITY

MASTER BATH

VANITY

BATH 2

W.C.

TUB/SHWR

SHWR

WHIRLPOOL TUB

W.C.

2 CAR GARAGE
22'0"X22'0"

STORAGE

DRIP/DRY

UTILITY
6'2"X7'6"

WASH

DRY

UP TO FUTURE REC. ROOM

SINK

SINK

D/W

REFG.

BREAKFAST AREA
10'6"X13'4"

FAMILY ROOM
16'0"X18'0"

ISLAND

BAR

WOOD BEAMS

OVENS

KITCHEN
11'2"X12'0"

PORCH

MUD ROOM

PANTRY

W.C.

VANITY

P'DR ROOM

DOWN TO BASE

BRM. CLOSET

PKT. DOORS

DINING ROOM
12'0"X14'0"

UP

FOYER

LIVING ROOM/ LIBRARY
16'0"X13'4"

STOOP

MAIN LEVEL: 1,414 SQUARE FEET
UPPER LEVEL: 1,082 SQUARE FEET
TOTAL: 2,496 SQUARE FEET
FUTURE RECREATION ROOM: 308 SQUARE FEET
Optional basement plan is included

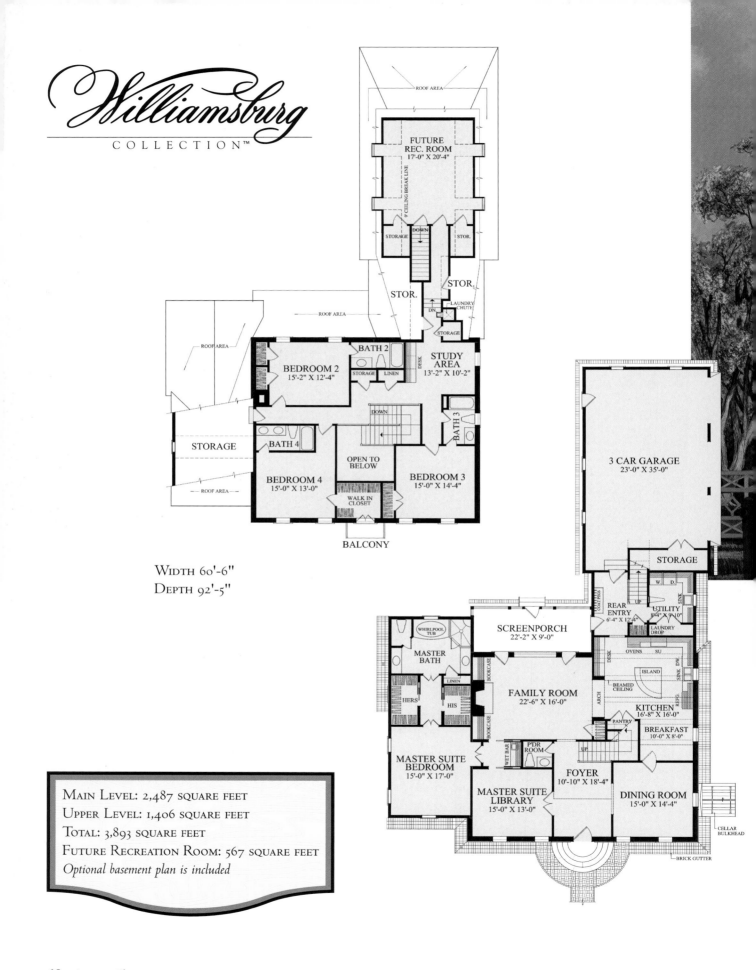

Williamsburg
COLLECTION™

ROOF AREA

FUTURE REC. ROOM
17'-0" X 20'-4"

9' CEILING BREAK LINE

DOWN

STORAGE   STOR.

ROOF AREA

STOR.

STOR.

LAUNDRY CHUTE

DN

STORAGE

ROOF AREA

ROOF AREA

BATH 2

STORAGE   LINEN

DESK

STUDY AREA
13'-2" X 10'-2"

BEDROOM 2
15'-2" X 12'-4"

DOWN

BATH 3

BATH 4

STORAGE

OPEN TO BELOW

BEDROOM 4
15'-0" X 13'-0"

BEDROOM 3
15'-0" X 14'-4"

ROOF AREA

WALK IN CLOSET

BALCONY

WIDTH 60'-6"
DEPTH 92'-5"

3 CAR GARAGE
23'-0" X 35'-0"

STORAGE

W. D.

COAT PEGS

REAR ENTRY
6'-4" X 12'-4"

UP

SINK

UTILITY
8'-4" X 9'-10"

LAUNDRY DROP

SCREENPORCH
22'-2" X 9'-0"

WHIRLPOOL TUB

MASTER BATH

LINEN

FAMILY ROOM
22'-6" X 16'-0"

BOOKCASE

DESK

OVENS   SU

DW.

ISLAND   SINK

BEAMED CEILING

KITCHEN
16'-8" X 16'-0"

REFG.

ARCH

HERS   HIS

BOOKCASE

PANTRY

BREAKFAST
10'-0" X 8'-0"

WET BAR

P'DR ROOM

UP

MASTER SUITE BEDROOM
15'-0" X 17'-0"

MASTER SUITE LIBRARY
15'-0" X 13'-0"

FOYER
10'-10" X 18'-4"

DINING ROOM
15'-0" X 14'-4"

CELLAR BULKHEAD

BRICK GUTTER

MAIN LEVEL: 2,487 SQUARE FEET
UPPER LEVEL: 1,406 SQUARE FEET
TOTAL: 3,893 SQUARE FEET
FUTURE RECREATION ROOM: 567 SQUARE FEET
Optional basement plan is included

Lightfoot House

Lightfoot House (c. 1730-50) The Lightfoot house—with its hipped roof and classical proportions—is an elegant example of Georgian architecture. The central portion of this home design is an authentic replication of the original Lightfoot house in Williamsburg. The side wing is a contemporary addition, designed to blend aesthetically with the period architecture while providing space for a well-appointed master bedroom suite. Built around 1760, the house was the Williamsburg town home of the prominent Lightfoot family of Tidewater Virginia. Colonel Philip Lightfoot I, was a wealthy merchant and landowner. In 1940, the mansion was restored and furnished with fine antiques to serve as a guesthouse for international dignitaries visiting Colonial Williamsburg.

Palmetto

DESIGN HPT770023

There is a very special home that sits on a corner of Meeting Street in Charleston, South Carolina. While overshadowed by larger and more grandiose homes, the Palmetto speaks softly, yet takes no backseat to another. The delicate proportions and simplistic charm of this home purport a simple dignity that captures one's very heart. Is it any wonder that all who return can hardly wait to hear the familiar, "welcome home"?

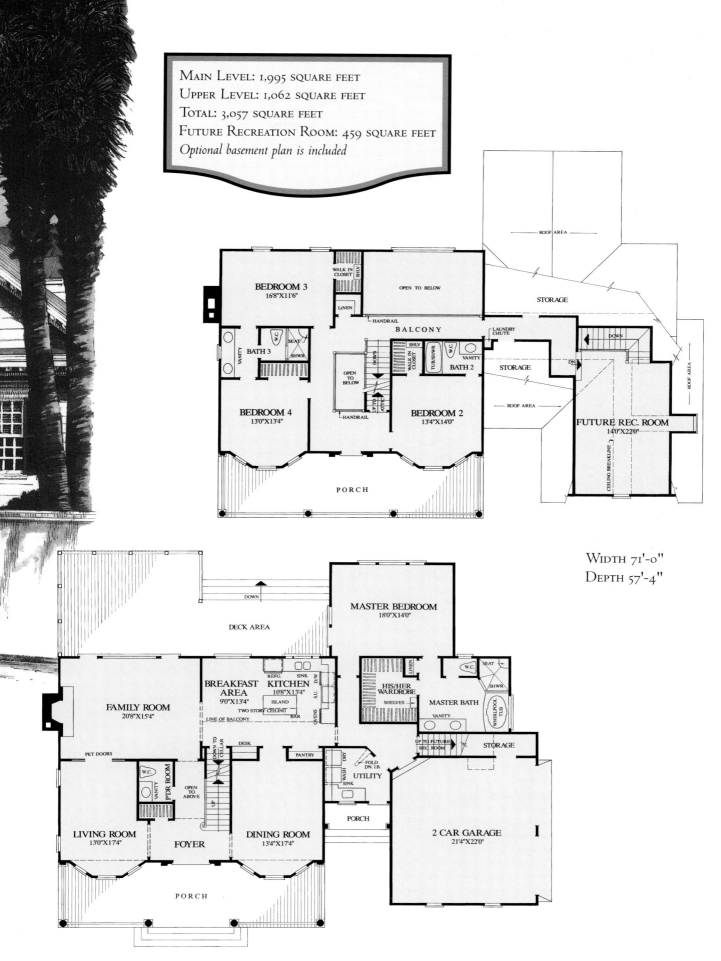

MAIN LEVEL: 1,995 SQUARE FEET
UPPER LEVEL: 1,062 SQUARE FEET
TOTAL: 3,057 SQUARE FEET
FUTURE RECREATION ROOM: 459 SQUARE FEET
Optional basement plan is included

ROOF AREA

STORAGE

BEDROOM 3
16'8"X11'6"

WALK IN CLOSET

SHLV

OPEN TO BELOW

LINEN

HANDRAIL

BALCONY

LAUNDRY CHUTE

SHLV

DOWN

TUB/SHWR

W.C.

STORAGE

DOWN

BATH 3

SEAT

SHWR

VANITY

WALK IN CLOSET

VANITY

BATH 2

STORAGE

DN.

ROOF AREA

OPEN TO BELOW

UP TO ATTIC

ROOF AREA

FUTURE REC. ROOM
14'0"X22'0"

BEDROOM 4
13'0"X13'4"

HANDRAIL

BEDROOM 2
13'4"X14'0"

CEILING BREAKLINE

PORCH

WIDTH 71'-0"
DEPTH 57'-4"

DOWN

MASTER BEDROOM
18'0"X14'0"

DECK AREA

REFG. SINK

LINEN

W.C.

SEAT

FAMILY ROOM
20'8"X15'4"

BREAKFAST AREA
9'0"X13'4"

KITCHEN
10'8"X13'4"

D/W

S.U.

HIS/HER WARDROBE

SHWR

ISLAND

OVENS

BAR

TWO STORY CEILING

SHELVES

MASTER BATH

WHIRLPOOL TUB

LINE OF BALCONY

VANITY

PKT DOORS

W.C.

DESK

DOWN TO CELLAR

PANTRY

WASH DRY

FOLD DN. I.B.

UP TO FUTURE REC. ROOM

STORAGE

VANITY

OPEN TO ABOVE

SINK

UTILITY

LIVING ROOM
13'0"X17'4"

FOYER

UP

DINING ROOM
13'4"X17'4"

PORCH

2 CAR GARAGE
21'4"X22'0"

PORCH

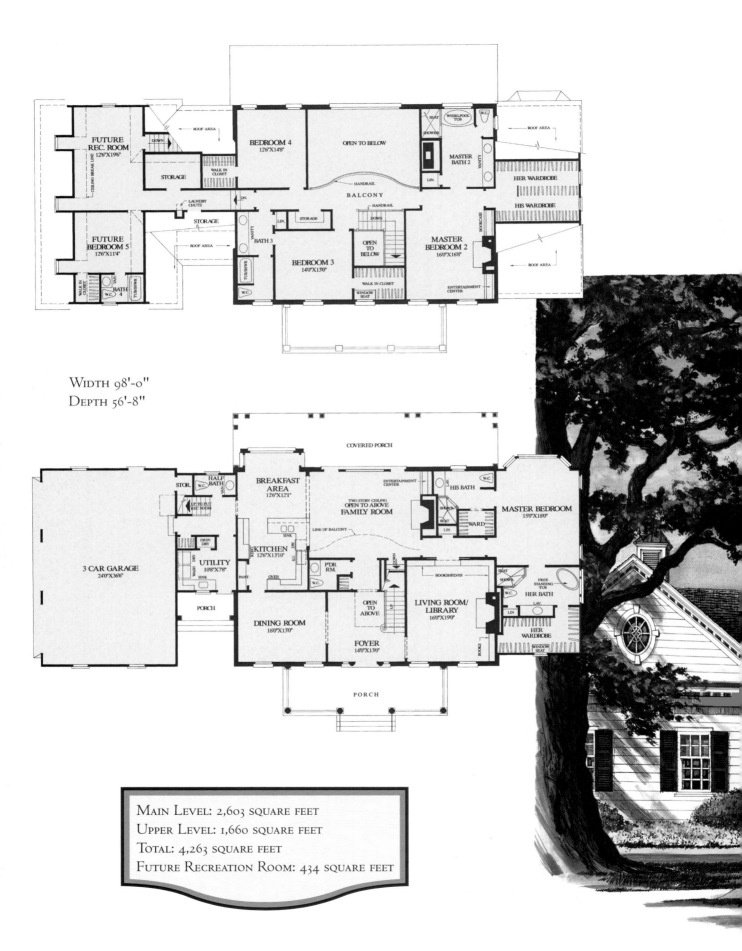

WIDTH 98'-0"
DEPTH 56'-8"

FUTURE REC. ROOM 12'6"X19'6"

STORAGE

FUTURE BEDROOM 5 12'6"X11'4"

WALK IN CLOSET

BATH 4

W.C.

LAUNDRY CHUTE

STORAGE

BATH 3

VANITY

TUB/SHWR

W.C.

ROOF AREA

DN.

LIN.

STORAGE

BEDROOM 4 12'6"X14'8"

WALK IN CLOSET

OPEN TO BELOW

HANDRAIL

BALCONY

HANDRAIL

OPEN TO BELOW

DOWN

BEDROOM 3 14'0"X13'0"

WALK IN CLOSET

WINDOW SEAT

SEAT

SHOWER

WHIRLPOOL TUB

W.C.

MASTER BATH 2

VANITY

LIN.

BOOKCASE

MASTER BEDROOM 2 16'0"X16'8"

ENTERTAINMENT CENTER

ROOF AREA

HER WARDROBE

HIS WARDROBE

ROOF AREA

3 CAR GARAGE 24'0"X36'6"

STOR.

HALF BATH

W.C.

VAN.

UP TO FUT. REC. ROOM

DRIP/ DRY

UTILITY 10'8"X7'8"

WASH DRY

SINK

PANT.

PORCH

DINING ROOM 16'0"X13'0"

COVERED PORCH

BREAKFAST AREA 12'6"X12'1"

SINK

KITCHEN 12'6"X13'0"

OVEN

PDR. RM.

W.C.

TWO STORY CEILING OPEN TO ABOVE FAMILY ROOM

LINE OF BALCONY

ENTERTAINMENT CENTER

LAV.

HIS BATH

W.C.

SHOWR.

SEAT

WARD.

LIN.

MASTER BEDROOM 15'0"X18'0"

OPEN TO ABOVE

DOWN

UP

FOYER 14'0"X13'0"

BOOKSHELVES

LIVING ROOM/ LIBRARY 16'0"X19'0"

BOOKS

SEAT

SHOWER

W.C.

LIN.

LAV.

FREE STANDING TUB

HER BATH

HER WARDROBE

WINDOW SEAT

PORCH

MAIN LEVEL: 2,603 SQUARE FEET
UPPER LEVEL: 1,660 SQUARE FEET
TOTAL: 4,263 SQUARE FEET
FUTURE RECREATION ROOM: 434 SQUARE FEET

Shepperd House

Purpose is in the air. Workmen are everywhere. This fine old home is being brought back to life after having been deserted for years. One day, quite by chance, a couple happened by, fell in love with its "bones" and possibilities and decided to restore the Shepperd House to its former glory. Some stories really do have happy endings. This one surely shall...

The Hamilton

"*Quality versus quantity.*" *This guiding rule was not only drilled into my head when growing up, but, in my maturing years observed and acknowledged as a wise and lasting truth. Details make all the difference and in homes they are the defining difference that sometimes dictate less in square footage in order to complete our total vision—details that enhance and solidify our home for the memories we make. The Hamilton typifies the translation from grand estate to the human scale and is more worthy of this old adage.*

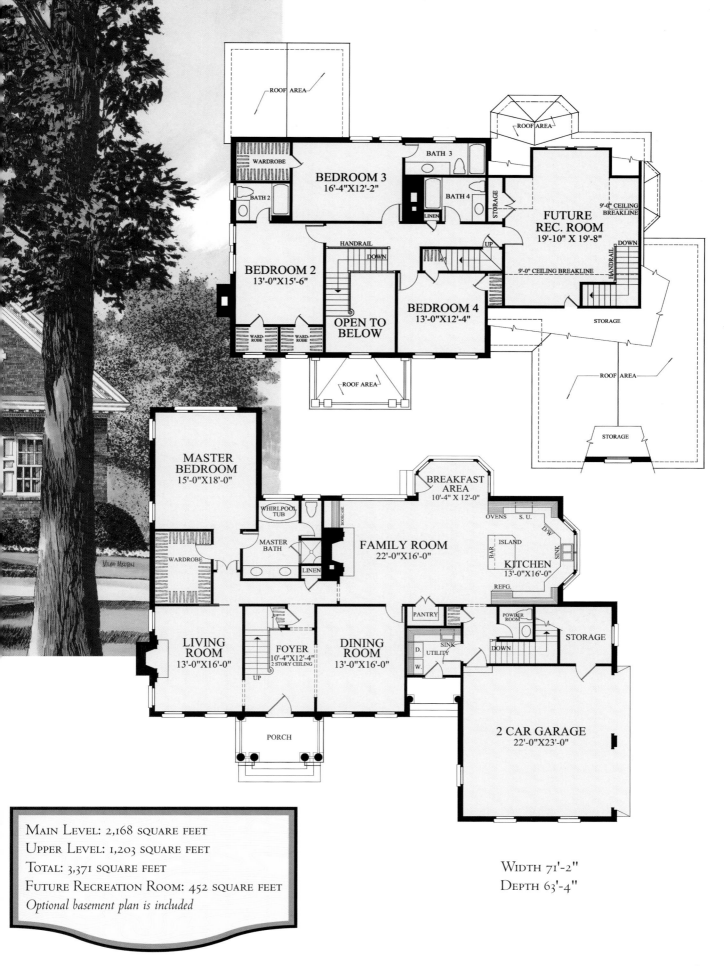

WARDROBE

BEDROOM 3
16'-4"X12'-2"

BATH 3

BATH 2

BATH 4

STORAGE

ROOF AREA

9'-0" CEILING BREAKLINE

FUTURE
REC. ROOM
19'-10" X 19'-8"

DOWN

LINEN

BEDROOM 2
13'-0"X15'-6"

HANDRAIL

DOWN

UP

9'-0" CEILING BREAKLINE

HANDRAIL

WARD-ROBE

WARD-ROBE

OPEN TO
BELOW

BEDROOM 4
13'-0"X12'-4"

STORAGE

ROOF AREA

ROOF AREA

STORAGE

MASTER
BEDROOM
15'-0"X18'-0"

WHIRLPOOL
TUB

MASTER
BATH

BOOKCASE

FAMILY ROOM
22'-0"X16'-0"

BREAKFAST
AREA
10'-4" X 12'-0"

OVENS

S. U.

BAR

ISLAND

DW

SINK

KITCHEN
13'-0"X16'-0"

WARDROBE

LINEN

REFG.

PANTRY

POWDER
ROOM

STORAGE

LIVING
ROOM
13'-0"X16'-0"

FOYER
10'-4"X12'-4"
2 STORY CEILING

UP

DINING
ROOM
13'-0"X16'-0"

D.
W.

SINK

UTILITY

DOWN

2 CAR GARAGE
22'-0"X23'-0"

PORCH

MAIN LEVEL: 2,168 square feet

UPPER LEVEL: 1,203 square feet

TOTAL: 3,371 square feet

FUTURE RECREATION ROOM: 452 square feet

Optional basement plan is included

WIDTH 71'-2"

DEPTH 63'-4"

James Anderson House

Design HPT770026

Williamsburg
COLLECTION™

MAIN LEVEL: 2,189 SQUARE FEET
UPPER LEVEL: 1,326 SQUARE FEET
TOTAL: 3,515 SQUARE FEET
FUTURE RECREATION ROOM: 441 SQUARE FEET
Optional basement plan is included

WIDTH 62'-2"
DEPTH 76'-4"

James Anderson House (c. 1770) This beautiful two-story is the reconstructed home of James Anderson, who is credited with building the original house and forge around 1770. James Anderson ran a successful blacksmithing operation and served as Virginia's public armorer for many years. He died in 1803, leaving the house to two of his eight children. In 1842, a tragic fire destroyed the house and all buildings on the property. In 1934, architects identified the original foundations of James Anderson's house and forge. Historians used insurance records and inventories and called upon the memories of longtime Williamsburg residents to determine the appearance of the house and reconstruct it on its original foundations. Today, visitors to Anderson's operating forge witness costumed tradesmen using 18th-Century tools and techniques to demonstrate the art of colonial blacksmithing.

Waverly

DESIGN HPT770027

The Waverly is a classical Georgian home that, from all appearances, could be either the newest dwelling on the block or the old historic home on whose grounds the surrounding neighborhood was conceived and developed. Proportions and authentic details so handsomely depicted, anchored by twin chimneys on either side of the impressive center structure, give one reflective pause upon approaching The Waverly for the first time—as well as all the times in the future when feeling truly welcomed home.

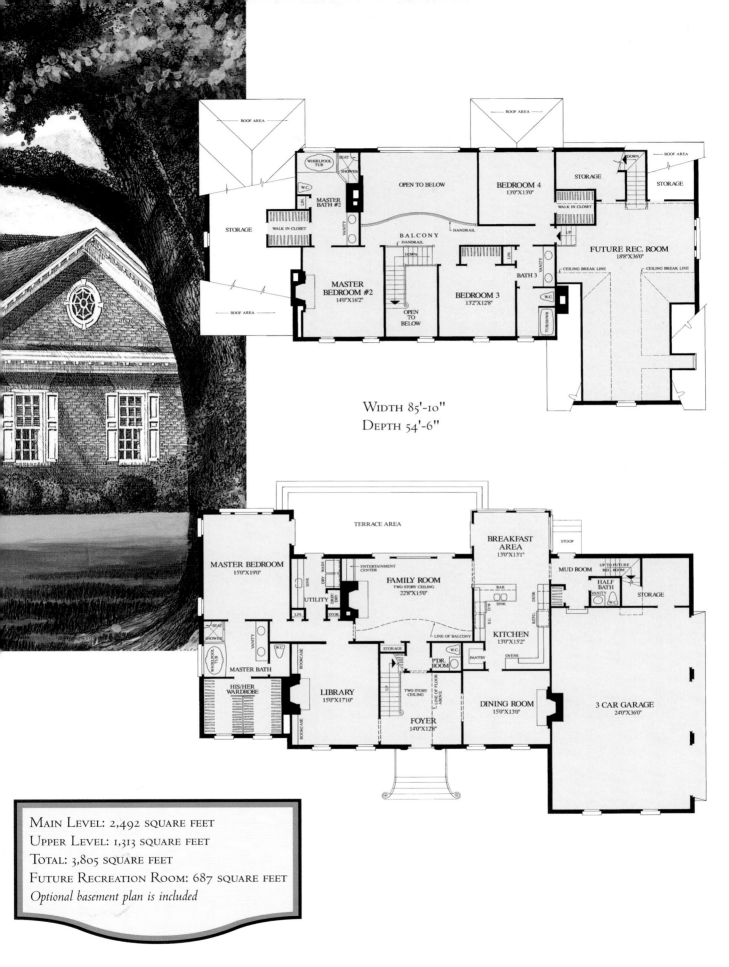

ROOF AREA

ROOF AREA

WHIRLPOOL TUB
SEAT
SHOWER
W.C.
MASTER BATH #2
OPEN TO BELOW
BEDROOM 4
13'0"X13'0"
STORAGE
DOWN
ROOF AREA
STORAGE

STORAGE
LIN
WALK IN CLOSET
VANITY
WALK IN CLOSET
UP
FUTURE REC. ROOM
18'8"X36'0"

BALCONY
HANDRAIL
HANDRAIL
DOWN
LIN
VANITY

MASTER BEDROOM #2
14'0"X16'2"
OPEN TO BELOW
BEDROOM 3
13'2"X12'8"
BATH 3
W.C.
CEILING BREAK LINE
CEILING BREAK LINE

ROOF AREA
TUB/SHWR

WIDTH 85'-10"
DEPTH 54'-6"

TERRACE AREA

BREAKFAST AREA
13'0"X13'1"
STOOP

MASTER BEDROOM
15'0"X19'0"
SINK
WASH
DRY
ENTERTAINMENT CENTER
FAMILY ROOM
TWO STORY CEILING
22'8"X15'0"
BAR
SINK
MUD ROOM
UP TO FUTURE REC. ROOM
HALF BATH
VANITY
W.C.
STORAGE

UTILITY
LIN
DRIP DRY
STOR.
DW
SLU
DESK
REFG.

SEAT
SHOWER
VANITY
W.C.
LINE OF BALCONY
KITCHEN
13'0"X15'2"
OVENS

WHIRLPOOL TUB
MASTER BATH
BOOKCASE
STORAGE
W.C.
P'DR. ROOM
PANTRY

HIS/HER WARDROBE
LIBRARY
15'0"X17'10"
UP
TWO STORY CEILING
FOYER
14'0"X12'8"
LINE OF FLOOR ABOVE
DINING ROOM
15'0"X13'0"
3 CAR GARAGE
24'0"X36'0"

BOOKCASE

MAIN LEVEL: 2,492 SQUARE FEET
UPPER LEVEL: 1,313 SQUARE FEET
TOTAL: 3,805 SQUARE FEET
FUTURE RECREATION ROOM: 687 SQUARE FEET
Optional basement plan is included

Twin Oaks

As the day dawned on their anniversary, her husband suggested a drive in the country. The car turned down a tree-lined drive and there, in front of her, was Twin Oaks—the handsome brick Federal home she had always loved. Now it is theirs, the best gift he could have given her. Evenings are quietly spent sharing the day's events, reading in companionable silence and enjoying the soothing melodies of Beethoven's Moonlight Sonata. This is as good as life gets, and she is in love for the first and last time in her life.

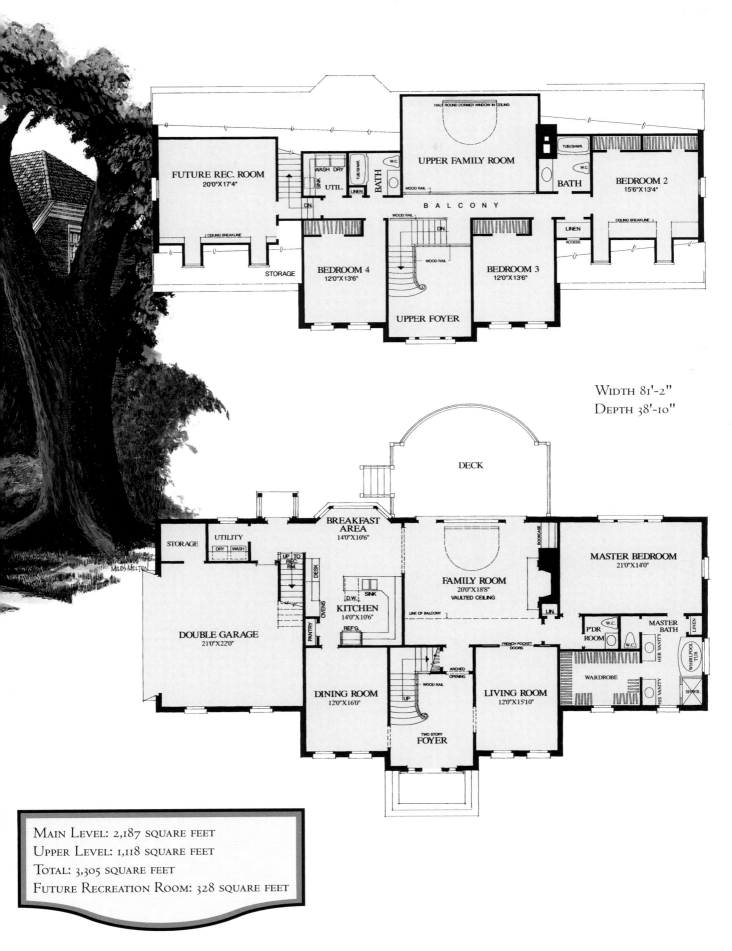

FUTURE REC. ROOM
20'0"X17'4"

WASH DRY
SINK
UTIL.
LINEN
TUB/SHWR

W.C.

BATH

HALF ROUND DORMER WINDOW IN CEILING

UPPER FAMILY ROOM

TUB/SHWR

W.C.

BATH

BEDROOM 2
15'6"X13'4"

CEILING BREAKLINE

DN.

STORAGE

WOOD RAIL

BALCONY

LINEN

ACCESS

CEILING BREAKLINE

WOOD RAIL

BEDROOM 4
12'0"X13'6"

DN.

WOOD RAIL

BEDROOM 3
12'0"X13'6"

UPPER FOYER

WIDTH 81'-2"
DEPTH 38'-10"

DECK

STORAGE

UTILITY
DRY WASH

UP TO
REC.
RM.

DN.

DESK

BREAKFAST
AREA
14'0"X10'6"

FAMILY ROOM
20'0"X18'8"
VAULTED CEILING

BOOKCASE

MASTER BEDROOM
21'0"X14'0"

DOUBLE GARAGE
21'0"X22'0"

PANTRY

OVENS

D.W.
SINK

KITCHEN
14'0"X10'6"

REF'G

LINE OF BALCONY

LIN.

MILES MELTON

WOOD RAIL

UP

ARCHED
OPENING

DINING ROOM
12'0"X16'0"

TWO STORY
FOYER

FRENCH POCKET
DOORS

LIVING ROOM
12'0"X15'10"

WARDROBE

P'DR
ROOM

W.C.

W.C.

MASTER
BATH

HER VANITY

LINEN

WHIRLPOOL
TUB

HIS VANITY

SHWR.

MAIN LEVEL: 2,187 SQUARE FEET
UPPER LEVEL: 1,118 SQUARE FEET
TOTAL: 3,305 SQUARE FEET
FUTURE RECREATION ROOM: 328 SQUARE FEET

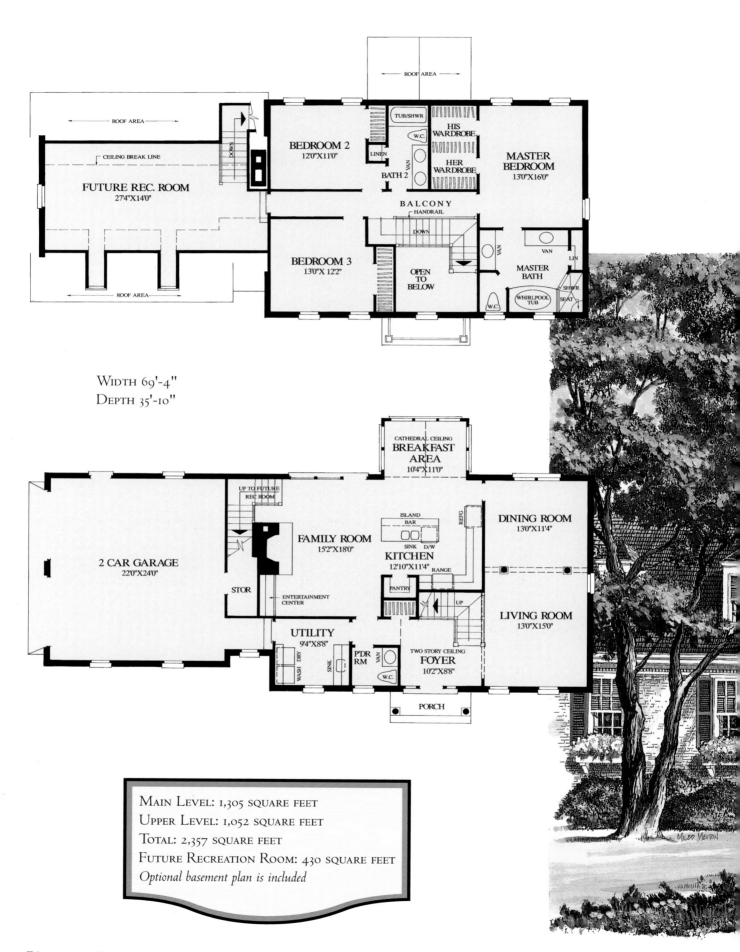

ROOF AREA

ROOF AREA

CEILING BREAK LINE

DOWN

FUTURE REC. ROOM
27'4"X14'0"

ROOF AREA

BEDROOM 2
12'0"X11'0"

TUB/SHWR

W.C.

LINEN

VAN

BATH 2

HIS WARDROBE

HER WARDROBE

MASTER BEDROOM
13'0"X16'0"

B A L C O N Y

HANDRAIL

BEDROOM 3
13'0"X 12'2"

DOWN

OPEN TO BELOW

VAN

VAN

LIN

MASTER BATH

WHIRLPOOL TUB

SHWR

SEAT

W.C.

WIDTH 69'-4"
DEPTH 35'-10"

CATHEDRAL CEILING
BREAKFAST AREA
10'4"X11'0"

UP TO FUTURE
REC ROOM

2 CAR GARAGE
22'0"X24'0"

STOR

FAMILY ROOM
15'2"X18'0"

ENTERTAINMENT CENTER

ISLAND BAR

SINK   D/W

KITCHEN
12'10"X11'4"

RANGE

REFG

DINING ROOM
13'0"X11'4"

PANTRY

UP

LIVING ROOM
13'0"X15'0"

UTILITY
9'4"X8'8"

WASH DRY

SINK

P'DR RM

VAN

W.C.

TWO STORY CEILING
FOYER
10'2"X8'8"

PORCH

MILES MELTON

Main Level: 1,305 square feet
Upper Level: 1,052 square feet
Total: 2,357 square feet
Future Recreation Room: 430 square feet
Optional basement plan is included

Myers Park

Everybody's dream...an old neighborhood right in the center of things. Good schools, lush plantings and big old trees, solid homes that appear to have stories to tell, porches where neighbors meet, sidewalks up and down the street—Myers Park, forever home.

The Brewton House

Classical old Southern houses are national treasures and an integral part of our heritage. Such is The Brewton House in Charleston, South Carolina. The history of this house, the town, the family and the folk from the surrounding area is both fascinating and illuminating—one more connection with our past that remains as a lasting glimpse into our yesteryears.

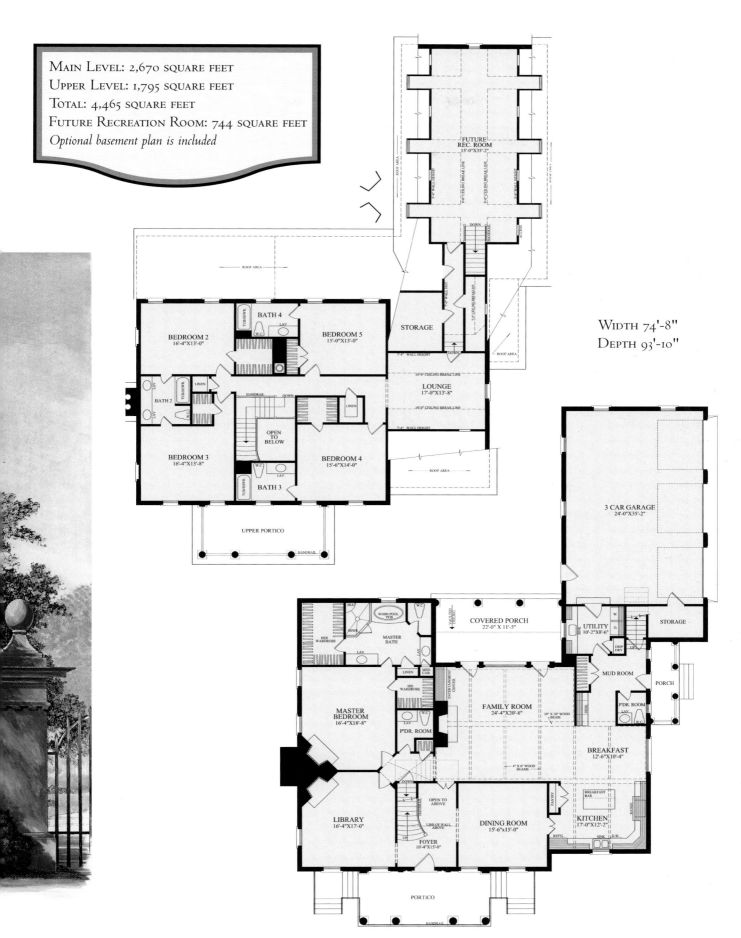

MAIN LEVEL: 2,670 SQUARE FEET
UPPER LEVEL: 1,795 SQUARE FEET
TOTAL: 4,465 SQUARE FEET
FUTURE RECREATION ROOM: 744 SQUARE FEET
Optional basement plan is included

FUTURE
REC. ROOM
15'-0"X35'-2"

WIDTH 74'-8"
DEPTH 93'-10"

STORAGE

LOUNGE
17'-0"X13'-8"

BEDROOM 2
16'-4"X13'-0"

BATH 4

BEDROOM 5
15'-0"X13'-0"

BATH 2

LINEN

OPEN
TO
BELOW

BEDROOM 3
16'-4"X13'-8"

BEDROOM 4
15'-6"X14'-0"

BATH 3

UPPER PORTICO

HANDRAIL

3 CAR GARAGE
24'-0"X35'-2"

SEAT

WHIRLPOOL
TUB

W.C.

COVERED PORCH
22'-0" X 11'-5"

UTILITY
10'-2"X8'-6"

STORAGE

HER
WARDROBE

MASTER
BATH

LINEN

MED.
CAB.

ENTERTAINMENT
CENTER

FAMILY ROOM
24'-4"X20'-8"

MUD ROOM

PORCH

MASTER
BEDROOM
16'-4"X18'-8"

HIS
WARDROBE

P'DR.
ROOM

P'DR. ROOM

BREAKFAST
12'-6"X10'-4"

OPEN TO
ABOVE

PANTRY

BREAKFAST
BAR

LIBRARY
16'-4"X17'-0"

DINING ROOM
15'-6"x15'-0"

KITCHEN
17'-0"X12'-2"

FOYER
10'-4"X15'-0"

PORTICO

HANDRAIL

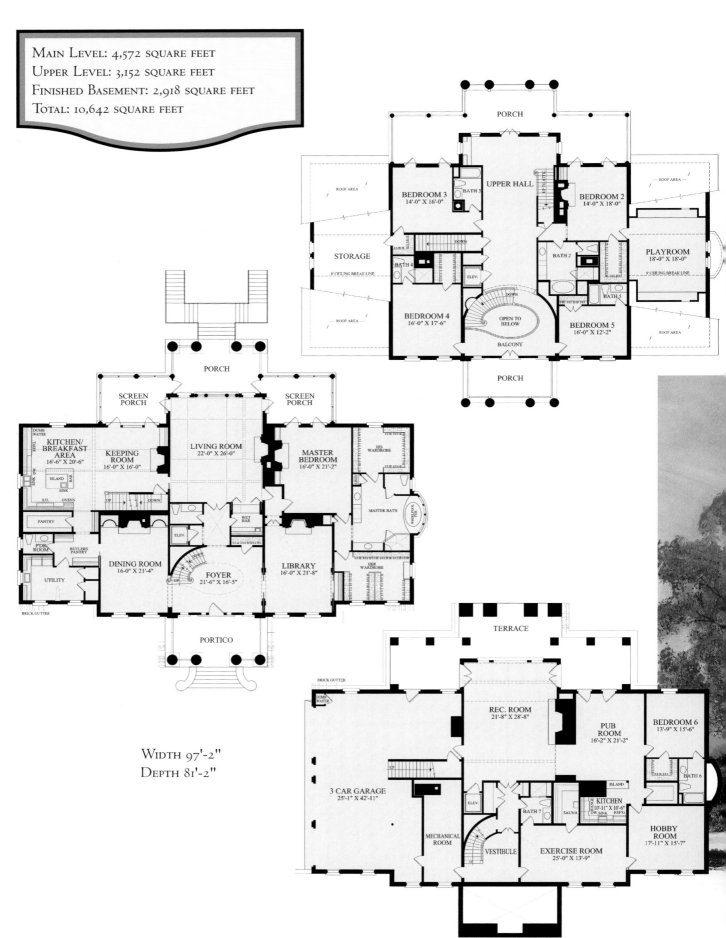

Main Level: 4,572 square feet
Upper Level: 3,152 square feet
Finished Basement: 2,918 square feet
Total: 10,642 square feet

PORCH

BEDROOM 3
14'-0" X 16'-0"

BATH 3

UPPER HALL

BEDROOM 2
14'-0" X 18'-0"

ROOF AREA

ROOF AREA

STORAGE

8' CEILING BREAK LINE

BATH 4

ELEV.

BATH 2

PLAYROOM
18'-0" X 18'-0"

8' CEILING BREAK LINE

ROOF AREA

BEDROOM 4
16'-0" X 17'-6"

DOWN

OPEN TO
BELOW

BALCONY

BEDROOM 5
16'-0" X 12'-2"

BATH 5

ROOF AREA

PORCH

PORCH

SCREEN
PORCH

SCREEN
PORCH

DUMB
WAITER

REFG.

KITCHEN/
BREAKFAST
AREA
16'-6" X 20'-6"

SINK DW

ISLAND BAR

SINK

S.U. OVENS

PANTRY

P'DR.
ROOM

BUTLERS
PANTRY

UTILITY

BRICK GUTTER

KEEPING
ROOM
16'-0" X 16'-0"

UP

DOWN

ELEV.

LIVING ROOM
22'-0" X 26'-0"

WET
BAR

DINING ROOM
16'-0" X 21'-4"

FOYER
21'-6" X 16'-5"

UP

MASTER
BEDROOM
16'-0" X 21'-2"

HIS
WARDROBE

MASTER BATH

WHIRLPOOL
TUB

LIBRARY
16'-0" X 21'-8"

HER
WARDROBE

PORTICO

WIDTH 97'-2"
DEPTH 81'-2"

TERRACE

BRICK GUTTER

DUMB
WAITER

REC. ROOM
21'-8" X 28'-8"

PUB
ROOM
16'-2" X 21'-2"

BEDROOM 6
13'-9" X 15'-6"

3 CAR GARAGE
25'-1" X 42'-11"

UP

ELEV.

ISLAND

BATH 7

RANGE KITCHEN
10'-11" X 10'-6"
DW SINK REFG.

SAUNA

BATH 6

MECHANICAL
ROOM

VESTIBULE

EXERCISE ROOM
25'-0" X 13'-9"

HOBBY
ROOM
17'-11" X 15'-7"

Sycamores

"Of course I know you two. You're the girls who live at Sycamores." Nodding our heads in the affirmative, we smiled and waited patiently astride our mounts while she went inside to prepare us a snack. Unbeknownst to us, she called our aunt. In short order there was a squeal of tires, a churning of dust and a roar of a car charging up the drive. We had, earlier that morning, impulsively decided to travel a bit, so we bridled the mules and rode bareback down a country road until we became hungry. Our aunt saw to it that our traveling days were over for the rest of that summer and, if you've ever ridden a mule, then you know our sitting days were over for a good while too.

Richmond Hill

*H*igh atop a hill overlooking the James River sits a grand and glorious plantation house. The spectacular views of stars, moon and twinkling lights from the town below entrance visitors from far and near as they gather each evening to recount the adventures of their day and delight in the glories of the night.

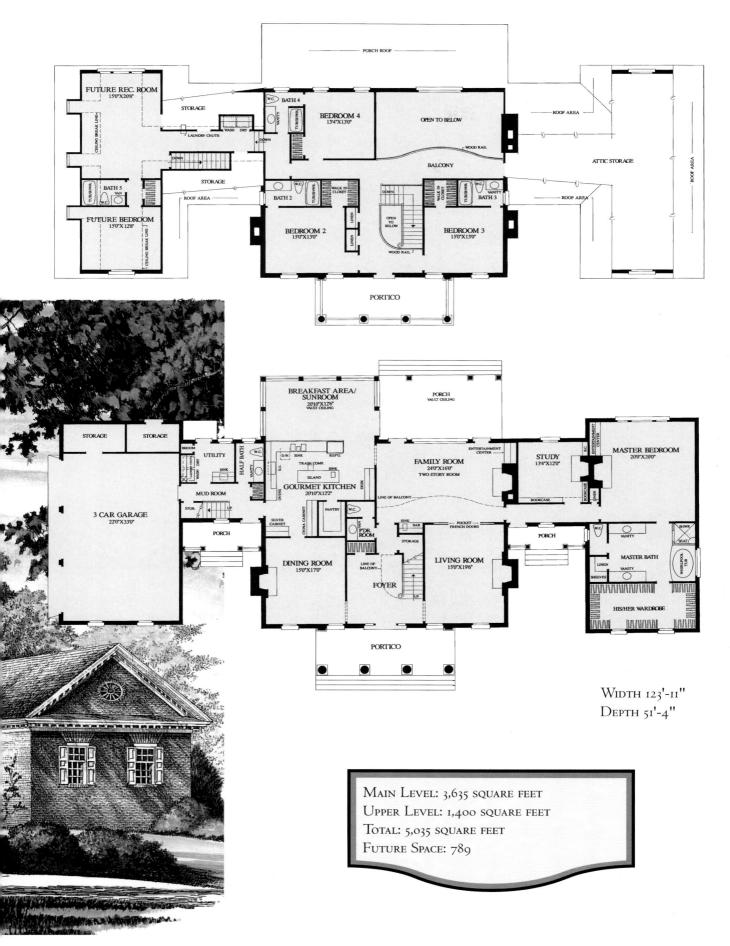

Upper Level

FUTURE REC. ROOM
15'0"X20'8"

STORAGE

BATH 4
W.C.
VANITY
TUB/SHWR.

BEDROOM 4
13'4"X13'0"

OPEN TO BELOW

ROOF AREA

CEILING BREAK LINE

WASH DRY

LAUNDRY CHUTE

DOWN

WOOD RAIL

ATTIC STORAGE

ROOF AREA

DOWN

STORAGE

BALCONY

BATH 5
TUB/SHWR.
W.C.
VAN

STORAGE

ROOF AREA

BATH 2
W.C.
TUB/SHWR.
VANITY

WALK IN CLOSET

LINEN

LINEN

DOWN

OPEN TO BELOW

WALK IN CLOSET

TUB/SHWR.
W.C.
VANITY
BATH 3

ROOF AREA

FUTURE BEDROOM
15'0"X12'8"

BEDROOM 2
15'0"X13'0"

WOOD RAIL

BEDROOM 3
15'0"X13'0"

CEILING BREAK LINE

PORTICO

PORCH ROOF

Main Level

STORAGE

STORAGE

3 CAR GARAGE
22'0"X33'0"

BROOM

UTILITY

HALF BATH

W.C.

WASH DRY

SINK

BREAKFAST AREA/
SUNROOM
20'10"X12'6"
VAULT CEILING

D.W. SINK

REFG.

TRASH COMP.

ISLAND

SINK

GOURMET KITCHEN
20'10"X12'2"

DESK

PANTRY

W.C.

ENTERTAINMENT CENTER

FAMILY ROOM
24'0"X16'0"
TWO STORY ROOM

ENTERTAINMENT CENTER

STUDY
13'4"X12'0"

B.C.

BOOKCASE

LINEN

MASTER BEDROOM
20'0"X20'0"

LINE OF BALCONY

BOOKCASE

MUD ROOM

STOR.

UP

SILVER CABINET

CHINA CABINET

PDR. ROOM

VAN.

SINK

BAR

STORAGE

POCKET FRENCH DOORS

W.C.

VANITY

PORCH

PORCH

SHWR.

SEAT

DINING ROOM
15'0"X17'0"

LINE OF BALCONY

FOYER

UP

LIVING ROOM
15'0"X19'6"

PORCH

LINEN

SHELVES

VANITY

MASTER BATH

WHIRLPOOL TUB

HIS/HER WARDROBE

PORTICO

WIDTH 123'-11"
DEPTH 51'-4"

MAIN LEVEL: 3,635 SQUARE FEET
UPPER LEVEL: 1,400 SQUARE FEET
TOTAL: 5,035 SQUARE FEET
FUTURE SPACE: 789

Savannah

Can you hear it? It's the soft rustle of crinolines beneath the fashionable watered-silk gowns of the county's young Southern belles. As they sashay through the grand entrance of the Savannah their thoughts turn to the forthcoming festivities. Backyard barbecues held at this stately home are often weekend events that hold a wealth of possibilities. Peeking past the rim of her parasol, she smiles a coy smile—the gentleman with the rogue's reputation from Charleston is making his way toward her. The genteel, Southern way of life is alive at the Savannah.

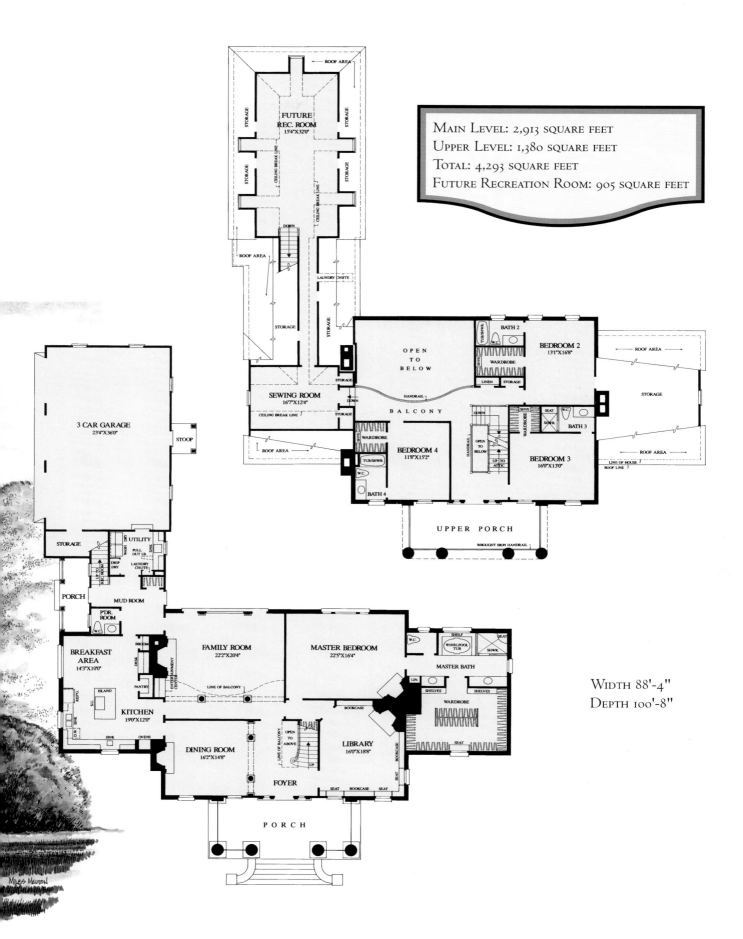

FUTURE
REC. ROOM
15'4"X32'0"

ROOF AREA

STORAGE

STORAGE

STORAGE

STORAGE

CEILING BREAK LINE

CEILING BREAK LINE

DOWN

ROOF AREA

STORAGE

LAUNDRY CHUTE

STORAGE

STORAGE

Main Level: 2,913 square feet
Upper Level: 1,380 square feet
Total: 4,293 square feet
Future Recreation Room: 905 square feet

BATH 2
TUB/SHWR
W.C.
SHVS
WARDROBE
LINEN   STORAGE

BEDROOM 2
13'1"X16'8"

ROOF AREA

STORAGE

OPEN
TO
BELOW

HANDRAIL

BALCONY

SHVS
SEAT
W.C.
WARDROBE
SHWR
BATH 3

SEWING ROOM
16'7"X12'4"

DOWN

STORAGE

CEILING BREAK LINE

STORAGE

ROOF AREA

SHVS
WARDROBE

BEDROOM 4
11'8"X15'2"

DOWN

HANDRAIL

OPEN TO BELOW

UP TO ATTIC

BEDROOM 3
16'0"X13'0"

ROOF AREA

LINE OF HOUSE
ROOF LINE

3 CAR GARAGE
23'4"X36'0"

STOOP

TUB/SHWR
W.C.
BATH 4

UPPER PORCH

WROUGHT IRON HANDRAIL

STORAGE

UP TO REC ROOM
WASH DRY UTILITY
DRIP DRY
PULL OUT LB.
SINK
LAUNDRY CHUTE

PORCH

MUD ROOM

P'DR.
ROOM
W.C.

BREAKFAST
AREA
14'3"X10'0"

BROOM
DESK
PANTRY
ENTERTAINMENT CENTER

FAMILY ROOM
22'2"X20'4"

LINE OF BALCONY

MASTER BEDROOM
22'5"X16'4"

W.C.

SHELF
WHIRLPOOL
TUB
SEAT
SHWR

MASTER BATH

LIN.
SHELVES
SHELVES

WARDROBE

SEAT

ISLAND

KITCHEN
19'0"X12'0"

REF'G.

SINK
D.W.
SINK   OVENS

DINING ROOM
16'2"X14'8"

FOYER

OPEN
TO
ABOVE
LINE OF BALCONY
UP

LIBRARY
16'0"X18'8"

BOOKCASE

SEAT   BOOKCASE   SEAT

BOOKCASE

PORCH

Width 88'-4"
Depth 100'-8"

MILES NELSON

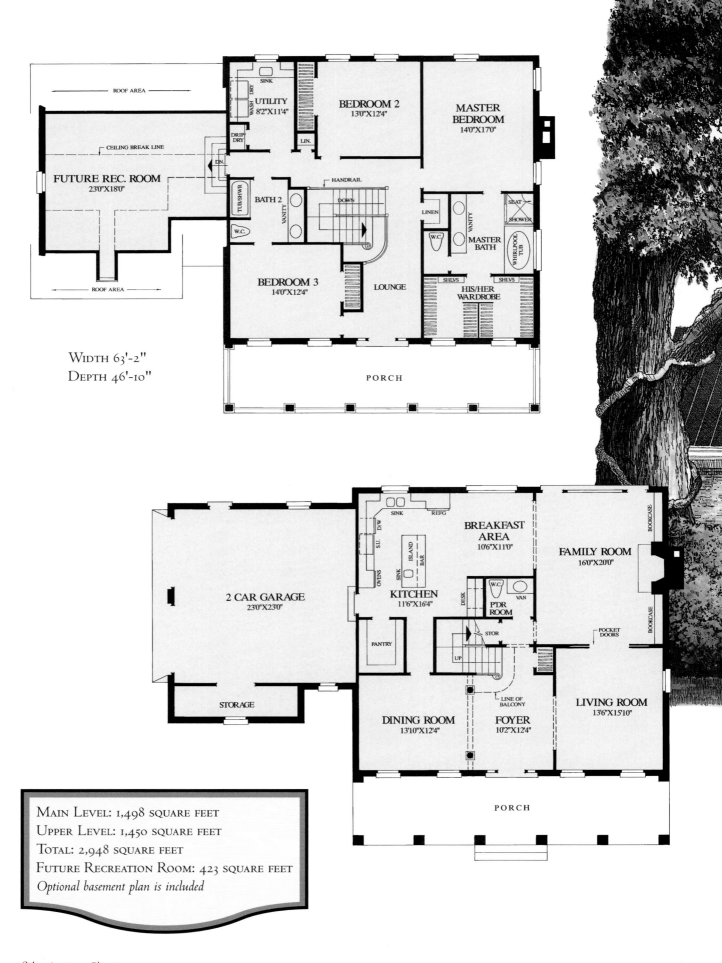

ROOF AREA

CEILING BREAK LINE

FUTURE REC. ROOM
23'0"X18'0"

ROOF AREA

WASH DRY
SINK

UTILITY
8'2"X11'4"

DRIP DRY

DN.

LIN.

BEDROOM 2
13'0"X12'4"

MASTER BEDROOM
14'0"X170"

HANDRAIL

TUB/SHWR

BATH 2

VANITY

W.C.

DOWN

LINEN

VANITY

SEAT
SHOWER

W.C.

MASTER BATH

WHIRLPOOL TUB

BEDROOM 3
14'0"X12'4"

LOUNGE

SHLVS

HIS/HER WARDROBE

SHLVS

WIDTH 63'-2"
DEPTH 46'-10"

PORCH

SINK   REFG

BREAKFAST AREA
10'6"X11'0"

FAMILY ROOM
16'0"X20'0"

BOOKCASE

D/W

S.U.

ISLAND BAR

OVENS   SINK

KITCHEN
11'6"X16'4"

DESK

W.C.

VAN

P'DR ROOM

BOOKCASE

2 CAR GARAGE
23'0"X23'0"

PANTRY

UP   STOR

POCKET DOORS

LINE OF BALCONY

LIVING ROOM
13'6"X15'10"

STORAGE

DINING ROOM
13'10"X12'4"

FOYER
10'2"X12'4"

PORCH

MAIN LEVEL: 1,498 SQUARE FEET
UPPER LEVEL: 1,450 SQUARE FEET
TOTAL: 2,948 SQUARE FEET
FUTURE RECREATION ROOM: 423 SQUARE FEET
Optional basement plan is included

Beaumont

DESIGN HPT770034

Wisteria vines wind 'round the huge trunk of the old live oak. Butterflies flit amid the buttercups, birds chirp to greet the morn and all awaken to the sweet smell of honeysuckle. The Beaumont stirs with these awakenings and busies itself preparing for another day.

The Josiah Smith House

DESIGN HPT770035

Would you believe that in the early days of building townhouses in Charleston, South Carolina, brick was more economical (to say nothing of being more fireproof) than wood? As the story goes, when The Josiah Smith House was constructed, the owner resisted all the enticing wiles of his wife and did the embarassing, socially incorrect thing by building his home of brick. As usual, she had the last say. Upon his untimely death, his fortune was put to good use framing over the entire structure with costly lumber. Whoever said "women always get their way" certainly knew what they were talking about. There must be a moral to this story—somewhere.

ROOF AREA

OPEN TO
SUN ROOM
BELOW

UTILITY

WASH
DRY

STORAGE

SINK

FUT. REC. ROOM
20'0"X20'0"

WOOD RAIL

BALCONY

DOWN

WOOD RAIL

SEAT

SHWR

WHIRLPOOL
TUB

WARDROBE

LINEN

BEDROOM 2
14'0"X12'6"

CEILING BREAK LINE

ROOF AREA

LINE OF HOUSE

MASTER BATH

LINEN

BIDET

W.C.

PIAZZA
10'8"X34'0"

LINEN

LINEN

MASTER BEDROOM
14'0"X20'0"

DOWN

OPEN TO
FOYER BELOW

WOOD RAIL

BATH 2

W.C.

WIDTH 84'-8"
DEPTH 65'-0"

BEDROOM 3
14'0"X12'0"

SHWR

DOWN

ROOF AREA

CIRCLE HEAD WINDOWS

TERRACE

SUNROOM
12'6"X19'0"
VALTED CEILING

KITCHEN
12'6"X19'0"

REF'G.

SINK

SINK

D.W.

STORAGE

CARRIAGE HOUSE
GARAGE
24'0"X24'0"

BREAKFAST
BAR

OVENS

SLU

UP TO FUT.
REC. ROOM

LINE OF BALCONY

DESK

PANTRY

DOWN

FAMILY ROOM
26'4"X15'4"

ENTERTAINMENT CENTER
BOOKCASE

DINING ROOM
14'0"X16'0"

PORCH

PIAZZA
10'8"X34'0"

DORIC COLUMNS

TUB/SHWR

BATH 3

STORAGE

DOWN TO
CELLAR

LIVING ROOM
14'0"X20'0"

UP

LIBRARY/
BEDROOM 4
14'0"X12'0"

UP

TWO STORY
FOYER

PORTICO

MAIN LEVEL: 2,064 SQUARE FEET
UPPER LEVEL: 1,521 SQUARE FEET
TOTAL: 3,585 SQUARE FEET
FUTURE RECREATION ROOM: 427 SQUARE FEET

The Pillow House

This wonderful old estate home has been the cornerstone of social, political and family power for generations. All aspects of these functions were built on a foundation (like the house) as solid as our constitution and, within these walls, power for good and just causes still resonates. In the small community outside its boundaries, tales are told and retold about the generations who lived, loved and toiled at The Pillow House in the rolling hills of Tennessee.

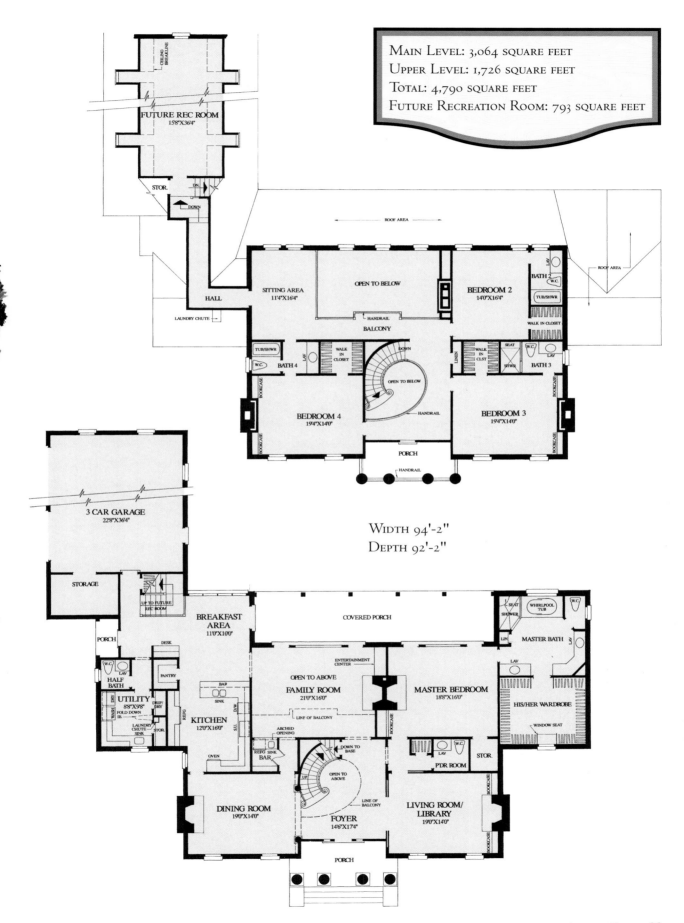

FUTURE REC ROOM
15'8"X36'4"

STOR.

DN.

DOWN

CEILING BREAKLINE

MAIN LEVEL: 3,064 SQUARE FEET
UPPER LEVEL: 1,726 SQUARE FEET
TOTAL: 4,790 SQUARE FEET
FUTURE RECREATION ROOM: 793 SQUARE FEET

ROOF AREA

ROOF AREA

SITTING AREA
11'4"X16'4"

OPEN TO BELOW

BEDROOM 2
14'0"X16'4"

BATH 2
W.C.
LAV

HALL

TUB/SHWR

WALK IN CLOSET

LAUNDRY CHUTE

HANDRAIL

BALCONY

TUB/SHWR
W.C.
BATH 4
LAV

WALK IN CLOSET

DOWN

OPEN TO BELOW

BOOKCASE

BEDROOM 4
19'4"X14'0"

HANDRAIL

OPEN TO BELOW

PORCH

HANDRAIL

LINEN

WALK IN CLST

SEAT

SHWR

W.C.
LAV
BATH 3

BOOKCASE

BEDROOM 3
19'4"X14'0"

BOOKCASE

3 CAR GARAGE
22'8"X36'4"

WIDTH 94'-2"

DEPTH 92'-2"

STORAGE

UP TO FUTURE REC ROOM

BREAKFAST AREA
11'0"X10'0"

COVERED PORCH

SEAT
SHOWER

WHIRLPOOL TUB

W.C.

PORCH

W.C.
LAV
HALF BATH

DESK

PANTRY

ENTERTAINMENT CENTER

LIN

MASTER BATH

LAV

UTILITY
8'8"X9'8"

WASH
DRY

FOLD DOWN
IB.

DRIP/DRY

BAR

SINK

D/W

OPEN TO ABOVE

FAMILY ROOM
21'0"X16'0"

LAV

HIS/HER WARDROBE

MASTER BEDROOM
18'8"X16'0"

REFG.

LINE OF BALCONY

LAUNDRY CHUTE
SINK

STOR.

KITCHEN
12'0"X16'0"

DN/UP

ARCHED OPENING

REFG. SINK
BAR

OVEN

UP

DOWN TO BASE

OPEN TO ABOVE

BOOKCASE

WINDOW SEAT

LAV
W.C.

STOR.

PDR ROOM

BOOKCASE

DINING ROOM
19'0"X14'0"

FOYER
14'6"X17'4"

LINE OF BALCONY

LIVING ROOM/
LIBRARY
19'0"X14'0"

PORCH

Neighborhood Homes

Peaceful, tree-lined streetscapes provide a perfect setting for gracious homes that are reminiscent of simpler times. Splendid mixes of styles inspired by yesterday recall our best childhood memories and offer more than just a glimpse of all of life's possibilities.

Neighborhood Homes is a diverse portfolio of truly high-quality designs that will fit comfortably within a classic town or village—even in the wide-open spaces. Country farmhouses, Victorian and Southern styles with finely crafted facades and breezy front porches invite enjoyment of the outdoors and foster a sense of community.

The Chevy Chase (page 114) is an example of this graceful, timeless architecture. Charming yet not a bit shy, this character-rich design lends an aura of hospitality to any neighborhood—whether it's a country meadow or a city street. An enchanting casual space boasts a breathtaking view of the back property.

Rugged stone and rustic shingles play well against a chic stucco gable with Blackberry Lane (page 122), creating wonderful curb appeal. Perfect proportions conceal a deeply comfortable interior that features open formal rooms and a casual living area enhanced by a rear deck.

Here's a portfolio of livable homes that boast spacious outdoor retreats, street-friendly facades and plenty of places to both relax and entertain—houses that pay homage to the past yet easily step into the future.

W.C.

MASTER BATH

WHIRLPOOL TUB

SHOWER

LINEN

WARDROBE

STORAGE

FOLD DK LR

UTILITY

DRY WASH SINK

2-CAR GARAGE
23'8"X22'0"

MASTER BEDROOM
13'0"X17'0"

DECK

DOWN

SINK   D.W.   REFG.

ISLAND   SINK

KITCHEN
14'0"X14'6"

OVENS

BROOM

BREAKFAST AREA
10'10"X14'6"

ENTERTAINMENT CENTER

FAMILY ROOM
16'8"X19'0"
TRAY CEILING

DESK

LINEN

BEDROOM 2
14'10"X12'0"

BATH 3

W.C.

WARDROBE

TUB/SHWR.

WARDROBE

DINING ROOM
12'6"X13'0"

PANTRY

LIVING ROOM
12'0"X16'2"

FOYER

BEDROOM 3
12'0"X11'8"

BATH 2

TUB/SHWR.

W.C.

PORCH

WIDTH 82'-6"
DEPTH 52'-8"

SQUARE FOOTAGE: 2,394

Somerset

DESIGN HPT770037

As a child she made up stories. Summers were spent gazing at the sky, creating cloud pictures and stories to go with them. The wind presented an everchanging canvas, transforming the billowing clouds from one image to another. The stories penned in her child-scrawl were packed away, but as a young woman, she never lost her dream of becoming an author. Today, she lingers over a cup of tea in the breakfast room, her mind developing the plot for her latest novel. Dreams do come true in the Somerset—her home.

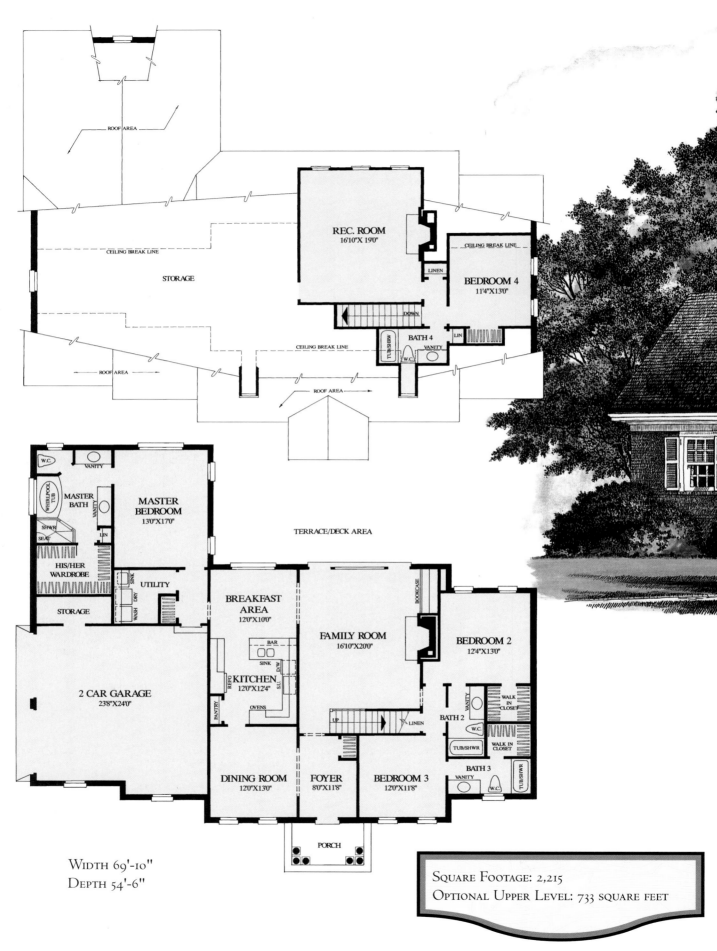

ROOF AREA

CEILING BREAK LINE

STORAGE

REC. ROOM
16'10"X 19'0"

CEILING BREAK LINE

LINEN

BEDROOM 4
11'4"X13'0"

DOWN

ROOF AREA

CEILING BREAK LINE

TUB/SHWR

BATH 4

VANITY

W.C.

LIN

ROOF AREA

W.C.

VANITY

WHIRLPOOL TUB

MASTER BATH

VANITY

MASTER BEDROOM
13'0"X17'0"

TERRACE/DECK AREA

SHWR

SEAT

LIN

HIS/HER WARDROBE

STORAGE

SINK

UTILITY

WASH DRY

BREAKFAST AREA
12'0"X10'0"

BAR

SINK D/W

KITCHEN
12'0"X12'4"

OVENS

FAMILY ROOM
16'10"X20'0"

BOOKCASE

BEDROOM 2
12'4"X13'0"

VANITY

WALK IN CLOSET

BATH 2

W.C.

2 CAR GARAGE
23'8"X24'0"

PANTRY

REFG

SU

UP

LINEN

TUB/SHWR

WALK IN CLOSET

DINING ROOM
12'0"X13'0"

FOYER
8'0"X11'8"

BEDROOM 3
12'0"X11'8"

VANITY

BATH 3

W.C.

TUB/SHWR

PORCH

Width 69'-10"

Depth 54'-6"

Square Footage: 2,215
Optional Upper Level: 733 square feet

Valdosta

Design HPT770038

Miss Margaret has lived here all her life–along with her brothers, sisters, cousins and grandparents. The Valdosta has been their home forever. It is with many fond memories that she bids a final farewell to the Valdosta and wishes happiness and joy for the new family ready to begin their sojourn within.

Back Bay Cottage

DESIGN HPT770039

Near Edisto Island, South Carolina, small backwater communities filled with low country cottages are dotted here, there and everywhere. Some have manicured lawns. Some have finely raked patterns in the bare, sandy soil. Some are freshly painted. Some are so weathered that they appear never to have known the art of cosmetic covering. However, all are abundantly filled with the colors and fragrances of beautiful flowers. There is no doubt that these homes are old with many a story to tell and they are clearly so well loved and cared for (whatever the circumstances of their owners) that although these cottages bespeak country, it is with quiet and genteel sophistication.

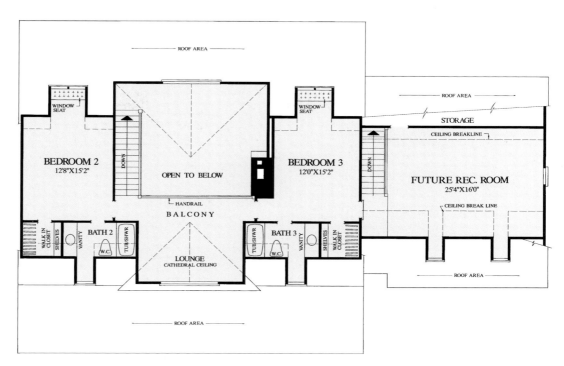

Upper Level

ROOF AREA

WINDOW SEAT

BEDROOM 2
12'8"X15'2"

OPEN TO BELOW

DOWN

ROOF AREA

STORAGE

CEILING BREAKLINE

DOWN

FUTURE REC. ROOM
25'4"X16'0"

CEILING BREAK LINE

WINDOW SEAT

BEDROOM 3
12'0"X15'2"

HANDRAIL

BALCONY

WALK IN CLOSET

SHELVES

VANITY

BATH 2

W.C.

TUB/SHWR

TUB/SHWR

W.C.

BATH 3

VANITY

SHELVES

WALK IN CLOSET

LOUNGE
CATHEDRAL CEILING

ROOF AREA

ROOF AREA

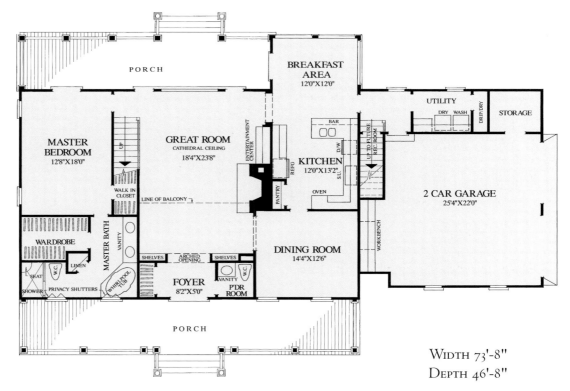

PORCH

BREAKFAST AREA
12'0"X12'0"

UTILITY

DRY

WASH

DRIP/DRY

STORAGE

MASTER BEDROOM
12'8"X18'0"

UP

WALK IN CLOSET

LINE OF BALCONY

GREAT ROOM
CATHEDRAL CEILING
18'4"X23'8"

ENTERTAINMENT CENTER

BAR

D/W

REFG

S.U.

KITCHEN
12'0"X13'2"

PANTRY

OVEN

UP TO FUTURE REC. ROOM

2 CAR GARAGE
25'4"X22'0"

WORKBENCH

WARDROBE

MASTER BATH

VANITY

W.C.

LINEN

SEAT

SHOWER

PRIVACY SHUTTERS

WHIRLPOOL TUB

SHELVES

ARCHED OPENING

SHELVES

FOYER
8'2"X5'0"

VANITY

P'DR ROOM

W.C.

DINING ROOM
14'4"X12'6"

PORCH

WIDTH 73'-8"
DEPTH 46'-8"

MAIN LEVEL: 1,713 SQUARE FEET
UPPER LEVEL: 885 SQUARE FEET
TOTAL: 2,598 SQUARE FEET
FUTURE RECREATION ROOM: 433 SQUARE FEET
Optional basement plan is included

The Airlie

In a tranquil setting down by the waterway is The Airlie. Weddings in the chapel, festivities on the grounds and strolls among the gardens are memories to be treasured by more than just a few. Huge live oaks, masses of azaleas in an amazing array of color and open patches of sun-drenched grassy areas surround this lovely home.

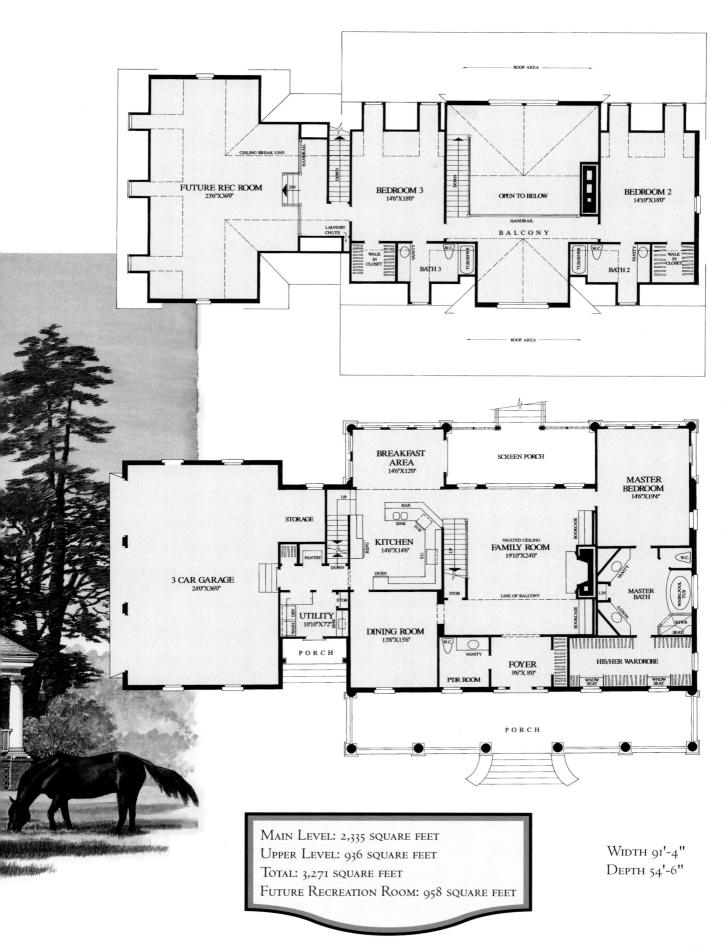

ROOF AREA

FUTURE REC ROOM
23'6"X36'0"

CEILING BREAK LINE

HANDRAIL

DOWN

DN

LAUNDRY CHUTE

BEDROOM 3
14'6"X18'0"

DOWN

OPEN TO BELOW

BEDROOM 2
14'10"X18'0"

HANDRAIL

B A L C O N Y

WALK IN CLOSET

VANITY

BATH 3

W.C.

TUB/SHWR

TUB/SHWR

W.C.

BATH 2

VANITY

WALK IN CLOSET

ROOF AREA

BREAKFAST AREA
14'6"X12'0"

SCREEN PORCH

MASTER BEDROOM
14'6"X19'4"

STORAGE

UP

3 CAR GARAGE
24'0"X36'0"

PANTRY

DOWN

REFG

BAR

SINK

D/W

KITCHEN
14'6"X14'6"

STS.

OVEN

UP

STOR

VAULTED CEILING
FAMILY ROOM
19'10"X24'0"

BOOKCASE

LINE OF BALCONY

BOOKCASE

VANITY

LIN.

MASTER BATH

W.C.

WHIRLPOOL TUB

LIN.

SHWR SEAT

STOR

WASH DRY

SINK

UTILITY
10'10"X7'2"

PORCH

DINING ROOM
13'8"X15'6"

PDR ROOM

W.C.

VANITY

FOYER
9'6"X 8'0"

HIS/HER WARDROBE

WNDW SEAT

WNDW SEAT

P O R C H

MAIN LEVEL: 2,335 SQUARE FEET
UPPER LEVEL: 936 SQUARE FEET
TOTAL: 3,271 SQUARE FEET
FUTURE RECREATION ROOM: 958 SQUARE FEET

WIDTH 91'-4"
DEPTH 54'-6"

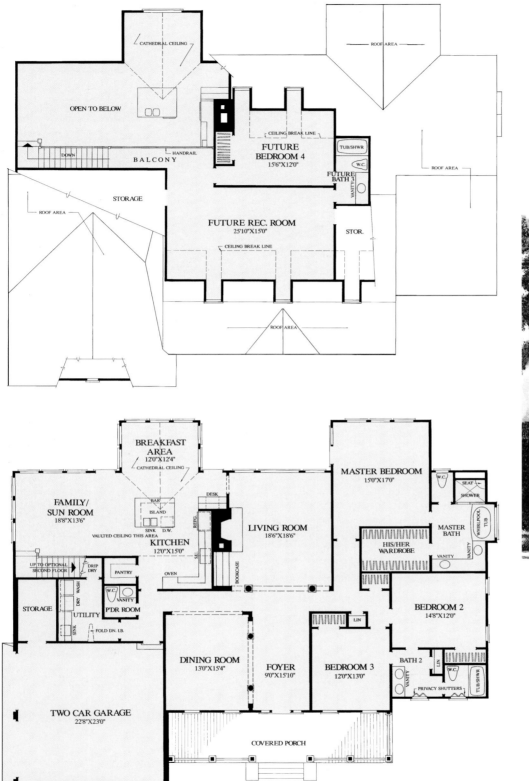

CATHEDRAL CEILING

OPEN TO BELOW

ROOF AREA

CEILING BREAK LINE

FUTURE BEDROOM 4
15'6"X12'0"

TUB/SHWR

W.C.

FUTURE BATH 3

VANITY

ROOF AREA

HANDRAIL

DOWN

BALCONY

STORAGE

ROOF AREA

FUTURE REC. ROOM
25'10"X15'0"

CEILING BREAK LINE

STOR.

ROOF AREA

MILES MASTON

BREAKFAST AREA
12'0"X12'4"
CATHEDRAL CEILING

MASTER BEDROOM
15'0"X17'0"

W.C.

SEAT
SHOWER

DESK

FAMILY/ SUN ROOM
18'8"X13'6"

BAR
ISLAND
SINK   D.W.
VAULTED CEILING THIS AREA

REFG.

LIVING ROOM
18'6"X18'6"

WHIRLPOOL
TUB

MASTER BATH

KITCHEN
12'0"X15'0"

VANITY

HIS/HER WARDROBE

UP TO OPTIONAL SECOND FLOOR

DRIP DRY

PANTRY

OVEN

BOOKCASE

VANITY

DRY WASH

W.C.
VANITY

P'DR ROOM

LIN

BEDROOM 2
14'8"X12'0"

STORAGE

UTILITY

SINK

FOLD DN. I.B.

DINING ROOM
13'0"X15'4"

FOYER
9'0"X15'10"

BEDROOM 3
12'0"X13'0"

BATH 2

LIN

W.C.

VANITY

TUB/SHWR

TWO CAR GARAGE
22'8"X23'0"

PRIVACY SHUTTERS

COVERED PORCH

WIDTH 75'-6"

DEPTH 60'-2"

TOTAL: 2,777 SQUARE FEET
FUTURE RECREATION ROOM: 818 SQUARE FEET
Optional basement plan is included

Bowling Green

Can you not just see it—sloping green lawns all the way to the river, sprawling wildflower gardens, rose trellises and white fences galore? Bowling Green, a place to nestle into, a place called home. Children running, playing, calling cheerfully to all who will listen; grown-ups strolling about visiting with one another until—at last, the newlyweds appear for all to toast with good wishes and loving entreaties for their frequent returns to Bowling Green.

FUTURE REC. ROOM
15'0"X22'0"

CEILING BREAK LINE

CEILING BREAK LINE

LAUNDRY CHUTE

DOWN

STORAGE

ROOF AREA

ROOF AREA

DOWN

STORAGE

BATH 3

SHOWER

W.C.

LINEN

WARDROBE

BEDROOM 2
15'5"X13'1"

RAIL

OPEN
TO
BELOW

DOWN

BEDROOM 3
16'7"X13'1"

CEILING BREAK LINE

ROOF AREA

BEDROOM 4
13'2"X12'9"

CEILING BREAK LINE

STOR.

TUB/SHWR.

BATH 2

W.C.

LINEN

WARDROBE

ROOF AREA

WIDTH 63'-4"
DEPTH 75'-5"

MAIN LEVEL: 2,193 SQUARE FEET
UPPER LEVEL: 1,179 SQUARE FEET
TOTAL: 3,372 SQUARE FEET
FUTURE RECREATION ROOM: 558 SQUARE FEET

2 - CAR GARAGE
22'0"X22'0"

UTILITY
11'0"X7'8"

SINK

DRY WASH FREEZ

STORAGE

UP

W.C.

PORCH

MUD ROOM

1/2 BATH

PORCH

BREAKFAST
AREA
10'8"X11'0"

PANTRY

ENT CENTER

DESK

FAMILY ROOM
21'1"X14'6"

HIS WARDROBE

W.C.

PDR. ROOM

LINEN

W.C.

WHIRLPOOL TUB

SHWR.

MASTER BATH

HER WARDROBE

MASTER BEDROOM
16'2"X16'0"

OVENS

SINK

ISLAND

S.U.

KITCHEN
14'8"X10'10"

D.W.

SINK

REFG.

DINING ROOM
15'0"X12'6"

DOWN

FOYER
TWO STORY CEILING

UP

LIVING ROOM/
LIBRARY
16'2"X16'0"

FRONT PORCH

Sunnyside

Fine china and milk-laced tea, melt-in-your-mouth shortbread cookies and cocoa-dusted meringues—for two little girls dressed in their Sunday best—this was the epitome of elegance. Our weekly afternoon tea with Grammie was a ritual never missed. Sunnyside—her Tidewater Virginian farmhouse—is a quietly elegant home with a warm, welcoming porch that invites tea parties and other lasting traditions.

Upper Level Floor Plan

SHLV / WARDROBE

CEILING BREAK LINE

FUTURE REC. ROOM
21'0"X17'0"

CEILING BREAK LINE

DN.

ROOF AREA

CEILING BREAK LINE

BEDROOM 3
12'0"X13'6"

OPEN TO BELOW

DN.

UP.

STORAGE

SHLV

WARDROBE

BEDROOM 2
12'0"X15'0"

CEILING BREAK LINE

BALCONY

HANDRAIL

LOUNGE

STORAGE

TUB/SHWR.

VANITY

BATH 2

W.C.

ROOF AREA

WIDTH 71'-8"
DEPTH 49'-4"

Main Level Floor Plan

SCREEN PORCH

2 CAR GARAGE
21'0"X26'0"

UP

BREAKFAST AREA
12'0"X9'0"

BAR

SINK

D/W

VAULTED CEILING

GREAT ROOM
18'0"X17'4"

S.U.

OVENS

UP

MASTER BEDROOM
12'0"X17'0"

STOR.

KITCHEN
12'0"X12'0"

REFG.

ENTERTAINMENT CENTER

PANTRY

UTILITY

DRY

WASH

P'DR ROOM

W.C.

SHLV.

DINING ROOM
12'4"X11'0"

COLUMNS

FOYER
5'8"X11'0"

WARDROBE

SHWR

W.C.

LIN.

INTERIOR PRIVACY SHUTTERS

VANITY

MASTER BATH

WHIRLPOOL TUB

COVERED PORCH

MAIN LEVEL: 1,370 SQUARE FEET
UPPER LEVEL: 668 SQUARE FEET
TOTAL: 2,038 SQUARE FEET
FUTURE RECREATION ROOM: 421 SQUARE FEET

Shenandoah II

DESIGN HPT770043

The Shenandoah II is a home built for celebrations. They began the day our family moved into this wonderful home and continue through the years. The crisp air of autumn finds a lineup of smiling Jack-O-lanterns, and soon it will be time to wind the stately columns with twinkling lights that brighten the snowy, silent nights. In a blink of an eye, the first signs of spring provide a colorful backdrop for hidden Easter eggs. And on the Fourth of July, the Stars and Stripes will proudly wave. At Shenandoah II each day is a celebration of home and family. May the celebrations live on—here's to a wonderful life!

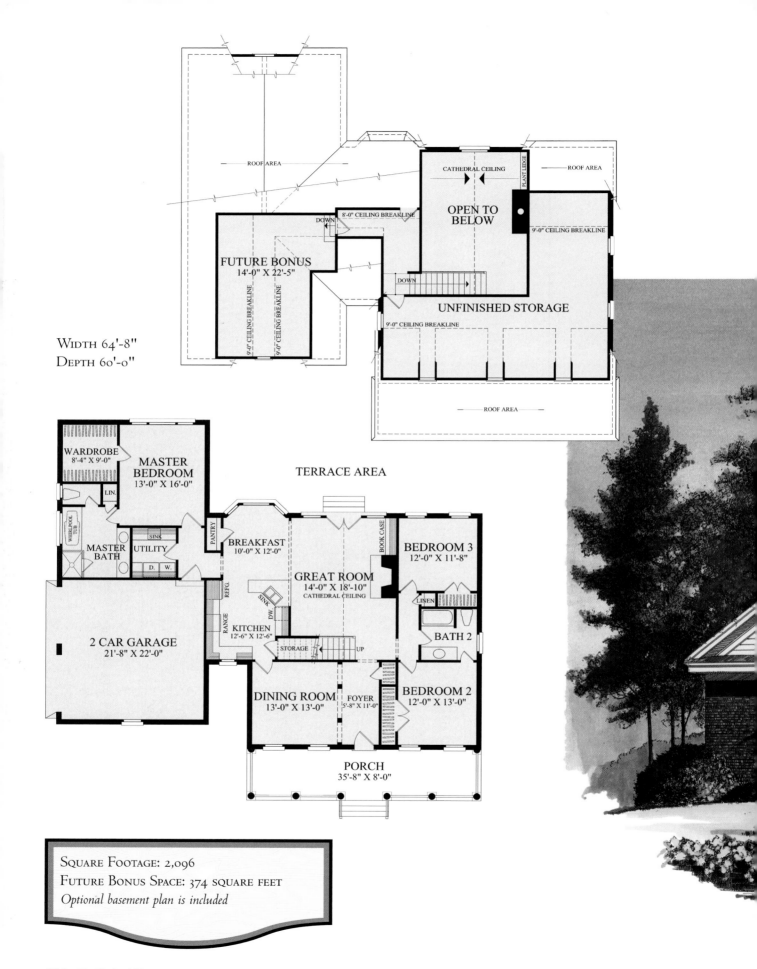

ROOF AREA

CATHEDRAL CEILING — ROOF AREA

PLANT LEDGE

8'-0" CEILING BREAKLINE

DOWN

OPEN TO BELOW

9'-0" CEILING BREAKLINE

FUTURE BONUS
14'-0" X 22'-5"

9'-4" CEILING BREAKLINE

9'-0" CEILING BREAKLINE

DOWN

UNFINISHED STORAGE

9'-0" CEILING BREAKLINE

ROOF AREA

WIDTH 64'-8"
DEPTH 60'-0"

WARDROBE
8'-4" X 9'-0"

MASTER
BEDROOM
13'-0" X 16'-0"

TERRACE AREA

LIN.

WHIRLPOOL TUB

MASTER BATH

SINK

UTILITY

D.   W.

PANTRY

BREAKFAST
10'-0" X 12'-0"

BOOK CASE

BEDROOM 3
12'-0" X 11'-8"

REFG.

GREAT ROOM
14'-0" X 18'-10"
CATHEDRAL CEILING

LINEN

SINK

DW

RANGE

KITCHEN
12'-6" X 12'-6"

STORAGE

UP

BATH 2

2 CAR GARAGE
21'-8" X 22'-0"

DINING ROOM
13'-0" X 13'-0"

FOYER
5'-8" X 11'-0"

BEDROOM 2
12'-0" X 13'-0"

PORCH
35'-8" X 8'-0"

SQUARE FOOTAGE: 2,096
FUTURE BONUS SPACE: 374 SQUARE FEET
Optional basement plan is included

Fairview

They were so glad to find this house. They had searched high and low for their perfect retirement home. Everything worked so perfectly all on one level and, as they quickly realized, had they begun married life here and expanded the upper level as children came along, it would have remained the perfect home for them—both then and now.

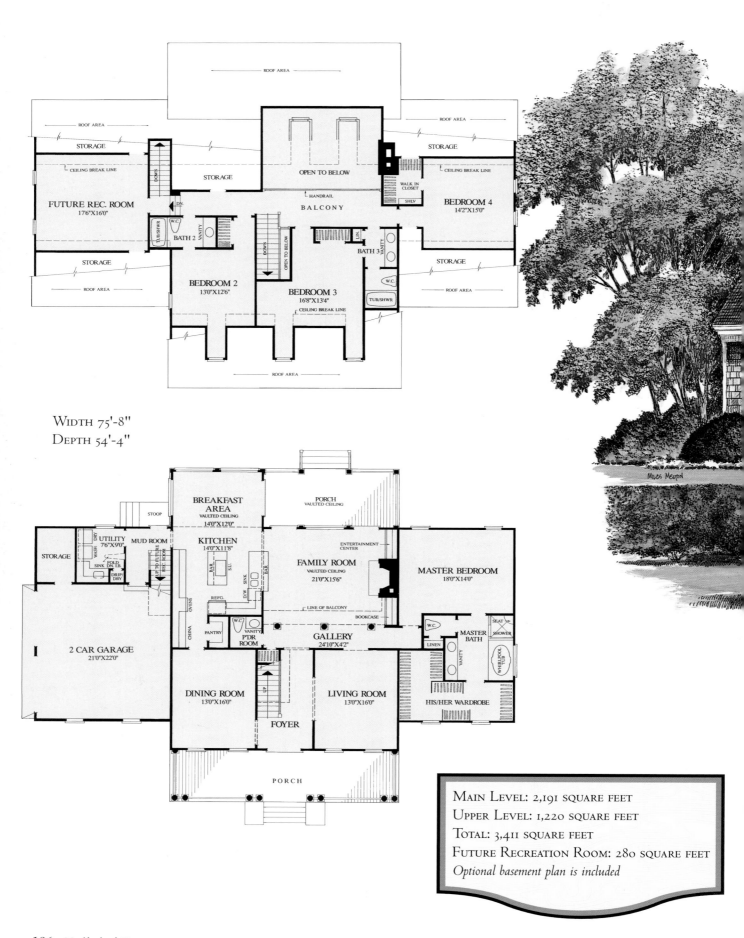

ROOF AREA

ROOF AREA

STORAGE

CEILING BREAK LINE

STORAGE

ROOF AREA

STORAGE

OPEN TO BELOW

FUTURE REC. ROOM
17'6"X16'0"

STORAGE

ROOF AREA

WALK IN
CLOSET

SHLV

ROOF AREA

STORAGE

CEILING BREAK LINE

BEDROOM 4
14'2"X15'0"

STORAGE

ROOF AREA

HANDRAIL

BALCONY

TUB/SHWR

W.C

BATH 2

VANITY

OPEN TO BELOW

DN.

DOWN

LIN

BATH 3

VANITY

W.C

BEDROOM 2
13'0"X12'6"

BEDROOM 3
16'8"X13'4"

TUB/SHWR

CEILING BREAK LINE

ROOF AREA

WIDTH 75'-8"
DEPTH 54'-4"

BREAKFAST
AREA
VAULTED CEILING
14'0"X12'0"

PORCH
VAULTED CEILING

STOOP

UTILITY
7'6"X9'0"

DRY

WASH

MUD ROOM

KITCHEN
14'0"X11'8"

SINK DN. LB.

FOLD

DRIP/
DRY

STORAGE

UP TO FUTURE
REC ROOM

BAR

S.U.

D.W

SINK

BAR

ENTERTAINMENT
CENTER

FAMILY ROOM
VAULTED CEILING
21'0"X15'6"

MASTER BEDROOM
18'0"X14'0"

REFG.

OVENS

CHINA

PANTRY

W.C

VANITY

P'DR
ROOM

LINE OF BALCONY

BOOKCASE

W.C

MASTER
BATH

SEAT

SHOWER

2 CAR GARAGE
21'0"X22'0"

GALLERY
24'10"X4'2"

LINEN

VANITY

WHIRLPOOL
TUB

DINING ROOM
13'0"X16'0"

UP

FOYER

LIVING ROOM
13'0"X16'0"

HIS/HER WARDROBE

PORCH

MAIN LEVEL: 2,191 SQUARE FEET
UPPER LEVEL: 1,220 SQUARE FEET
TOTAL: 3,411 SQUARE FEET
FUTURE RECREATION ROOM: 280 SQUARE FEET
Optional basement plan is included

Biloxi

All along the Gulf Coast highway one cannot help but admire the beautiful homes that seemingly go on forever. Shingled cottages (with columned porches sitting amid flowing lawns with large shade trees) hold out an inviting hand to come and dream your dreams right there—in a large old rocking chair with a cool glass of lemonade and an unending view of the sea. Neighbors are friendly, visitors are welcome, "ma'am" and "sir" are the norm and life is good—as it should be, at home in the Biloxi.

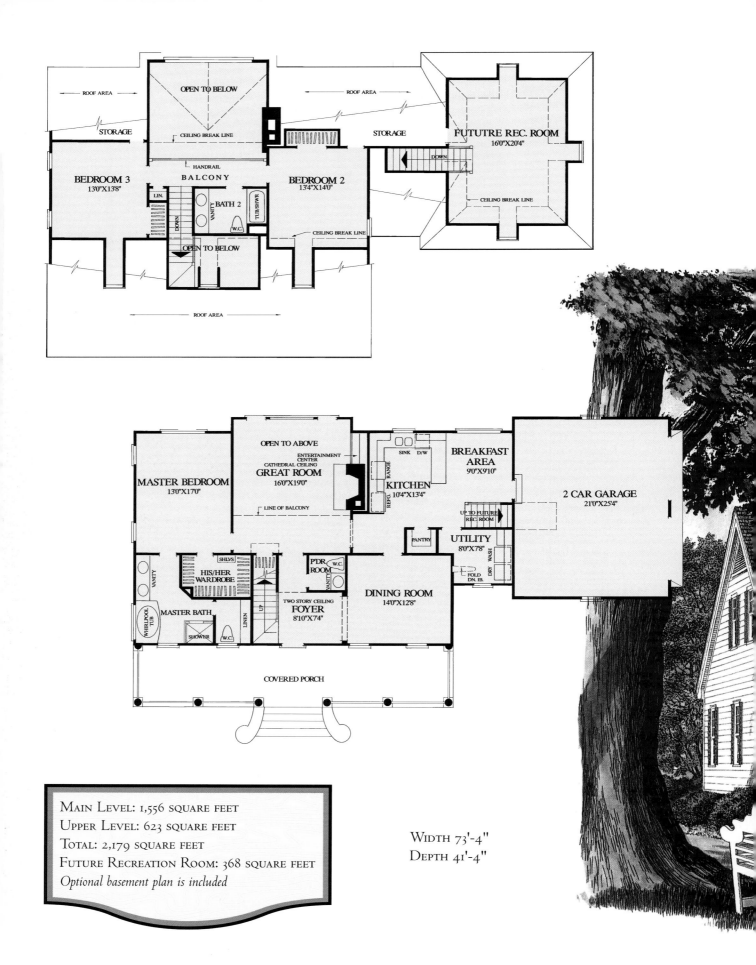

ROOF AREA

STORAGE

BEDROOM 3
13'0"X13'8"

OPEN TO BELOW

CEILING BREAK LINE

HANDRAIL

BALCONY

LIN.

DOWN

VANITY

BATH 2

TUB/SHWR

W.C.

OPEN TO BELOW

ROOF AREA

STORAGE

BEDROOM 2
13'4"X14'0"

CEILING BREAK LINE

DOWN

FUTUTRE REC. ROOM
16'0"X20'4"

CEILING BREAK LINE

MASTER BEDROOM
13'0"X17'0"

OPEN TO ABOVE

CATHEDRAL CEILING
GREAT ROOM
16'0"X19'0"

ENTERTAINMENT
CENTER

LINE OF BALCONY

SINK   D/W

RANGE

KITCHEN
10'4"X13'4"

REFG.

BREAKFAST AREA
9'0"X9'10"

UP TO FUTURE
REC ROOM

2 CAR GARAGE
21'0"X25'4"

VANITY

SHLVS

HIS/HER WARDROBE

UP

MASTER BATH

WHIRLPOOL TUB

SHOWER   W.C.

LINEN

FOYER
8'10"X7'4"

TWO STORY CEILING

P'DR
ROOM

W.C.

VANITY

PANTRY

DINING ROOM
14'0"X12'8"

UTILITY
8'0"X7'8"

DRY   WASH

FOLD
DN. IB.

COVERED PORCH

MAIN LEVEL: 1,556 SQUARE FEET
UPPER LEVEL: 623 SQUARE FEET
TOTAL: 2,179 SQUARE FEET
FUTURE RECREATION ROOM: 368 SQUARE FEET
Optional basement plan is included

WIDTH 73'-4"
DEPTH 41'-4"

Planter's Cottage

DESIGN HPT770046

Planter's cottages were raised, one and a half-story homes that overlooked the rivers and captured their breezes. Though life was hard in those early times, each day began fresh amid the first rays of light and closed with the promise of another peaceful night.

Connecticut Cottage

DESIGN HPT770047

An endearing and enduring American original—our Connecticut Cottage. Straightforward and of spare design, yet warm, cozy and uncomplicated...this home snaps things of the past into sharp focus for the pure pleasure of today. The Connecticut Cottage is a home that fits your very soul.

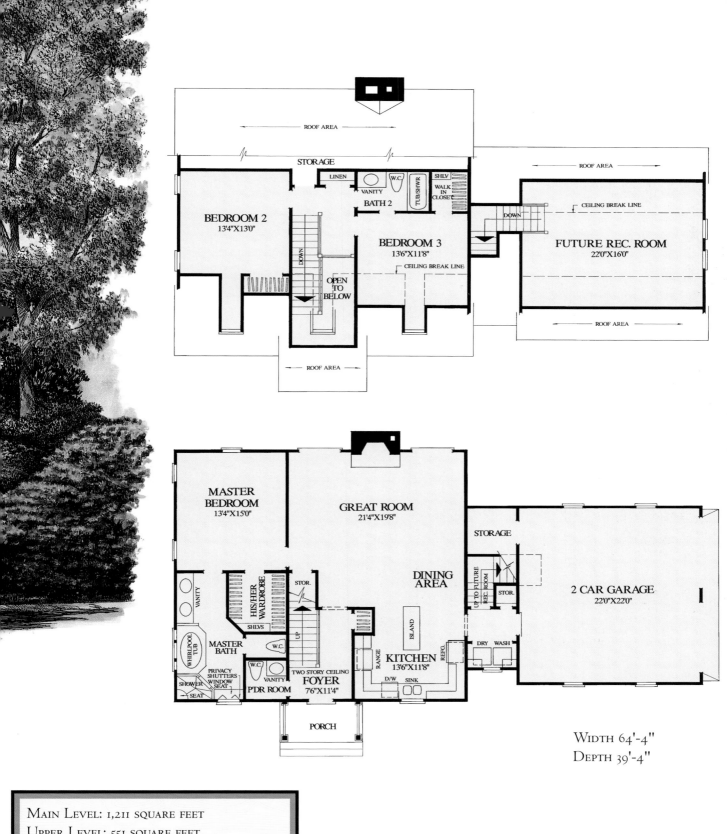

ROOF AREA

STORAGE

LINEN

VANITY

W.C.

BATH 2

TUB/SHWR

SHLV

WALK IN CLOSET

ROOF AREA

DOWN

CEILING BREAK LINE

BEDROOM 2
13'4"X13'0"

DOWN

BEDROOM 3
13'6"X11'8"

FUTURE REC. ROOM
22'0"X16'0"

OPEN TO BELOW

CEILING BREAK LINE

ROOF AREA

ROOF AREA

MASTER BEDROOM
13'4"X15'0"

GREAT ROOM
21'4"X19'8"

STORAGE

2 CAR GARAGE
22'0"X22'0"

UP TO FUTURE REC. ROOM

STOR.

VANITY

HIS/HER WARDROBE

STOR.

DINING AREA

ISLAND

SHLVS

WHIRLPOOL TUB

MASTER BATH

W.C.

DRY

WASH

PRIVACY SHUTTERS

WINDOW SEAT

SHOWER

SEAT

W.C.

VANITY

P'DR ROOM

TWO STORY CEILING

FOYER
7'6"X11'4"

RANGE

KITCHEN
13'6"X11'8"

REFG.

D/W

SINK

UP

PORCH

WIDTH 64'-4"
DEPTH 39'-4"

MAIN LEVEL: 1,211 SQUARE FEET
UPPER LEVEL: 551 SQUARE FEET
TOTAL: 1,762 SQUARE FEET
FUTURE RECREATION ROOM: 378 SQUARE FEET
Optional basement plan is included

Carolina Coastal Cottage

Restoration is afoot. Charming cottages being refurbished with loving care abound. However, if the idea of restoration is not your "cup of tea," so to speak, the Carolina Coastal Cottage is just for you. Built correctly, it will stand the test of time just as well as those that came before it. Enjoy!

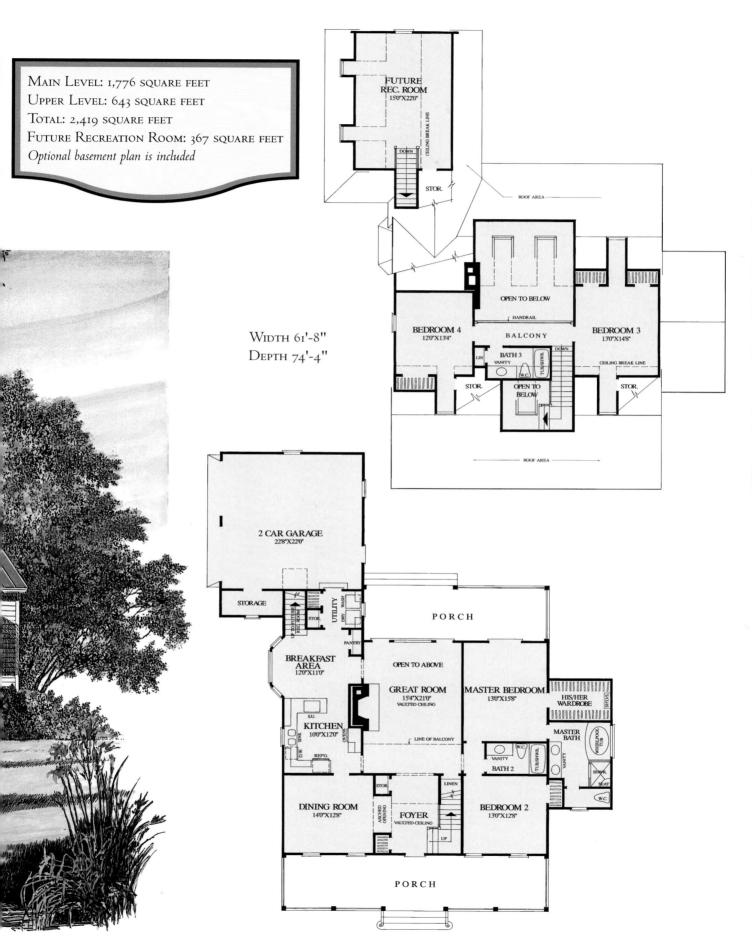

Main Level: 1,776 square feet
Upper Level: 643 square feet
Total: 2,419 square feet
Future Recreation Room: 367 square feet
Optional basement plan is included

Width 61'-8"
Depth 74'-4"

FUTURE
REC. ROOM
15'0"X22'0"

DOWN

STOR.

ROOF AREA

OPEN TO BELOW

HANDRAIL

BEDROOM 4
12'0"X13'4"

BALCONY

BEDROOM 3
13'0"X14'8"

LIN

BATH 3
VANITY

DOWN

W.C.

STOR.

OPEN TO
BELOW

STOR.

CEILING BREAK LINE

STOR.

ROOF AREA

2 CAR GARAGE
22'8"X22'0"

STORAGE

UP TO FUTURE
REC. ROOM

STOR.

UTILITY

WASH

DRY

PANTRY

PORCH

BREAKFAST
AREA
12'0"X11'0"

OPEN TO ABOVE

S.U.

GREAT ROOM
15'4"X21'0"
VAULTED CEILING

MASTER BEDROOM
13'0"X15'8"

HIS/HER
WARDROBE

SH/FIX.

KITCHEN
10'0"X12'0"

OVENS

LINE OF BALCONY

MASTER
BATH

WHIRLPOOL
TUB

SINK

D.W.

REF'G.

BATH 2

VANITY

W.C.

TUB/SHWR.

VANITY

SHWR.

SEAT

DINING ROOM
14'0"X12'8"

STOR.

ARCHED OPENING

FOYER
VAULTED CEILING

LINEN

BEDROOM 2
13'0"X12'8"

W.C.

UP

PORCH

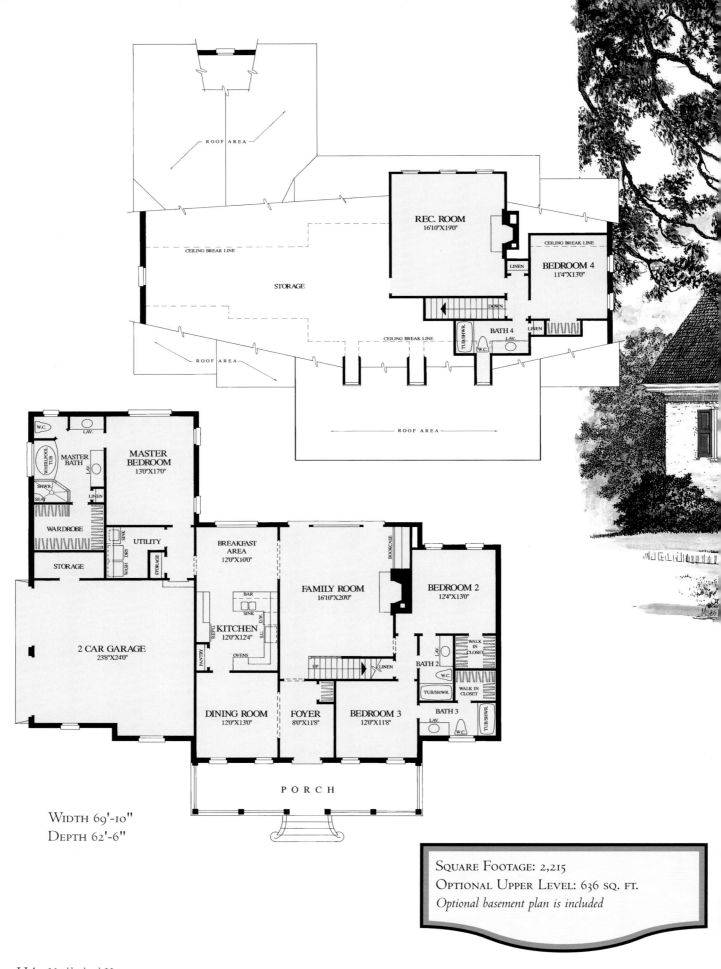

ROOF AREA

CEILING BREAK LINE

STORAGE

REC. ROOM
16'10"X19'0"

CEILING BREAK LINE

LINEN

BEDROOM 4
11'4"X13'0"

DOWN

CEILING BREAK LINE

TUB/SHWR.

BATH 4

LINEN

LAV.

W.C.

ROOF AREA

ROOF AREA

W.C.

LAV.

MASTER
BATH

WHIRLPOOL TUB

MASTER
BEDROOM
13'0"X17'0"

SHWR.

SEAT

LINEN

WARDROBE

SINK

UTILITY

STORAGE

WASH DRY

STORAGE

2 CAR GARAGE
23'8"X24'0"

PANTRY

BREAKFAST
AREA
12'0"X10'0"

BAR

SINK

KITCHEN
12'0"X12'4"

REFG.

D.W.

OVENS

FAMILY ROOM
16'10"X20'0"

BOOKCASE

BEDROOM 2
12'4"X13'0"

WALK
IN
CLOSET

LAV.

BATH 2

W.C.

TUB/SHWR.

WALK IN
CLOSET

UP

LINEN

DINING ROOM
12'0"X13'0"

FOYER
8'0"X11'8"

BEDROOM 3
12'0"X11'8"

BATH 3

LAV.

W.C.

TUB/SHWR.

PORCH

WIDTH 69'-10"
DEPTH 62'-6"

SQUARE FOOTAGE: 2,215
OPTIONAL UPPER LEVEL: 636 SQ. FT.
Optional basement plan is included

Chevy Chase

DESIGN HPT770049

Administrations change. History is made. Policies are set. Technology advances. The pace is fast—the future unknown. The result: stress. Yet solace—that elusive element in our lives, is found each day in the circle of friends and family, in the space of home—at Chevy Chase.

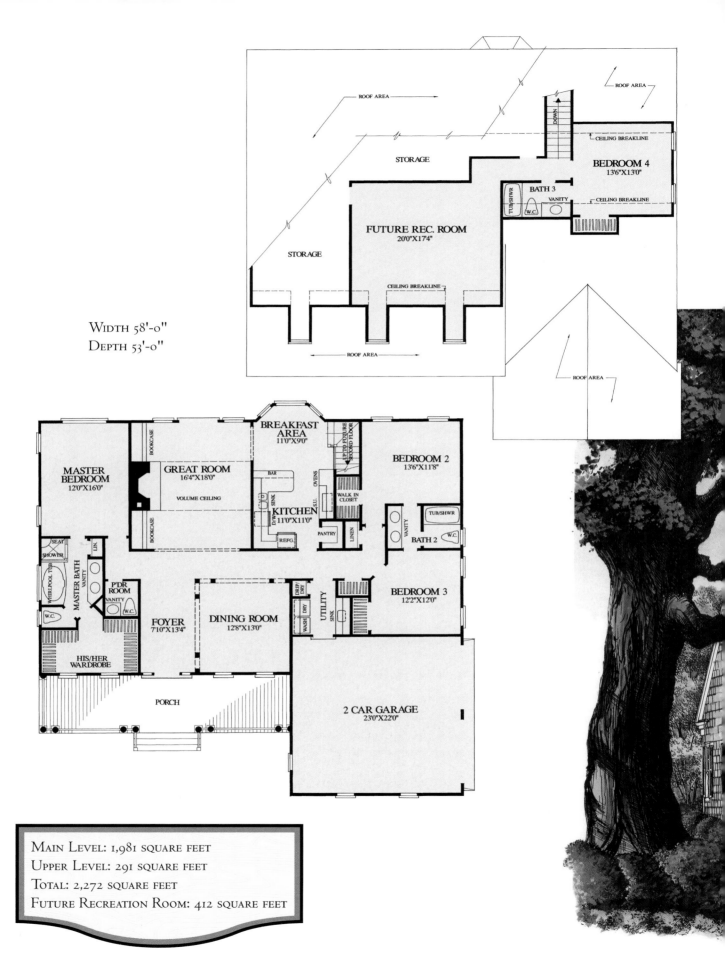

ROOF AREA

ROOF AREA

STORAGE

BEDROOM 4
13'6"X13'0"

CEILING BREAKLINE

DOWN

CEILING BREAKLINE

TUB/SHWR

BATH 3

VANITY

W.C.

FUTURE REC. ROOM
20'0"X17'4"

STORAGE

CEILING BREAKLINE

WIDTH 58'-0"
DEPTH 53'-0"

ROOF AREA

ROOF AREA

BREAKFAST AREA
11'0"X9'0"

MASTER BEDROOM
12'0"X16'0"

GREAT ROOM
16'4"X18'0"

VOLUME CEILING

BOOKCASE

BOOKCASE

BAR

SINK

D/WSHR

UP TO FUTURE SECOND FLOOR

OVENS

S.U.

WALK IN CLOSET

BEDROOM 2
13'6"X11'8"

KITCHEN
11'0"X11'0"

REFG.

PANTRY

LINEN

VANITY

TUB/SHWR

BATH 2

W.C.

SEAT

SHOWER

LIN.

WHIRLPOOL TUB

MASTER BATH

VANITY

P'DR ROOM

VANITY

W.C.

W.C.

FOYER
7'10"X13'4"

DINING ROOM
12'8"X13'0"

DRIP/DRY

DRY

WASH

UTILITY

SINK

BEDROOM 3
12'2"X12'0"

HIS/HER WARDROBE

PORCH

2 CAR GARAGE
23'0"X22'0"

MAIN LEVEL: 1,981 SQUARE FEET

UPPER LEVEL: 291 SQUARE FEET

TOTAL: 2,272 SQUARE FEET

FUTURE RECREATION ROOM: 412 SQUARE FEET

Culpeper Cottage

If it's perfect, it can also be simple. And that is exactly what this quaint, shingle-style cottage is. Listening to the excited voices of children as he walks up the path strewn with tricycles, balls, baby dolls and wagons, is it any wonder that the postman smiles broadly at this charm in disarray. The youngsters all rush to him, each eagerly beseeching to be the one to take a letter to mama.

Marshlands

DESIGN HPT770051

While taking a ride on the "Natchez," a paddle wheel boat on the lower Mississippi, the shoreline on either side of the river becomes vivid with both past and present. The Marshlands, in its understated solid beauty, sits agelessly and serenely in a field of colorful wildflowers. Beckoning up memories of how, as children, we would run with the butterflies, wade in the river and picnic on the rocks–Oh, what this raised cottage on the Old Mississippi reawakened in me…

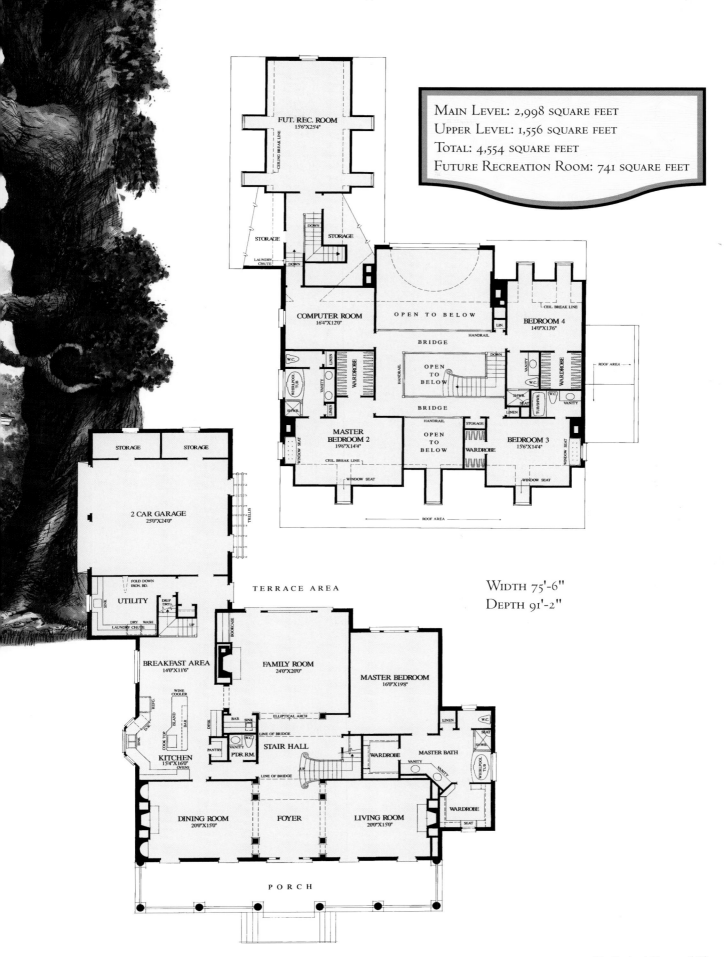

FUT. REC. ROOM
15'6"X25'4"

CEILING BREAK LINE

STORAGE

DOWN

STORAGE

LAUNDRY CHUTE

DOWN

COMPUTER ROOM
16'4"X12'0"

OPEN TO BELOW

CEIL BREAK LINE

BEDROOM 4
14'0"X13'6"

LIN.

HANDRAIL

W.C.

LINEN

WARDROBE

VANITY

WARDROBE

ROOF AREA

WHIRLPOOL TUB

VANITY

BRIDGE

OPEN
TO
BELOW

DOWN

SHWR.
SEAT

TUB/SHWR.

W.C.

SHWR.

LINEN

HANDRAIL

HANDRAIL

VANITY

LINEN

BRIDGE

HANDRAIL

MASTER
BEDROOM 2
19'6"X14'4"

OPEN
TO
BELOW

STORAGE

WARDROBE

BEDROOM 3
15'6"X14'4"

WINDOW SEAT

CEIL BREAK LINE

WINDOW SEAT

WINDOW SEAT

WINDOW SEAT

ROOF AREA

MAIN LEVEL: 2,998 SQUARE FEET
UPPER LEVEL: 1,556 SQUARE FEET
TOTAL: 4,554 SQUARE FEET
FUTURE RECREATION ROOM: 741 SQUARE FEET

STORAGE

STORAGE

2 CAR GARAGE
25'0"X24'0"

TRELLIS

FOLD DOWN
IRON. BD.

SINK

UTILITY

DRIP
DRY

DRY   WASH

LAUNDRY CHUTE

UP

TERRACE AREA

WIDTH 75'-6"
DEPTH 91'-2"

BREAKFAST AREA
14'0"X11'6"

BOOKCASE

FAMILY ROOM
24'0"X20'0"

MASTER BEDROOM
16'0"X19'8"

WINE
COOLER

REFG.

DESK

BAR   SINK

ELLIPTICAL ARCH

LINE OF BRIDGE

LINEN

W.C.

SHWR
SEAT

ISLAND

COOK TOP

BAR

DW

SINK

PANTRY

DESK

VANITY

W.C.

P'DR. RM.

STAIR HALL

WARDROBE

MASTER BATH

VANITY

WHIRLPOOL
TUB

KITCHEN
15'4"X16'0"

OVENS

LINE OF BRIDGE

UP

VANITY

DINING ROOM
20'0"X15'0"

FOYER

LIVING ROOM
20'0"X15'0"

WARDROBE

SEAT

PORCH

Adirondack Cottage

The large old Adirondack camps were the inspiration for this exquisite Adirondack Cottage. The sensitive use of twig design is delicately detailed in this lovely home. So right in the mountains, so right in the farmlands, so right in any setting where it can blend with the surrounding beauty of nature itself.

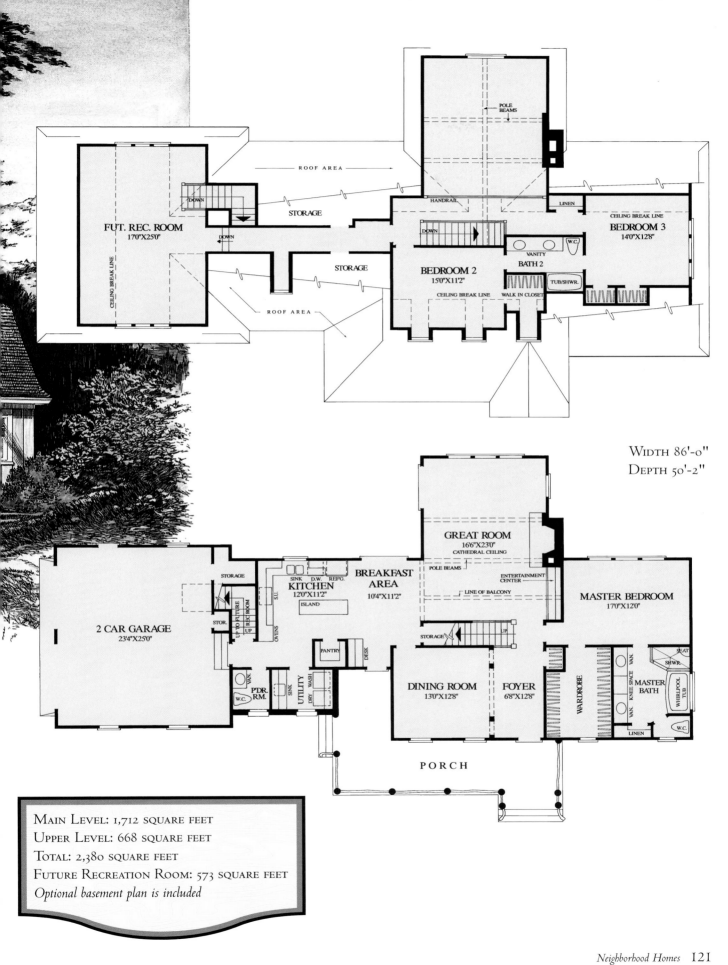

FUT. REC. ROOM
17'0"X25'0"

ROOF AREA

STORAGE

CEILING BREAK LINE

DOWN

DOWN

STORAGE

ROOF AREA

POLE
BEAMS

HANDRAIL

DOWN

VANITY

W.C.

LINEN

CEILING BREAK LINE

BEDROOM 3
14'0"X12'8"

BEDROOM 2
15'0"X11'2"

BATH 2

CEILING BREAK LINE

WALK IN CLOSET

TUB/SHWR.

WIDTH 86'-0"

DEPTH 50'-2"

GREAT ROOM
16'6"X23'0"
CATHEDRAL CEILING

POLE BEAMS

ENTERTAINMENT
CENTER

LINE OF BALCONY

MASTER BEDROOM
17'0"X12'0"

STORAGE

KITCHEN
12'0"X11'2"

BREAKFAST
AREA
10'4"X11'2"

SINK   D.W.   REFG.

ISLAND

STOR.

UP TO FUTURE REC ROOM

UP

OVENS

2 CAR GARAGE
23'4"X25'0"

VAN.

P'DR.
RM.

W.C.

SINK

UTILITY

DRY   WASH

PANTRY

DESK

DINING ROOM
13'0"X12'8"

STORAGE

UP

FOYER
6'8"X12'8"

WARDROBE

VAN.   KNEE SPACE   VAN.

LINEN

MASTER
BATH

WHIRLPOOL
TUB

SHWR.

SEAT

W.C.

PORCH

MAIN LEVEL: 1,712 SQUARE FEET
UPPER LEVEL: 668 SQUARE FEET
TOTAL: 2,380 SQUARE FEET
FUTURE RECREATION ROOM: 573 SQUARE FEET
Optional basement plan is included

Blackberry Lane

This "little jewel" of a home emanates a warmth and joy not soon to be forgotten. Cozy sunlit rooms filled with freshly cut flowers, smiling faces and the laughter of friends and family abound in the Blackberry Lane. Curved gables, wide trim, stone and shingle siding and colorful window boxes combined with absolutely perfect proportions truly make this home a neighborhood classic.

ROOF AREA

ROOF AREA

OPEN TO BELOW

BEDROOM 3
12'2"X11'0"

TUB/SHWR.

WC

VANITY

BATH 2

BEDROOM 2
11'8"X14'0"

HANDRAIL

BALCONY

BEDROOM 4
12'2"X11'0"

HANDRAIL

OPEN TO BELOW

DOWN

LINEN

DN

STOR

FUTURE REC. ROOM
20'8"X24'0"

CEILING BREAKLINE

Main Level: 1,627 square feet
Upper Level: 783 square feet
Total: 2,410 square feet
Future Recreation Room: 418 square feet

BREAKFAST AREA
12'8"X9'0"
CATHEDRAL CEILING

DECK

REFG.

BAR

D.W. SINK

RANGE

KITCHEN
12'6"X11'0"

PANTRY

FAMILY ROOM
15'6"X16'4"
VOLUME CEILING

MASTER BEDROOM
17'0"X12'10"

W.C

MASTER BATH

VANITY

Width 46'-0"
Depth 58'-6"

DINING ROOM
11'10"X12'6"

VANITY

P'DR ROOM

W.C.

ENT CENTER

LINEN

SHWR

UTILITY

WASH   DRY

WARDROBE

SEAT

WHIRLPOOL TUB

LIVING ROOM
15'6"X13'0"

TWO STORY CEILING
FOYER

UP

2 CAR GARAGE
20'8"X24'0"

PORCH

Thistlewood

DESIGN HPT770054

If fairy tales are to be believed, and of course they are, then The Thistlewood captures imaginations of romance and brings memories of delightful cottages and their stories to mind—Goldilocks and the Three Bears, Little Red Riding Hood, Snow White and the Seven Dwarfs, and Jack and the Beanstalk to name a few. The romance. The charm. The detail. What a delightful home—The Thistlewood.

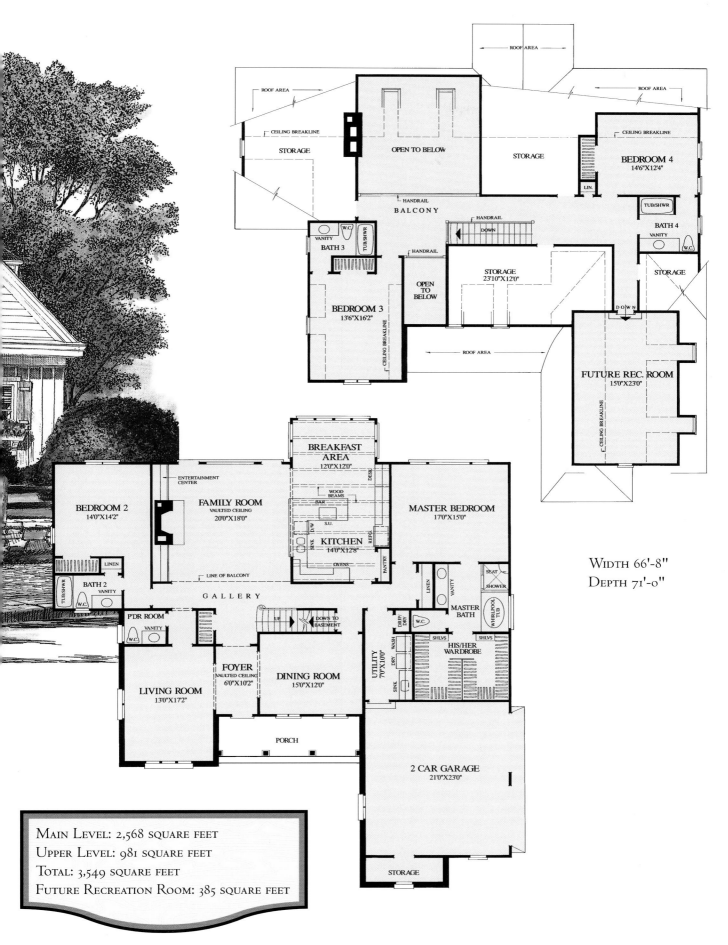

ROOF AREA

ROOF AREA

ROOF AREA

CEILING BREAKLINE

STORAGE

OPEN TO BELOW

STORAGE

CEILING BREAKLINE

BEDROOM 4
14'6"X12'4"

LIN.

TUB/SHWR

BATH 4

VANITY

W.C.

BALCONY

HANDRAIL

HANDRAIL

DOWN

VANITY

W.C.

TUB/SHWR

BATH 3

HANDRAIL

STORAGE

STORAGE
23'10"X12'0"

OPEN TO BELOW

BEDROOM 3
13'6"X16'2"

CEILING BREAKLINE

DOWN

ROOF AREA

FUTURE REC. ROOM
15'0"X23'0"

CEILING BREAKLINE

BREAKFAST AREA
12'0"X12'0"

DESK

WOOD BEAMS

BAR

S.U.

D/W

KITCHEN
14'0"X12'8"

SINK

OVENS

REFG.

PANTRY

ENTERTAINMENT CENTER

FAMILY ROOM
VAULTED CEILING
20'0"X18'0"

BEDROOM 2
14'0"X14'2"

LINEN

TUB/SHWR

BATH 2

VANITY

W.C.

LINE OF BALCONY

MASTER BEDROOM
17'0"X15'0"

LINEN

VANITY

SEAT

SHOWER

MASTER BATH

WHIRLPOOL TUB

W.C.

DRIP/DRY

SHLVS

SHLVS

HIS/HER WARDROBE

GALLERY

P'DR ROOM

W.C.

VANITY

UP

DOWN TO BASEMENT

UTILITY
7'0"X10'0"

WASH

DRY

SINK

FOYER
VAULTED CEILING
6'0"X10'2"

DINING ROOM
15'0"X12'0"

LIVING ROOM
13'0"X17'2"

PORCH

2 CAR GARAGE
21'0"X23'0"

STORAGE

Width 66'-8"
Depth 71'-0"

Main Level: 2,568 square feet
Upper Level: 981 square feet
Total: 3,549 square feet
Future Recreation Room: 385 square feet

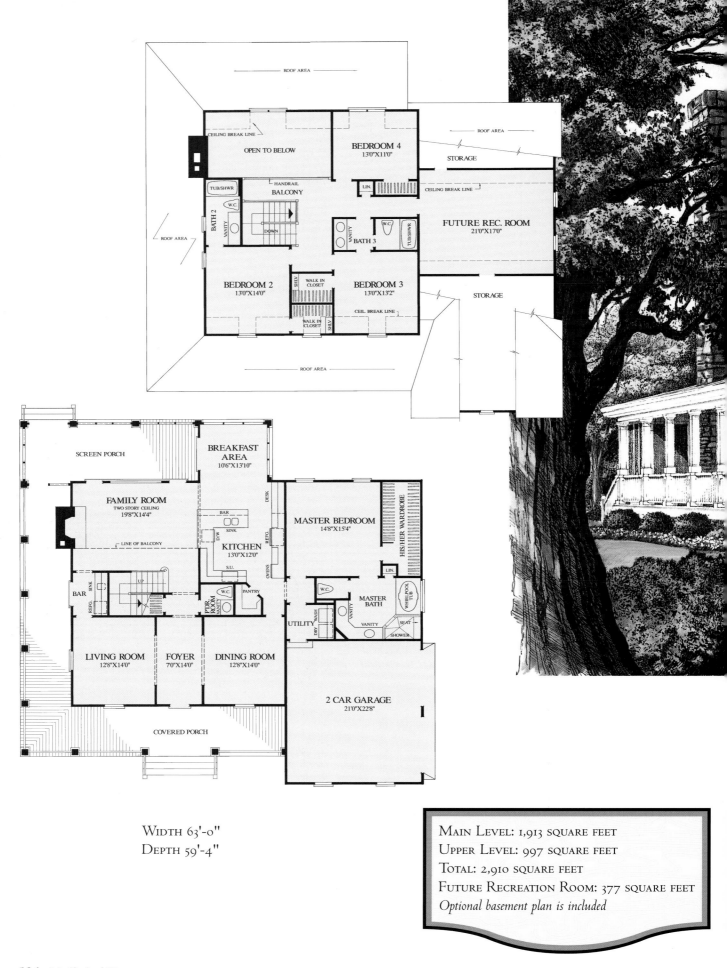

Width 63'-0"
Depth 59'-4"

Main Level: 1,913 square feet
Upper Level: 997 square feet
Total: 2,910 square feet
Future Recreation Room: 377 square feet
Optional basement plan is included

Homestead

DESIGN HPT770055

Rounding a curve near the Blue Ridge Parkway–there, straight ahead, nestled between adjacent ridges lies The Homestead. With a sudden catch in the throat, one is immediately immersed in images of the generations who have lived, loved and toiled there. Lullabies, folk tales and the clear lilt of a fiddle in the crisp evening air invade one's senses in a rush of nostalgic reverie. Imagine the stories that could be told!

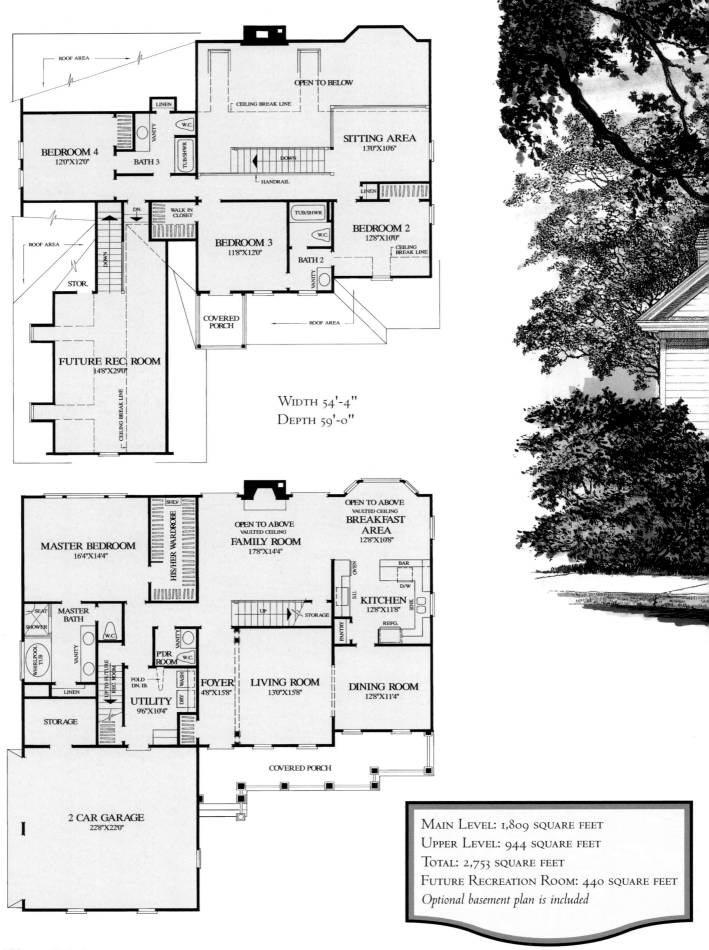

ROOF AREA

LINEN

BEDROOM 4
12'0"X12'0"

BATH 3

VANITY

W.C.

TUB/SHWR

OPEN TO BELOW

CEILING BREAK LINE

SITTING AREA
13'0"X10'6"

DOWN

HANDRAIL

LINEN

DN.

WALK IN CLOSET

DOWN

ROOF AREA

STOR.

FUTURE REC. ROOM
14'8"X29'0"

CEILING BREAK LINE

BEDROOM 3
11'8"X12'0"

TUB/SHWR

W.C.

BATH 2

VANITY

BEDROOM 2
12'8"X10'0"

CEILING BREAK LINE

COVERED PORCH

ROOF AREA

WIDTH 54'-4"
DEPTH 59'-0"

SHLV

MASTER BEDROOM
16'4"X14'4"

HIS/HER WARDROBE

OPEN TO ABOVE
VAULTED CEILING
FAMILY ROOM
17'8"X14'4"

OPEN TO ABOVE
VAULTED CEILING
BREAKFAST AREA
12'8"X10'8"

SEAT

SHOWER

MASTER BATH

WHIRLPOOL TUB

VANITY

W.C.

LINEN

UP TO FUTURE REC. ROOM

STORAGE

VANITY

P'DR ROOM

W.C.

FOLD DN. IB.

WASH

DRY

UTILITY
9'6"X10'4"

UP

STORAGE

FOYER
4'8"X15'8"

LIVING ROOM
13'0"X15'8"

OVEN

S.U.

BAR

D/W

KITCHEN
12'8"X11'8"

SINK

PANTRY

REFG.

DINING ROOM
12'8"X11'4"

2 CAR GARAGE
22'8"X22'0"

COVERED PORCH

MAIN LEVEL: 1,809 SQUARE FEET
UPPER LEVEL: 944 SQUARE FEET
TOTAL: 2,753 SQUARE FEET
FUTURE RECREATION ROOM: 440 SQUARE FEET
Optional basement plan is included

Cape May

DESIGN HPT770056

What a charming town. All along the streets sit cottages of exquisite detail—which one shall it be? Which one will shelter us in storms and hold us tenderly throughout our summer days? The Cape May, of course. None other could match its warmth, its intricate design, its romantic charm.

Rocky Springs

DESIGN HPT770057

Not far from our city, yet seemingly way out in the country, there is one community consisting of one street lined with quaint little houses that seem to glow with love. Among them sits my favorite. It would fit on any street anywhere and everyone would stop to admire the solid charm of the Rocky Springs.

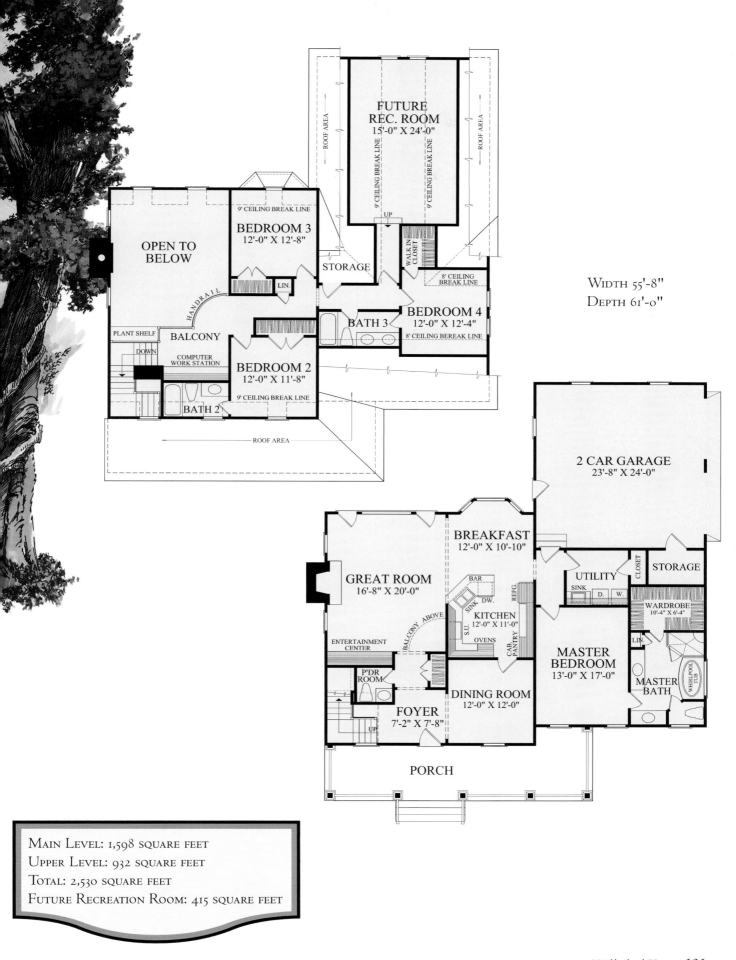

FUTURE
REC. ROOM
15'-0" X 24'-0"

ROOF AREA

9' CEILING BREAK LINE

9' CEILING BREAK LINE

ROOF AREA

UP

WALK IN CLOSET

9' CEILING BREAK LINE

OPEN TO BELOW

BEDROOM 3
12'-0" X 12'-8"

LIN.

STORAGE

8' CEILING BREAK LINE

BATH 3

BEDROOM 4
12'-0" X 12'-4"

8' CEILING BEREAK LINE

HANDRAIL

PLANT SHELF

BALCONY

DOWN

COMPUTER WORK STATION

BEDROOM 2
12'-0" X 11'-8"

9' CEILING BREAK LINE

BATH 2

ROOF AREA

WIDTH 55'-8"
DEPTH 61'-0"

2 CAR GARAGE
23'-8" X 24'-0"

BREAKFAST
12'-0" X 10'-10"

UTILITY

CLOSET

STORAGE

GREAT ROOM
16'-8" X 20'-0"

BAR

SINK   DW.

REFG.

SINK   D.   W.

WARDROBE
10'-4" X 6'-4"

KITCHEN
12'-0" X 11'-0"

S.U.

OVENS

ENTERTAINMENT CENTER

BALCONY ABOVE

CAB.
PANTRY

LIN.

MASTER BEDROOM
13'-0" X 17'-0"

WHIRLPOOL TUB

P'DR ROOM

DINING ROOM
12'-0" X 12'-0"

MASTER BATH

UP

FOYER
7'-2" X 7'-8"

PORCH

Main Level: 1,598 square feet

Upper Level: 932 square feet

Total: 2,530 square feet

Future Recreation Room: 415 square feet

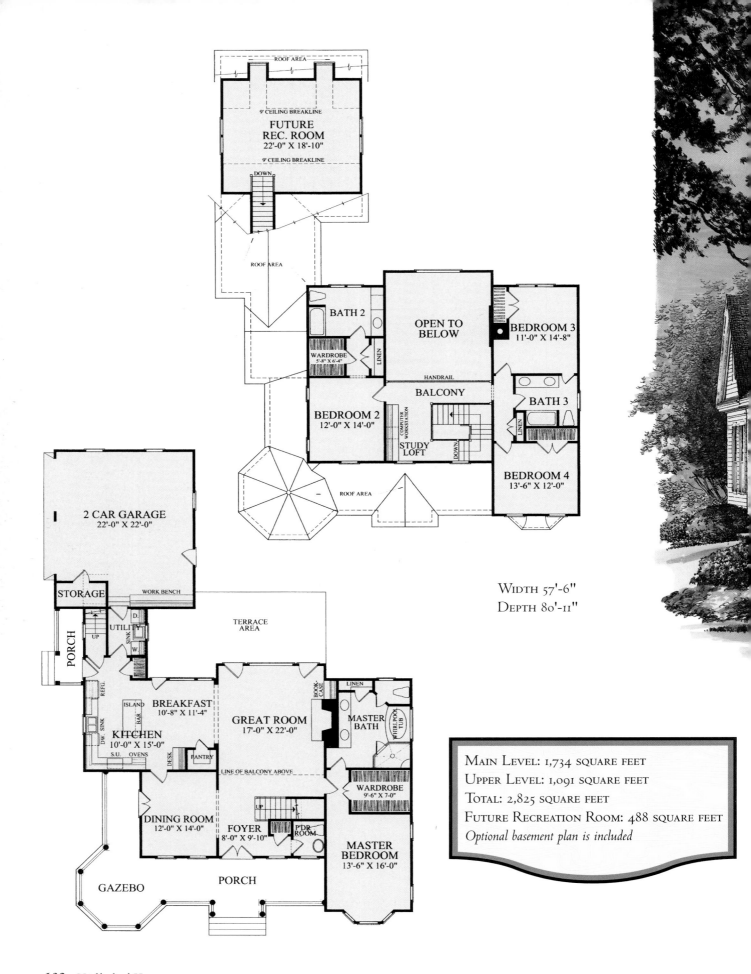

ROOF AREA

9' CEILING BREAKLINE

**FUTURE
REC. ROOM**
22'-0" X 18'-10"

9' CEILING BREAKLINE

DOWN

ROOF AREA

BATH 2

WARDROBE
5'-8" X 6'-4"

LINEN

**OPEN TO
BELOW**

HANDRAIL

BEDROOM 3
11'-0" X 14'-8"

BALCONY

BATH 3

BEDROOM 2
12'-0" X 14'-0"

COMPUTER WORKSTATION

LINEN

DOWN

**STUDY
LOFT**

ROOF AREA

BEDROOM 4
13'-6" X 12'-0"

2 CAR GARAGE
22'-0" X 22'-0"

STORAGE

WORK BENCH

PORCH

UP

UTILITY

SINK

W

TERRACE
AREA

REFG.

ISLAND

BAR

BREAKFAST
10'-8" X 11'-4"

GREAT ROOM
17'-0" X 22'-0"

BOOK-CASE

LINEN

**MASTER
BATH**

WHIRLPOOL TUB

DW. SINK

KITCHEN
10'-0" X 15'-0"

S.U.   OVENS

DESK

PANTRY

LINE OF BALCONY ABOVE

WARDROBE
9'-6" X 7-0"

DINING ROOM
12'-0" X 14'-0"

UP

FOYER
8'-0" X 9'-10"

P'DR
ROOM

**MASTER
BEDROOM**
13'-6" X 16'-0"

GAZEBO

PORCH

WIDTH 57'-6"
DEPTH 80'-11"

MAIN LEVEL: 1,734 SQUARE FEET
UPPER LEVEL: 1,091 SQUARE FEET
TOTAL: 2,825 SQUARE FEET
FUTURE RECREATION ROOM: 488 SQUARE FEET
Optional basement plan is included

Salisbury

DESIGN HPT770058

In a perfect little Southern town, "Aunt Bea" of "Mayberry" fame decided to spend the remainder of her life. After living in the imagery of sleepy Southern perfection, she wanted the real thing. This picturesque rendition of our Salisbury is, of course, a perfect fit and we all hope she found exactly what she was looking for.

Woodbridge

Design HPT770059

Wandering the back streets of Woodbridge, Connecticut, where we became lost amid all the myriad crooks and turns in the roads, we came upon a perfectly proportioned home. The Woodbridge is so intriguing that we looked, admired, walked on and returned yet again for another admiring glance. With the tolling of the church bells, instant thoughts of being in another era surfaced—thoughts of a simpler time and place.

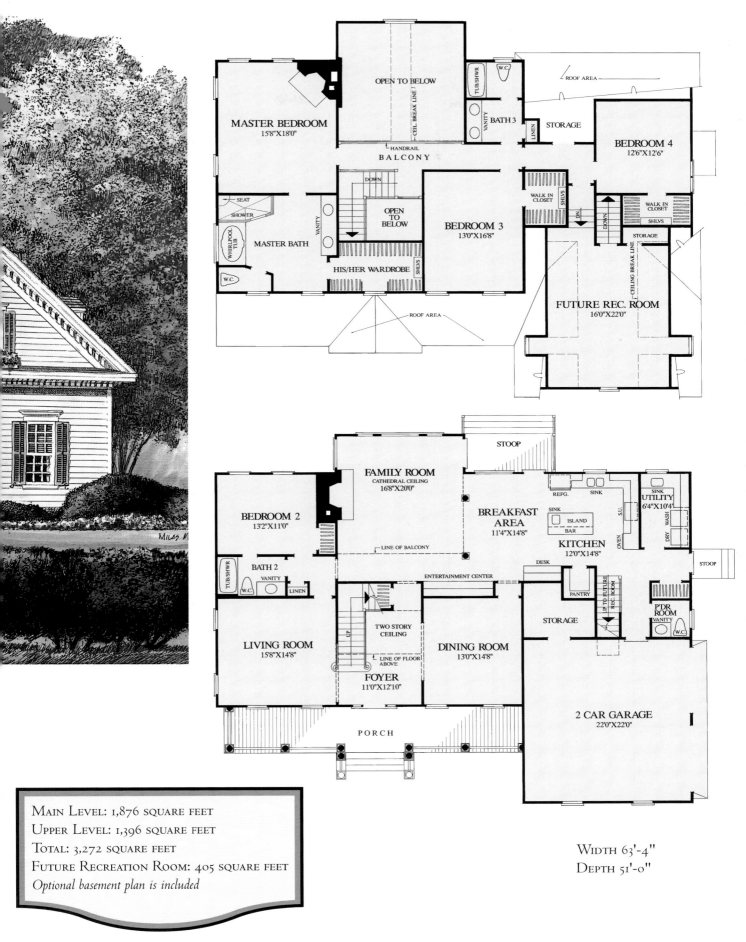

UPPER LEVEL

MASTER BEDROOM
15'8"X18'0"

OPEN TO BELOW

CEIL BREAK LINE

TUB/SHWR

W.C.

BATH 3

VANITY

LINEN

STORAGE

ROOF AREA

BEDROOM 4
12'6"X12'6"

HANDRAIL

B A L C O N Y

SEAT

SHOWER

WHIRLPOOL TUB

VANITY

DOWN

OPEN TO BELOW

MASTER BATH

W.C.

HIS/HER WARDROBE

SHLVS

BEDROOM 3
13'0"X16'8"

WALK IN CLOSET

SHLVS

DN.

DOWN

WALK IN CLOSET

SHLVS

STORAGE

CEILING BREAK LINE

FUTURE REC. ROOM
16'0"X22'0"

ROOF AREA

MAIN LEVEL

STOOP

FAMILY ROOM
CATHEDRAL CEILING
16'8"X20'0"

REFG.

SINK

SINK

UTILITY
6'4"X10'4"

WASH

DRY

BEDROOM 2
13'2"X11'0"

BREAKFAST AREA
11'4"X14'8"

SINK

ISLAND

BAR

S.U.

OVEN

KITCHEN
12'0"X14'8"

STOOP

LINE OF BALCONY

TUB/SHWR

BATH 2

W.C.

VANITY

LINEN

ENTERTAINMENT CENTER

DESK

PANTRY

UP TO FUTURE REC. ROOM

P'DR ROOM

VANITY

W.C.

LIVING ROOM
15'8"X14'8"

UP

TWO STORY CEILING

LINE OF FLOOR ABOVE

FOYER
11'0"X12'10"

DINING ROOM
13'0"X14'8"

STORAGE

2 CAR GARAGE
22'0"X22'0"

P O R C H

MILES

MAIN LEVEL: 1,876 SQUARE FEET
UPPER LEVEL: 1,396 SQUARE FEET
TOTAL: 3,272 SQUARE FEET
FUTURE RECREATION ROOM: 405 SQUARE FEET
Optional basement plan is included

WIDTH 63'-4"
DEPTH 51'-0"

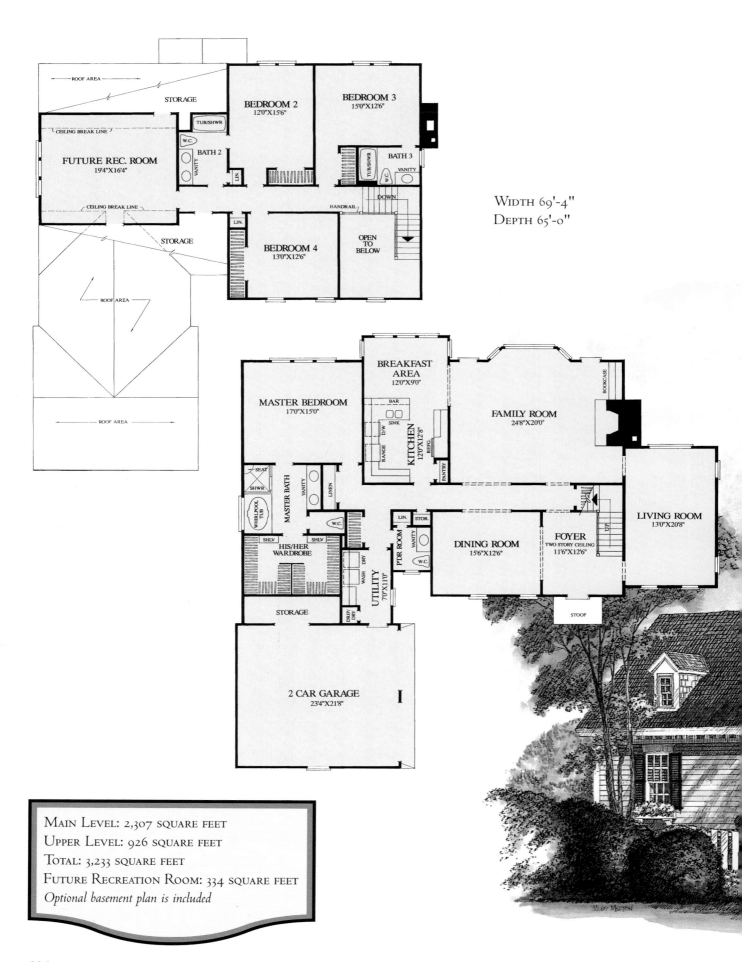

ROOF AREA

STORAGE

CEILING BREAK LINE

TUB/SHWR

W.C.

FUTURE REC. ROOM
19'4"X16'4"

BATH 2

VANITY

BEDROOM 2
12'0"X15'6"

BEDROOM 3
15'0"X12'6"

LIN.

TUB/SHWR

W.C.

BATH 3

VANITY

CEILING BREAK LINE

STORAGE

DOWN

HANDRAIL

LIN.

ROOF AREA

BEDROOM 4
13'0"X12'6"

OPEN TO BELOW

ROOF AREA

WIDTH 69'-4"
DEPTH 65'-0"

BREAKFAST AREA
12'0"X9'0"

BAR

SINK

D/W

RANGE

REFG.

MASTER BEDROOM
17'0"X15'0"

FAMILY ROOM
24'8"X20'0"

BOOKCASE

KITCHEN
12'0"X12'8"

PANTRY

SEAT

SHWR

VANITY

LINEN

WHIRLPOOL TUB

MASTER BATH

W.C.

LIN.

STOR.

ROOF AREA

LIVING ROOM
13'0"X20'8"

SHLV

SHLV

HIS/HER WARDROBE

WASH

DRY

UTILITY
7'0"X11'0"

PDR ROOM

VANITY

W.C.

DINING ROOM
15'6"X12'6"

FOYER
TWO STORY CEILING
11'6"X12'6"

UP

STORAGE

DRIP/DRY

STOOP

2 CAR GARAGE
23'4"X21'8"

MAIN LEVEL: 2,307 SQUARE FEET
UPPER LEVEL: 926 SQUARE FEET
TOTAL: 3,233 SQUARE FEET
FUTURE RECREATION ROOM: 334 SQUARE FEET
Optional basement plan is included

Cape Charles

What poise. What grace. What crisp, precise detail. What a stirring of nostalgic feelings upon seeing The Cape Charles just beyond—sitting regally but gracefully, shimmering at the water's edge. The proportions, the cedar shingles in the gabled ends, the chimney configuration—all this and more awaken dreams of "home" and all that it encompasses. Dreams really do come true—yours can too!

Baystreet

Design HPT770061

She grew up in this home. It was old long before she was born. There was no interior stairway then and no matter the weather or time of day, all ups and downs were by way of the front porch steps. She never questioned the function of the house (it was simply home to her), but her college friends thought it quaint. Today all renovations are complete, modern amenities discreetly abound and her children frolic all around—as well as up and down both staircases—one within and one without.

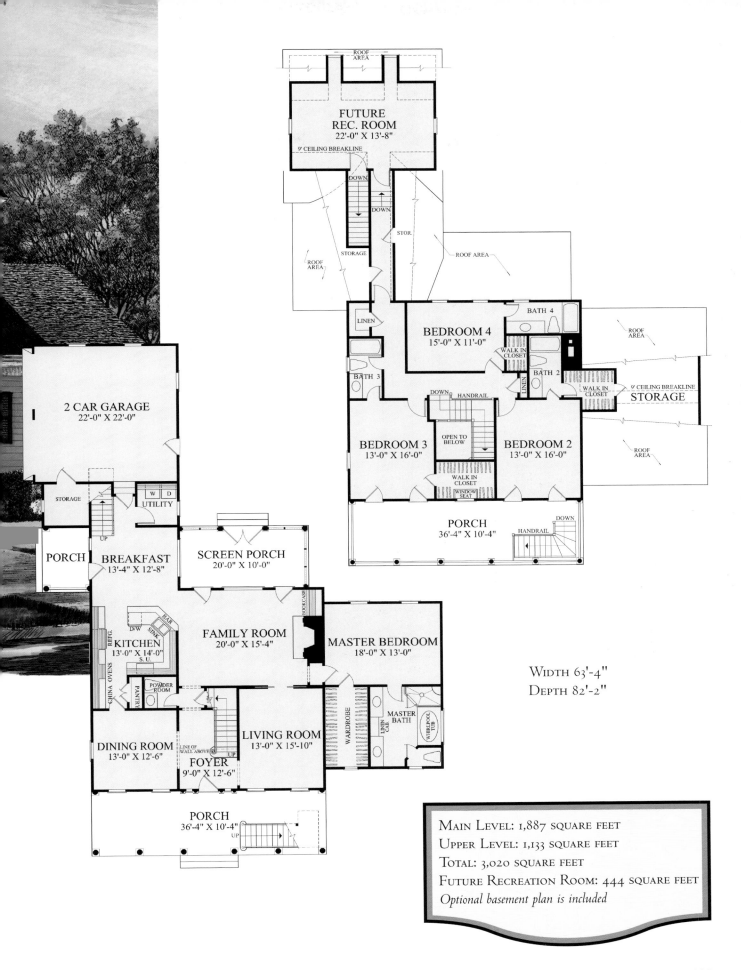

FUTURE
REC. ROOM
22'-0" X 13'-8"

ROOF
AREA

9' CEILING BREAKLINE

DOWN

DOWN

STOR.

ROOF
AREA

STORAGE

ROOF AREA

LINEN

BEDROOM 4
15'-0" X 11'-0"

BATH 4

WALK IN
CLOSET

ROOF
AREA

9' CEILING BREAKLINE

BATH
3

LINEN

BATH 2

WALK IN
CLOSET

STORAGE

DOWN   HANDRAIL

BEDROOM 3
13'-0" X 16'-0"

OPEN TO
BELOW

BEDROOM 2
13'-0" X 16'-0"

ROOF
AREA

WALK IN
CLOSET

WINDOW
SEAT

PORCH
36'-4" X 10'-4"

DOWN

HANDRAIL

2 CAR GARAGE
22'-0" X 22'-0"

STORAGE

W   D

UTILITY

UP

PORCH

BREAKFAST
13'-4" X 12'-8"

SCREEN PORCH
20'-0" X 10'-0"

REFG.

D/W   SINK

BAR

KITCHEN
13'-0" X 14'-0"

S.U.

CHINA OVENS

POWDER
ROOM

PANTRY

FAMILY ROOM
20'-0" X 15'-4"

BOOKCASE

MASTER BEDROOM
18'-0" X 13'-0"

WARDROBE

LINEN CAB.

MASTER
BATH

WHIRLPOOL
TUB

DINING ROOM
13'-0" X 12'-6"

LINE OF
WALL ABOVE

UP

FOYER
9'-0" X 12'-6"

LIVING ROOM
13'-0" X 15'-10"

PORCH
36'-4" X 10'-4"

UP

WIDTH 63'-4"
DEPTH 82'-2"

MAIN LEVEL: 1,887 SQUARE FEET
UPPER LEVEL: 1,133 SQUARE FEET
TOTAL: 3,020 SQUARE FEET
FUTURE RECREATION ROOM: 444 SQUARE FEET
Optional basement plan is included

Esprit de France

ABordeaux chateau in Haut Medoc or hillside retreats in Avignon—the charming houses and villages of France have influenced American residential design in powerful ways. Ateliers and terraces, stately turrets and timber trusses evoke all of the charm of these pastoral places.

Inspired by the rural and historic vernaculars of the French countryside, from Bretagne to Provence, Esprit de France captures the spirit of the region in 21st-century designs. Thick paneled doors and stone arches, beamed ceilings and hearth-warmed rooms enrich these home places.

A dignified, gentle Old World style steps into the future with Chateau de Bachen (page 156). Perched atop the rolling hills of Burgundy or perfectly set at the end of a driveway in Charleston, this classic manor says that you've truly arrived.

The Carmel Cottage (page 152) will help you to recall the lush green landscape of the European countryside. A charming outdoor dining terrace and foliage-covered trellis invite an enjoyment of nature, bringing the magic of a European ambience to your piece of heaven.

These extraordinary homes lend a splendid New World flavor to a myriad of French Country styles. Timeless grandeur and deeply comfortable amenities define this world-class collection of inviting luxury plans.

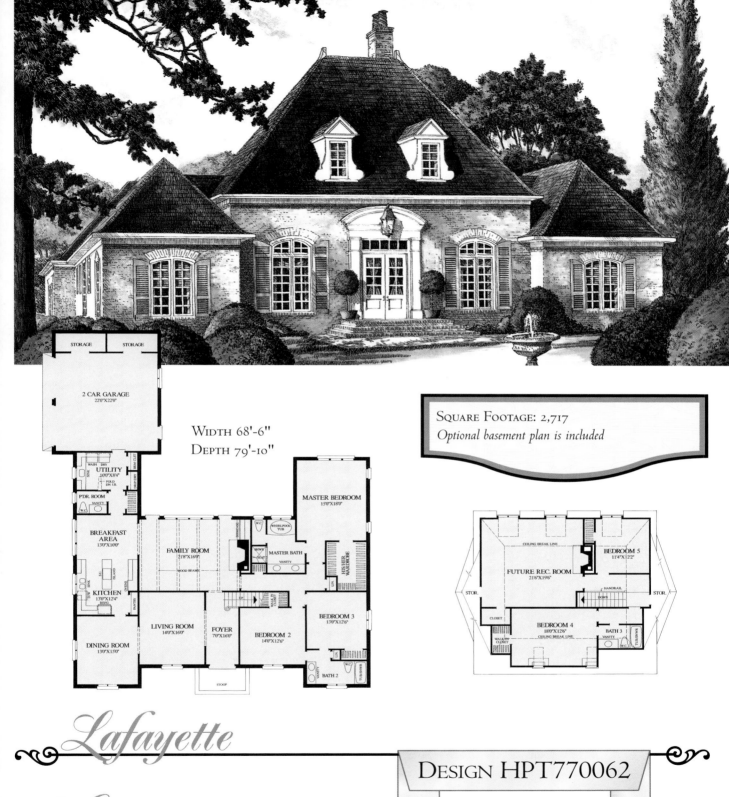

STORAGE STORAGE

2 CAR GARAGE
22'0"X22'0"

WASH DRY
UTILITY
10'0"X8'4"
FOLD
DN. LB.

PDR. ROOM
W.C.
VANITY

BREAKFAST
AREA
13'0"X10'0"

KITCHEN
13'0"X12'4"

DINING ROOM
13'0"X15'0"

FAMILY ROOM
21'8"X16'0"

WOOD BEAMS

LIVING ROOM
14'0"X16'0"

FOYER
7'0"X16'0"

MASTER BEDROOM
15'0"X18'0"

WHIRLPOOL
TUB

W.C.

MASTER BATH

VANITY

HIS HER WARDROBE

BEDROOM 3
13'0"X12'6"

BEDROOM 2
14'0"X12'6"

VANITY

BATH 2

W.C.

STOOP

WIDTH 68'-6"
DEPTH 79'-10"

SQUARE FOOTAGE: 2,717
Optional basement plan is included

CEILING BREAK LINE

FUTURE REC. ROOM
21'6"X19'6"

BEDROOM 5
11'4"X22'

STOR.

HANDRAIL

DOWN

STOR.

CLOSET

WALK-IN
CLOSET

BEDROOM 4
18'0"X12'6"
CEILING BREAK LINE

BATH 3

VANITY

W.C.

Lafayette

DESIGN HPT770062

Let me tell you a little known, but very true story. When our soldiers were overseas during World War I, they fell in love with the inviting, aged and patinaed old homes of France—homes that gave them feelings of warmth in their otherwise desolate days. Upon returning home after the war, they decided to build romantic cottages such as Lafayette for themselves; thus, introducing to our shores the symmetry, quaintness and detail of classical French architecture.

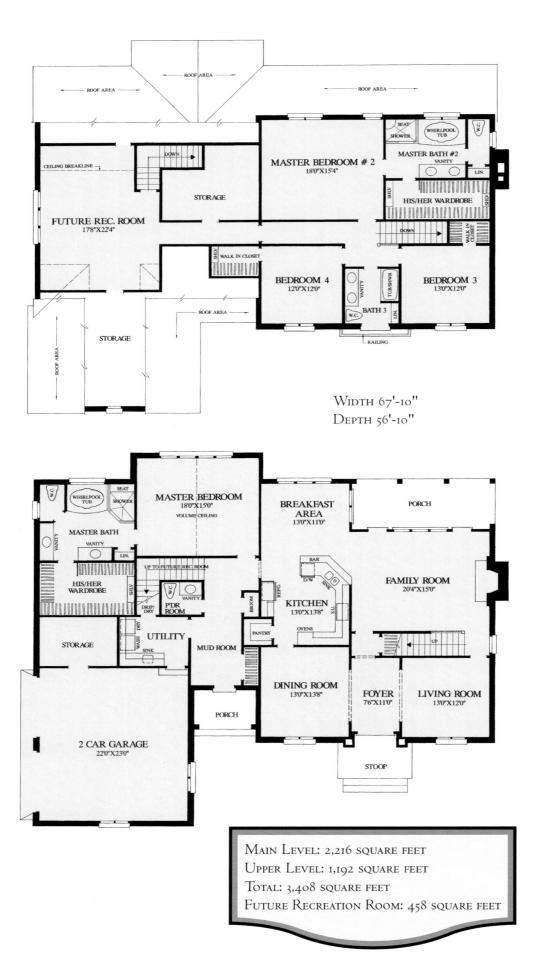

Upper Level

ROOF AREA

ROOF AREA

ROOF AREA

ROOF AREA

CEILING BREAKLINE

DOWN

STORAGE

MASTER BEDROOM # 2
18'0"X15'4"

SEAT
SHOWER

WHIRLPOOL TUB

W.C.

MASTER BATH #2

VANITY

LIN.

FUTURE REC. ROOM
17'8"X22'4"

SHLV

HIS/HER WARDROBE

SHLV

SHLV

WALK IN CLOSET

DOWN

WALK IN CLOSET

SHLV

WALK IN CLOSET

BEDROOM 4
12'0"X12'0"

VANITY

TUB/SHWR

BEDROOM 3
13'0"X12'0"

STORAGE

ROOF AREA

ROOF AREA

W.C.

BATH 3

LIN.

RAILING

WIDTH 67'-10"
DEPTH 56'-10"

Main Level

W.C.

WHIRLPOOL TUB

SEAT
SHOWER

MASTER BEDROOM
18'0"X15'0"
VOLUME CEILING

BREAKFAST AREA
13'0"X11'0"

PORCH

VANITY

MASTER BATH

VANITY

LIN.

UP TO FUTURE REC. ROOM

BAR

D/W

SINK

FAMILY ROOM
20'4"X15'0"

SHLV

W.C.

VANITY

REFG.

HIS/HER WARDROBE

DRIP/ DRY

P'DR ROOM

BROOM

KITCHEN
13'0"X13'8"

S.U.

STORAGE

WASH

SINK

UTILITY

PANTRY

OVENS

UP

MUD ROOM

DINING ROOM
13'0"X13'8"

FOYER
7'6"X11'0"

LIVING ROOM
13'0"X12'0"

PORCH

2 CAR GARAGE
22'0"X23'0"

STOOP

MAIN LEVEL: 2,216 SQUARE FEET
UPPER LEVEL: 1,192 SQUARE FEET
TOTAL: 3,408 SQUARE FEET
FUTURE RECREATION ROOM: 458 SQUARE FEET

Saint Remy

This elegant and tasteful, yet modest chateau is an exquisite rendition of "French country" that stands alone in both character and design. The French people, the land, the architecture and the cuisine come together in a harmony that exists so perfectly—perhaps nowhere else. The tranquil and natural approach to blending all that is indigenous to the land with thoughtful detail and a heartiness that is so satisfying to all the senses is uniquely Southern—in this case, the wine region of southern France.

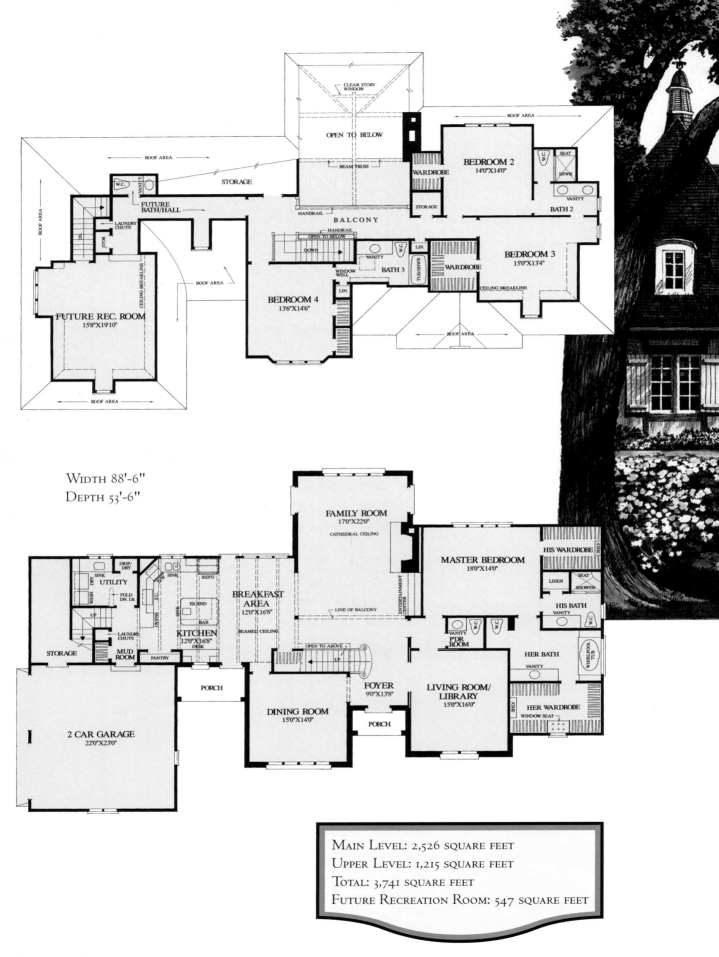

CLEAR STORY WINDOW

OPEN TO BELOW

ROOF AREA

STORAGE

BEAM TRUSS

ROOF AREA

BEDROOM 2
14'0"X14'0"

W.C.

SEAT

SHWR

WARDROBE

STORAGE

BATH 2

VANITY

W.C.

VANITY

FUTURE
BATH/HALL

ROOF AREA

HANDRAIL

BALCONY

LAUNDRY
CHUTE

STOR.

DN.

HANDRAIL

OPEN TO BELOW

DOWN

VANITY

W.C.

LIN.

WARDROBE

BEDROOM 3
15'0"X13'4"

CEILING BREAKLINE

ROOF AREA

WINDOW
WELL

BATH 3

TUB/SHWR

LIN.

CEILING BREAKLINE

FUTURE REC. ROOM
15'8"X19'10"

ROOF AREA

BEDROOM 4
13'6"X14'6"

ROOF AREA

ROOF AREA

WIDTH 88'-6"
DEPTH 53'-6"

FAMILY ROOM
17'0"X22'0"

CATHEDRAL CEILING

ROOF AREA

MASTER BEDROOM
18'0"X14'0"

HIS WARDROBE

DRIP/
DRY

SINK

UTILITY

REFG

LINEN

SEAT

SHOWER

SHLVS

WASH

DRY

FOLD
DN. LB.

OVENS

SINK

SINK

DW

BREAKFAST
AREA
12'0"X16'8"

LINE OF BALCONY

ENTERTAINMENT
CENTER

HIS BATH

VANITY

W.C.

LAUNDRY
CHUTE

ISLAND

BAR

KITCHEN
12'0"X16'8"

DESK

BEAMED CEILING

VANITY

W.C.

W.C.

PDR.
ROOM

WHIRLPOOL
TUB

HER BATH

VANITY

STORAGE

MUD
ROOM

PANTRY

OPEN TO ABOVE

UP

FOYER
9'0"X13'8"

LIVING ROOM/
LIBRARY
15'0"X16'0"

UP

PORCH

DINING ROOM
15'0"X14'0"

SHLV

HER WARDROBE

WINDOW SEAT

2 CAR GARAGE
22'0"X23'0"

PORCH

MAIN LEVEL: 2,526 SQUARE FEET
UPPER LEVEL: 1,215 SQUARE FEET
TOTAL: 3,741 SQUARE FEET
FUTURE RECREATION ROOM: 547 SQUARE FEET

Provence

What has come to be known as the "Country French" look is really the style of Provence. A farmhouse with French flourish, never contrived or pretentious, yet comfortable, exquisite and distinctive is this regional style. Rural traditions kept alive in small French villages vibrating with "white" sun, pulsating winds, olive groves and lavender fields embody all that is most French. Afternoons are spent with old and young alike exchanging stories while sipping wine beneath broad trees and at small sidewalk cafes–taking the moment to enjoy life, one day at a time.

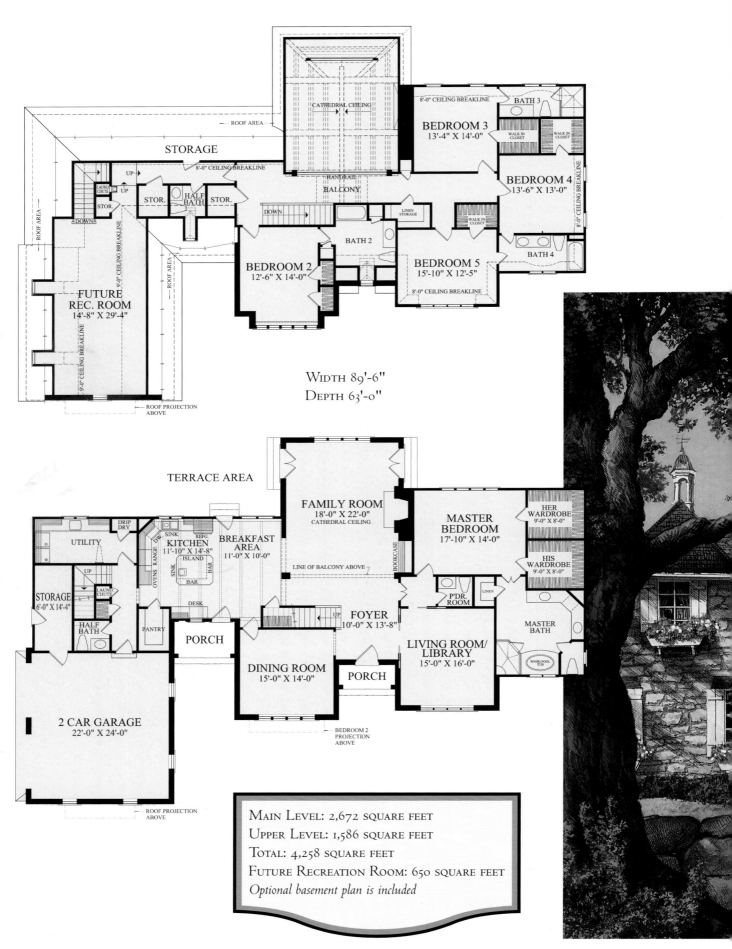

Manoir De Bais

The little sidewalk cafe was brimming with activity when excited voices at the next table caught our attention. Noting our interest, they invited us to join them and during the next hour regaled us with myths and legends of an old country home nearby. When, during our visit, we came upon Manoir de Bais, all the stories we had heard sprang to life. The romance of this old-world French manor remains with us to this very day.

Saint Clair

All it takes is a smile. This is a truth known everywhere, but we found it especially so in the tiny Normandy village of Saint Clair. Speaking no French other than "bonjour" or "merci", we discovered rather quickly that a word and a smile (coupled with the requisite hand gestures of course) was all it took for easy understanding. The people of Saint Clair made us feel right at home–"Southern Hospitality" at it's best.

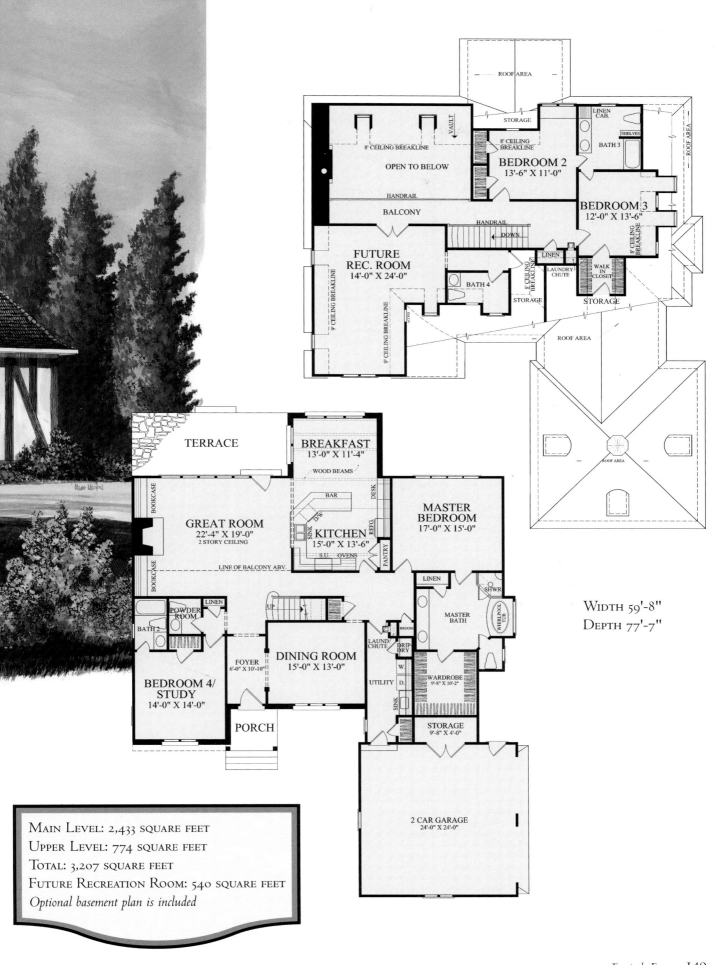

ROOF AREA

LINEN CAB.

STORAGE

SHELVES

BATH 3

8' CEILING BREAKLINE

VAULT

8' CEILING BREAKLINE

OPEN TO BELOW

ROOF AREA

BEDROOM 2
13'-6" X 11'-0"

BEDROOM 3
12'-0" X 13'-6"

8' CEILING BREAKLINE

HANDRAIL

BALCONY

HANDRAIL

DOWN

LINEN

FUTURE
REC. ROOM
14'-0" X 24'-0"

9' CEILING BREAKLINE

9' CEILING BREAKLINE

9' CEILING BREAKLINE

BATH 4

8' CEILING BREAKLINE

LAUNDRY CHUTE

WALK IN CLOSET

STORAGE

STORAGE

ROOF AREA

ROOF AREA

TERRACE

BREAKFAST
13'-0" X 11'-4"

WOOD BEAMS

BOOKCASE

GREAT ROOM
22'-4" X 19'-0"
2 STORY CEILING

BAR

DW

SINK

KITCHEN
15'-0" X 13'-6"

DESK

REFG.

MASTER
BEDROOM
17'-0" X 15'-0"

ROOF AREA

BOOKCASE

LINE OF BALCONY ABV.

S.U.   OVENS

PANTRY

LINEN

SHWR

POWDER ROOM

LINEN

UP

MASTER
BATH

WHIRLPOOL TUB

WIDTH 59'-8"
DEPTH 77'-7"

BATH 2

FOYER
6'-0" X 10'-10"

DINING ROOM
15'-0" X 13'-0"

LAUND.
CHUTE

DRIP DRY

BROOM

SINK

UTILITY

W.

D.

WARDROBE
9'-8" X 10'-2"

BEDROOM 4/
STUDY
14'-0" X 14'-0"

PORCH

STORAGE
9'-8" X 4'-0"

2 CAR GARAGE
24'-0" X 24'-0"

MAIN LEVEL: 2,433 SQUARE FEET
UPPER LEVEL: 774 SQUARE FEET
TOTAL: 3,207 SQUARE FEET
FUTURE RECREATION ROOM: 540 SQUARE FEET
Optional basement plan is included

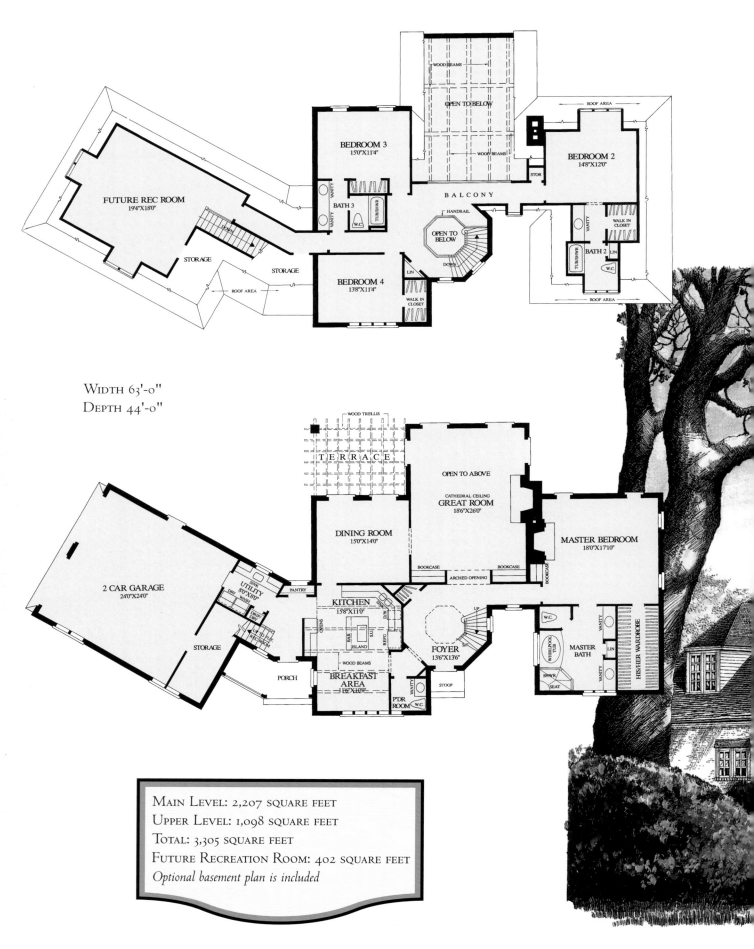

FUTURE REC ROOM
19'4"X18'0"

STORAGE

STORAGE

ROOF AREA

BEDROOM 3
15'0"X11'4"

VANITY

BATH 3

VANITY

W.C.

TUB/SHWR

OPEN TO BELOW

WOOD BEAMS

WOOD BEAMS

BALCONY

HANDRAIL

OPEN TO BELOW

DOWN

LIN

BEDROOM 4
13'8"X11'4"

WALK IN CLOSET

ROOF AREA

ROOF AREA

STOR

BEDROOM 2
14'8"X12'0"

VANITY

WALK IN CLOSET

TUB/SHWR

BATH 2

LIN

W.C.

ROOF AREA

WIDTH 63'-0"
DEPTH 44'-0"

WOOD TRELLIS

TERRACE

OPEN TO ABOVE

CATHEDRAL CEILING
GREAT ROOM
18'6"X26'0"

2 CAR GARAGE
24'0"X24'0"

STORAGE

UTILITY
8'0"X8'0"

SINK

DRY. WASH.

DRIP DRY

PANTRY

UP TO FUT. REC. ROOM

DINING ROOM
15'0"X14'0"

BOOKCASE

BOOKCASE

ARCHED OPENING

BOOKCASE

MASTER BEDROOM
18'0"X17'10"

KITCHEN
15'8"X11'0"

OVENS

BAR

ISLAND

SINK

D.W.

REFG.

SUB.

UP

W.C.

WHIRLPOOL TUB

VANITY

MASTER BATH

LIN

HIS/HER WARDROBE

WOOD BEAMS

FOYER
13'6"X13'6"

SHWR

SEAT

VANITY

PORCH

BREAKFAST AREA
11'6"X12'0"

VANITY

STOOP

PDR ROOM

W.C.

MAIN LEVEL: 2,207 SQUARE FEET
UPPER LEVEL: 1,098 SQUARE FEET
TOTAL: 3,305 SQUARE FEET
FUTURE RECREATION ROOM: 402 SQUARE FEET
Optional basement plan is included

Le Mans

The door opened and we were greeted by a most gracious and lovely lady, the owner of Le Mans. Indeed, her family had lived here for generations and it was only recently that she began using the first floor to display her antiques. Exquisite and elegant pieces—each a treasure, much like the home itself. A memory not to be forgotten, but displayed and enjoyed now and always.

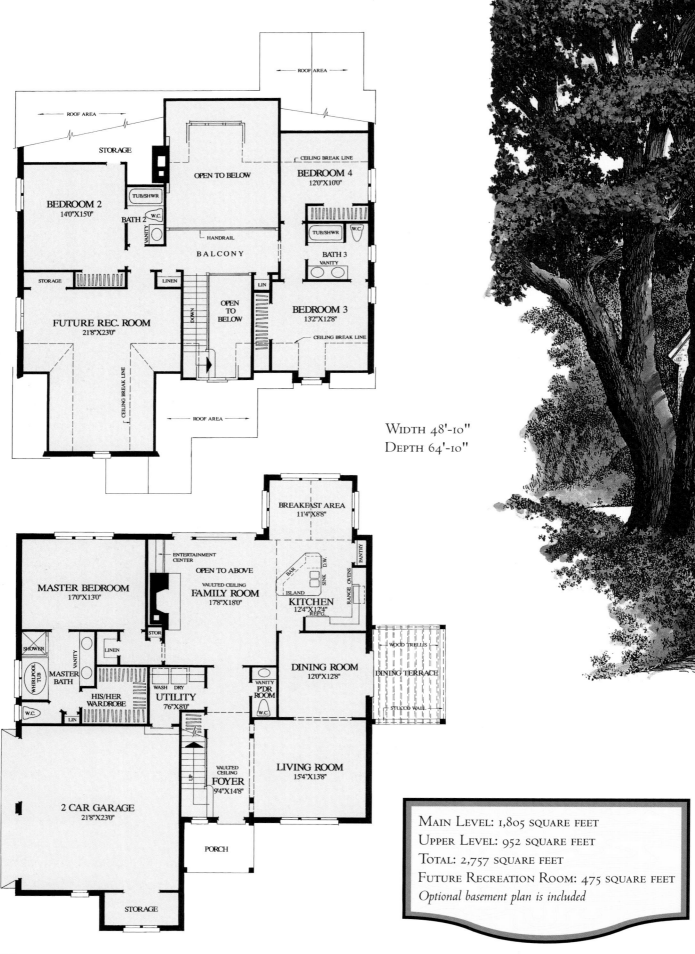

STORAGE

OPEN TO BELOW

BEDROOM 4
12'0"X10'0"

CEILING BREAK LINE

TUB/SHWR

W.C.

BEDROOM 2
14'0"X15'0"

BATH 2

W.C.

VANITY

HANDRAIL

TUB/SHWR

W.C.

BATH 3

VANITY

BALCONY

STORAGE

LINEN

LIN

OPEN TO BELOW

BEDROOM 3
13'2"X12'8"

FUTURE REC. ROOM
21'8"X23'0"

DOWN

CEILING BREAK LINE

CEILING BREAK LINE

ROOF AREA

WIDTH 48'-10"
DEPTH 64'-10"

BREAKFAST AREA
11'4"X8'8"

PANTRY

ENTERTAINMENT CENTER

BAR

SINK

D.W.

OPEN TO ABOVE

VAULTED CEILING
FAMILY ROOM
17'8"X18'0"

ISLAND

KITCHEN
12'4"X12'4"

RANGE

OVENS

MASTER BEDROOM
17'0"X13'0"

STOR

REFG.

SHOWER

LINEN

WOOD TRELLIS

MASTER BATH

VANITY

WHIRLPOOL TUB

WASH DRY

VANITY

DINING ROOM
12'0"X12'8"

DINING TERRACE

W.C.

HIS/HER WARDROBE

UTILITY
7'6"X8'0"

PDR ROOM

W.C.

STUCCO WALL

LIN

2 CAR GARAGE
21'8"X23'0"

UP

VAULTED CEILING
FOYER
9'4"X14'8"

LIVING ROOM
15'4"X13'8"

PORCH

STORAGE

MAIN LEVEL: 1,805 SQUARE FEET
UPPER LEVEL: 952 SQUARE FEET
TOTAL: 2,757 SQUARE FEET
FUTURE RECREATION ROOM: 475 SQUARE FEET
Optional basement plan is included

Carmel Cottage

The winding streets, the quaint little shops, the pounding surf, the tree-covered land—the setting for Carmel Cottage. Warm, weathered and welcoming, this home endures the test of time and embraces all who pause to admire.

Avignon

DESIGN HPT770069

In the south of France there is an old and ornate town that is over-flowing with art, beauty and history. My Wilmington friends, in order to make their travel connections elsewhere, needed to locate the train station in Avignon. They consulted their guidebook, they consulted their language translator, they attempted communication—all to no avail. Finally, Bobby, in desperation, approached an elderly man and motioned up and down with his right fist while saying "Choo-Choo." This was all that was needed for them to finally receive directions to the depot. "C'est la vie!"

ROOF AREA

ROOF AREA

STORAGE

OPEN TO FAMILY BELOW

BEDROOM 4
12'-8" X 11'-0"

9' CEILING BREAKLINE

HANDRAIL

BALCONY

HANDRAIL

BATH 2

DOWN

BATH3

FUTURE
REC. ROOM
21'-0" X 17'-0"

BEDROOM 2
13'-0" X 14'-0"

W.I.C.

BEDROOM 3
12'-8" X 13'-2"

STORAGE

W.I.C.

ROOF AREA

BALCONY

ROOF AREA

WIDTH 57'-2"
DEPTH 60'-2"

PORCH
19'-10" X 10'-0"

BREAKFAST
11'-8" X 14'-6"

DESK

FAMILY ROOM
19'-6" X 14'-4"
2 STORY CLG.

BAR

DW. SINK

MASTER
BEDROOM
14'-8" X 15'-4"

OVENS REFG.

KITCHEN
12'-8" X 11'-10"

S.U.

REFG. SINK

UP

LINEN

PWDR ROOM

MASTER
BATH
12'-3" X 9'-0"

WHIRLPOOL TUB

LIVING ROOM
12'-6" X 14'-0"

FOYER
6'-10" X 14'-0"

DINING ROOM
12'-6" X 14'-0"

UTILITY

2 CAR GARAGE
21'-0" X 22'-8"

STOOP

MAIN LEVEL: 1,973 SQUARE FEET
UPPER LEVEL: 1,062 SQUARE FEET
TOTAL: 3,035 SQUARE FEET
FUTURE RECREATION ROOM: 384 SQUARE FEET
Optional basement plan is included

MASTER BEDROOM
24'0"X17'2"

ROOF AREA

OPEN TO BELOW

BEDROOM 2
16'0"X16'0"

WALK IN CLOSET

BATH 2

CEILING BREAK LINE

POCKET DOORS

LINEN CABINET
LAUNDRY
CHUTE

BALCONY

HANDRAIL

DN.

STORAGE

TUB/SHWR

STORAGE

LINEN

TUB/SHWR

SEAT

SHOWER

VANITY

MASTER BATH

WHIRLPOOL
TUB

DOWN

WALK IN CLOSET

BATH 4

LIN

DOWN

VANITY

WALK IN CLOSET

SHWR

SEAT

BATH 3

W.C.

VANITY

VANITY

BIDET

W.C.

HER WARDROBE

DRESSING TABLE

HIS WARDROBE

BEDROOM 4
16'0"X14'0"

OPEN TO BELOW

UP TO ATTIC

BEDROOM 3
16'0"X13'8"

HANDRAIL

WNDW
SEAT

WNDW
SEAT

WNDW
SEAT

FUTURE ROOM
19'4"X12'4"

SITTING AREA

WIDTH 72'-0"
DEPTH 66'-6"

TERRACEE/DECK AREA

BATH 5

VAN

W.C.

BEDROOM 5
16'8"X17'0"

KITCHEN
15'0"X18'2"
VOLUME CEILING

D/W SINK REFG

BREAKFAST
AREA
9'0"X18'2"
VOLUME CEILING

FAMILY ROOM
24'8"X20'2"

BOOKCASE

TUB/SHWR

SINK

ISLAND

OVENS

WALK IN CLOSET

LINE OF BALCONY

WASH DRY

DRIP/
DRY

LAUNDRY
CHUTE

PANTRY

DESK

SINK

UTILITY
12'4"X8'0"

LINEN

BUTLERS
PANTRY

W.C.

P'DR ROOM

VANITY

BAR

SHELVES

BOOKCASE

STORAGE

UP

STORAGE

LINE OF BALCONY

UP

LIVING ROOM
16'0"X24'0"

3 CAR GARAGE
24'0"X34'10"

DINING ROOM
16'0"X18'0"

FOYER
14'0"X18'0"

STOOP

MAIN LEVEL: 2,870 SQUARE FEET
UPPER LEVEL: 2,502 SQUARE FEET
TOTAL: 5,372 SQUARE FEET
FUTURE BONUS SPACE: 271 SQUARE FEET
Optional basement plan is included

MILES MELTON

Chateau De Bachen

Evenly spaced trees lining the way, fields of lavender light and the smell of freshly cut hay–these sights and smells engulfed our senses as we approached Chateau De Bachen. The impressive simplicity, the massive presence, the natural melding of architecture and landscape seemed so right, so romantic, so perfect. An intimate getaway for our very first night together.

Philadelphia

DESIGN HPT770071

O̶ur Liberty Bell, Ben Franklin's print shop, the signing of the Declaration of Independence—what history one feels in the streets of Philadelphia. So many beginnings and so many endings in the foundation and growth of our country have their roots in this city. Classical and commanding, The Philadelphia is typical of many homes in the Historic District and would be majestic in any neighborhood, anywhere—today as well as yesterday and tomorrow.

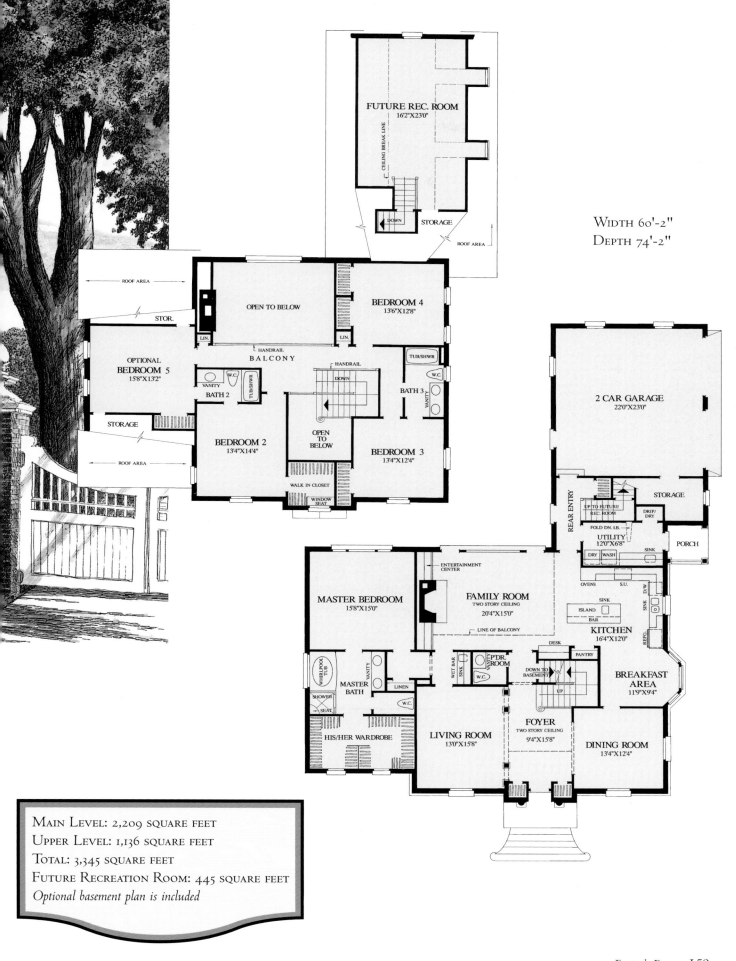

FUTURE REC. ROOM
16'2"X23'0"

CEILING BREAK LINE

DOWN

STORAGE

ROOF AREA

WIDTH 60'-2"
DEPTH 74'-2"

ROOF AREA

STOR.

OPEN TO BELOW

BEDROOM 4
13'6"X12'8"

LIN.

LIN.

OPTIONAL
BEDROOM 5
15'8"X13'2"

HANDRAIL
BALCONY

HANDRAIL

TUB/SHWR

W.C.

VANITY
BATH 2

TUB/SHWR

DOWN

W.C.

BATH 3

VANITY

STORAGE

BEDROOM 2
13'4"X14'4"

OPEN
TO
BELOW

BEDROOM 3
13'4"X12'4"

ROOF AREA

WALK IN CLOSET

WINDOW
SEAT

2 CAR GARAGE
22'0"X23'0"

REAR ENTRY

UP TO FUTURE
REC. ROOM

STORAGE

DRIP/
DRY

FOLD DN. I.B.

UTILITY
12'0"X6'8"

PORCH

DRY

WASH

SINK

ENTERTAINMENT
CENTER

OVENS

S.U.

SINK

D.W.

REFR.

MASTER BEDROOM
15'8"X15'0"

FAMILY ROOM
TWO STORY CEILING
20'4"X15'0"

ISLAND

SINK

BAR

KITCHEN
16'4"X12'0"

LINE OF BALCONY

WHIRLPOOL
TUB

MASTER
BATH

VANITY

WET BAR

SINK

P'DR.
ROOM

VANITY

W.C.

DESK

PANTRY

DOWN TO BASEMENT

UP

BREAKFAST
AREA
11'9"X9'4"

SHOWER

SEAT

LINEN

W.C.

HIS/HER WARDROBE

LIVING ROOM
13'0"X15'8"

FOYER
TWO STORY CEILING
9'4"X15'8"

DINING ROOM
13'4"X12'4"

MAIN LEVEL: 2,209 SQUARE FEET
UPPER LEVEL: 1,136 SQUARE FEET
TOTAL: 3,345 SQUARE FEET
FUTURE RECREATION ROOM: 445 SQUARE FEET
Optional basement plan is included

Bromley Court

Never have I seen such gentle and lush countryside as the rolling hills of England. It is today as it must have been throughout the yesterdays–sheep grazing, stone walls and quaint little villages along the way. Now and then a great house appears–classic, balanced, and elegant in detail. Such is the Bromley Court, a very English Georgian dwelling.

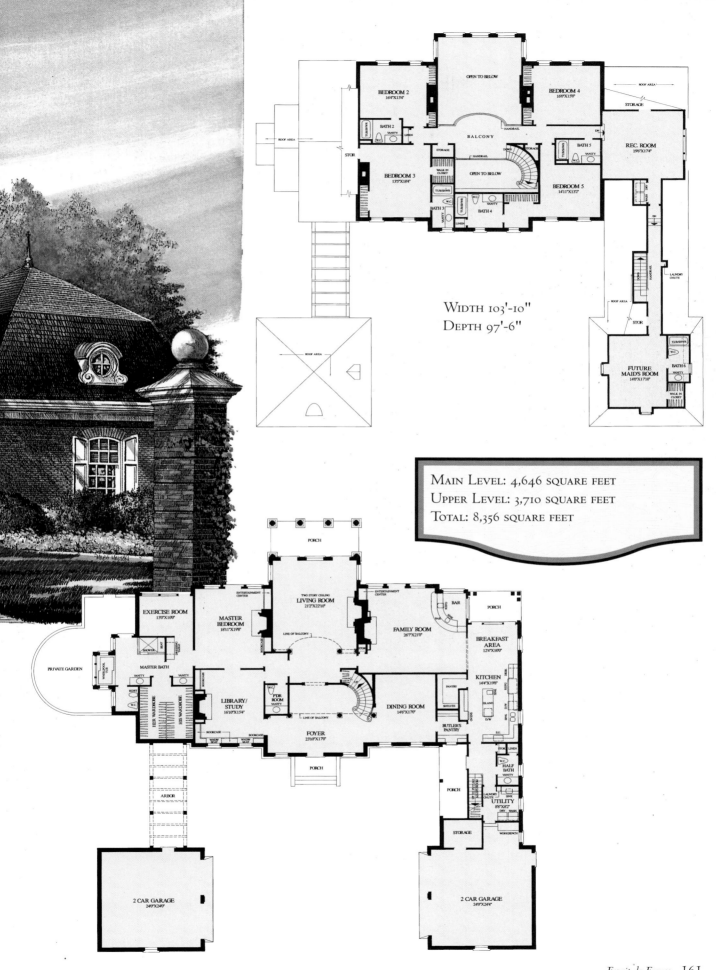

WIDTH 103'-10"
DEPTH 97'-6"

MAIN LEVEL: 4,646 SQUARE FEET
UPPER LEVEL: 3,710 SQUARE FEET
TOTAL: 8,356 SQUARE FEET

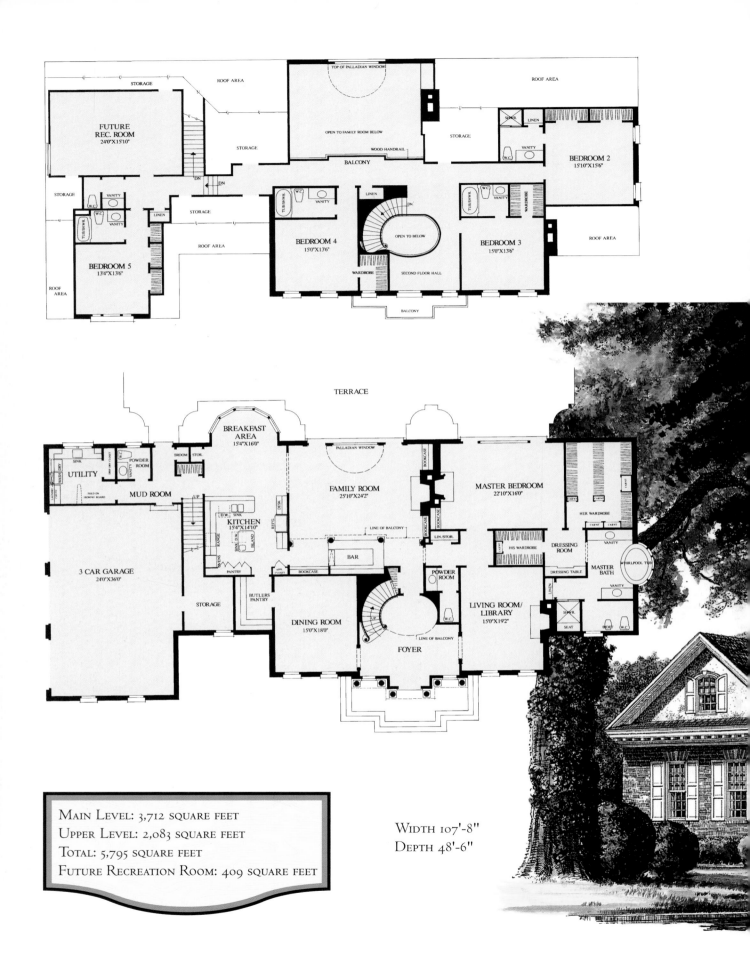

Upper Level

FUTURE REC. ROOM
24'0"X15'10"

ROOF AREA

STORAGE

TOP OF PALLADIAN WINDOW

ROOF AREA

OPEN TO FAMILY ROOM BELOW

STORAGE

SHWR. LINEN

VANITY

W.C.

BEDROOM 2
15'10"X15'6"

STORAGE

DN

DN

STORAGE

WOOD HANDRAIL

BALCONY

STORAGE

VANITY

W.C.

W.C.

VANITY

LINEN

STORAGE

ROOF AREA

BEDROOM 5
13'4"X13'6"

TUB/SHWR.

TUB/SHWR.

W.C.

VANITY

BEDROOM 4
15'0"X13'6"

LINEN

DN

OPEN TO BELOW

WARDROBE

W.C.

VANITY

TUB/SHWR.

WARDROBE

BEDROOM 3
15'0"X13'6"

ROOF AREA

ROOF AREA

WARDROBE

SECOND FLOOR HALL

BALCONY

Main Level

TERRACE

SINK

WASH DRY

POWDER ROOM

VANITY

W.C.

DRIP DRY CLOSET

UTILITY

FOLD DN IRONING BOARD

LAUNDRY CHUTE

MUD ROOM

BREAKFAST AREA
15'4"X16'0"

BROOM STOR.

PALLADIAN WINDOW

BOOKCASE

MASTER BEDROOM
22'10"X16'0"

CABINET

CABINET

CABINET

HER WARDROBE

CABINET

CABINET

VANITY

WHIRLPOOL TUB

UP

DESK

KITCHEN
15'4"X14'10"

O.W. SINK

RANGE

OVENS

ISLAND

REFG.

FAMILY ROOM
25'10"X24'2"

LINE OF BALCONY

BOOKCASE

BOOKCASE

LIN./STOR.

HIS WARDROBE

DRESSING ROOM

DRESSING TABLE

MASTER BATH

VANITY

3 CAR GARAGE
24'0"X36'0"

SINK

PANTRY

APPL. CLOSET

BOOKCASE

BAR

POWDER ROOM

W.C.

LIVING ROOM/ LIBRARY
15'0"X19'2"

LINEN

SHWR.

SEAT

BIDET

W.C.

STORAGE

BUTLERS PANTRY

DINING ROOM
15'0"X18'0"

UP

FOYER

LINE OF BALCONY

MAIN LEVEL: 3,712 SQUARE FEET
UPPER LEVEL: 2,083 SQUARE FEET
TOTAL: 5,795 SQUARE FEET
FUTURE RECREATION ROOM: 409 SQUARE FEET

WIDTH 107'-8"
DEPTH 48'-6"

The Southerly

The stately Southerly, a home with presence and impressive refinement, is the type of architecture brought to our shores by the more affluent English people in the later Georgian period. Formality at its best and classic detail that is difficult to surpass, combined with a floor plan which is both gracious and most of all functional—all of these elements merge in the Southerly, an English Georgian home.

UNFINISHED
ATTIC STORAGE

DOWN

ROOF AREA   ROOF AREA

ROOF AREA   ROOF AREA

Main Level: 3,027 square feet
Upper Level: 1,509 square feet
Total: 4,536 square feet
Optional basement plan is included

ROOF AREA   ROOF AREA

BATH 3

BEDROOM 3
17'-0" X 13'-0"

BEDROOM 4
17'-0" X 13'-0"

WALK-IN CLOSET   WALK-IN CLOSET

COPPER ROOF

STORAGE

WALK-IN CLOSET   LINEN

DOWN   HANDRAIL

BATH 4

STORAGE

BEDROOM 2
16'-0" X 15'-0"

OPEN TO BELOW

BEDROOM 5
14'-6" X 13'-0"

ROOF AREA

BATH 2

ROOF AREA

COPPER ROOF

2 CAR GARAGE
23'-0" X 35'-4"

WIDTH 85'-0"
DEPTH 82'-6"

STORAGE

STORAGE   STORAGE

UP

BREAKFAST
AREA
16'-0" X 12'-0"

REFG.   VEG. SINK

SINK   DW.

ISLAND   BAR

DESK

BOOKCASE

STORAGE

MASTER
BEDROOM
18'-0" X 16'-8"

FAMILY ROOM
23'-8" X 17'-0"

PDR.
ROOM

LIBRARY
13'-0" X 13'-0"

OVEN

KITCHEN
16'-0" X 14'-8"
S.U.

LINEN

MASTER
BATH

WHIRLPOOL TUB

WASH   DRY

FOLD DN.
IRON. BD.

PANTRY

DINING ROOM
16'-0" X 15'-0"

UP

LIVING ROOM
15'-0" X 15'-0"

BOOKCASE

STOR.

UTILITY

SINK

STORAGE

LINE OF WALL ABOVE

FOYER
12'-8" X 11'-2"

BOOKCASE

WARDROBE

PORCH
13'-0" X 6'-6"

Winchester

The family was gathering at the Winchester. As soon as the car doors opened, the children ran gleefully to see their Grandparents—leaving their Mother and Father to struggle with the luggage, toys and presents. It was a special homecoming (different from all the ones before) for it marked Mama and Papa's fiftieth anniversary and everyone was coming home to celebrate.

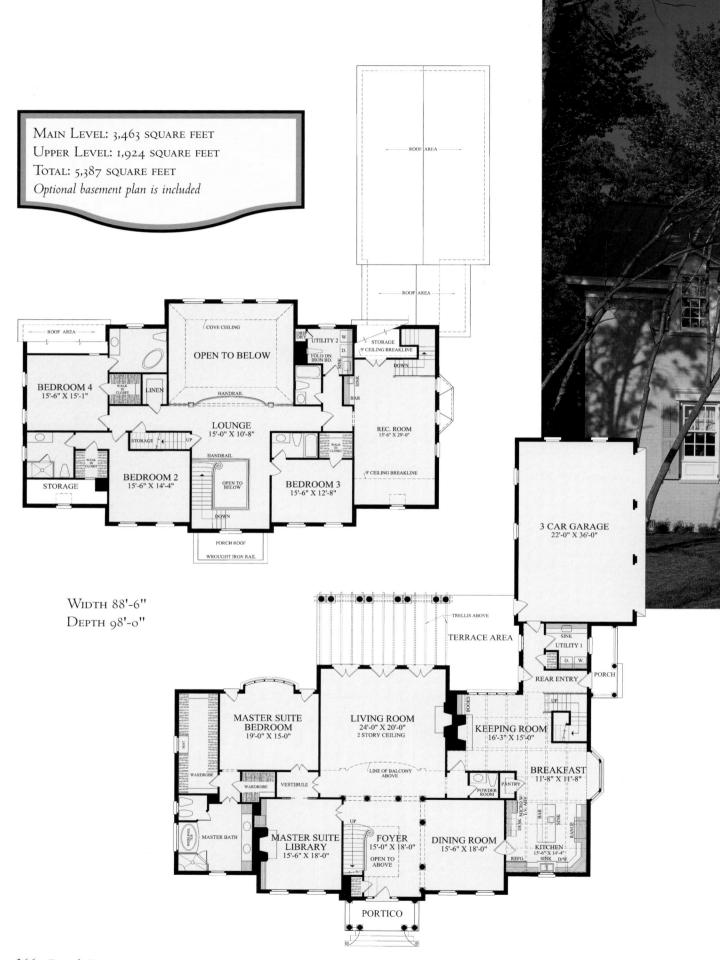

Main Level: 3,463 square feet
Upper Level: 1,924 square feet
Total: 5,387 square feet
Optional basement plan is included

ROOF AREA

ROOF AREA

ROOF AREA

COVE CEILING

OPEN TO BELOW

DRIP DRY

UTILITY 2

FOLD DN. IRON BD.

W.

D.

SINK

STORAGE

9' CEILING BREAKLINE

DOWN

BEDROOM 4
15'-6" X 15'-1"

WALK IN CLOSET

LINEN

SINK

BAR

HANDRAIL

LOUNGE
15'-0" X 10'-8"

REC. ROOM
15'-6" X 29'-0"

STORAGE

UP

HANDRAIL

WALK IN CLOSET

9' CEILING BREAKLINE

WALK IN CLOSET

BEDROOM 2
15'-6" X 14'-4"

OPEN TO BELOW

BEDROOM 3
15'-6" X 12'-8"

STORAGE

DOWN

PORCH ROOF

WROUGHT IRON RAIL

Width 88'-6"
Depth 98'-0"

3 CAR GARAGE
22'-0" X 36'-0"

TRELLIS ABOVE

TERRACE AREA

SINK

UTILITY 1

D.

W.

REAR ENTRY

PORCH

MASTER SUITE
BEDROOM
19'-0" X 15'-0"

LIVING ROOM
24'-0" X 20'-0"
2 STORY CEILING

BOOKS

KEEPING ROOM
16'-3" X 15'-0"

SEAT

WARDROBE

WARDROBE

VESTIBULE

LINE OF BALCONY
ABOVE

BREAKFAST
11'-8" X 11'-8"

PANTRY

POWDER ROOM

DESK

MICRO W/ OV. ABV.

BAR

SINK

RANGE

WHIRLPOOL TUB

MASTER BATH

MASTER SUITE
LIBRARY
15'-6" X 18'-0"

UP

FOYER
15'-0" X 18'-0"
OPEN TO ABOVE

DINING ROOM
15'-6" X 18'-0"

KITCHEN
15'-6" X 14'-4"

REF.

SINK

D/W

PORTICO

Photo by Jeffery S. Otto   This home, as shown in the photograph, may differ from the actual blueprints. For more detailed information, please check the floor plans carefully.

Longview

House Extraordinaire...with Regency and Colonial Revival architectural characteristics, the Longview is a home of elegance and comfort, a home that combines the best of architecture and design—a refined home that exudes both excitement and warmth. The Longview was designed and built as a Classic American Homes Lifestyle Showcase. Inside and out, the Longview is romantic and extraordinary and, because of the classical design of the home and furnishings, it is timeless—a trait that is distinctly "Poole."

St. Charles

New Orleans, famous for the French Quarter with its Dixieland jazz, Creole delights and beignets is an exhilarating experience. In contrast, the quiet Garden District with the streetcar ride to Audubon Park, ancient trees lining the avenues and gracious homes along the way are pure delight. Listen and you can hear hooves beating along the paths, children laughing at play and violins as the waltz begins—all from times past. The St. Charles is reminiscent of there and then, but is a home place for here and now.

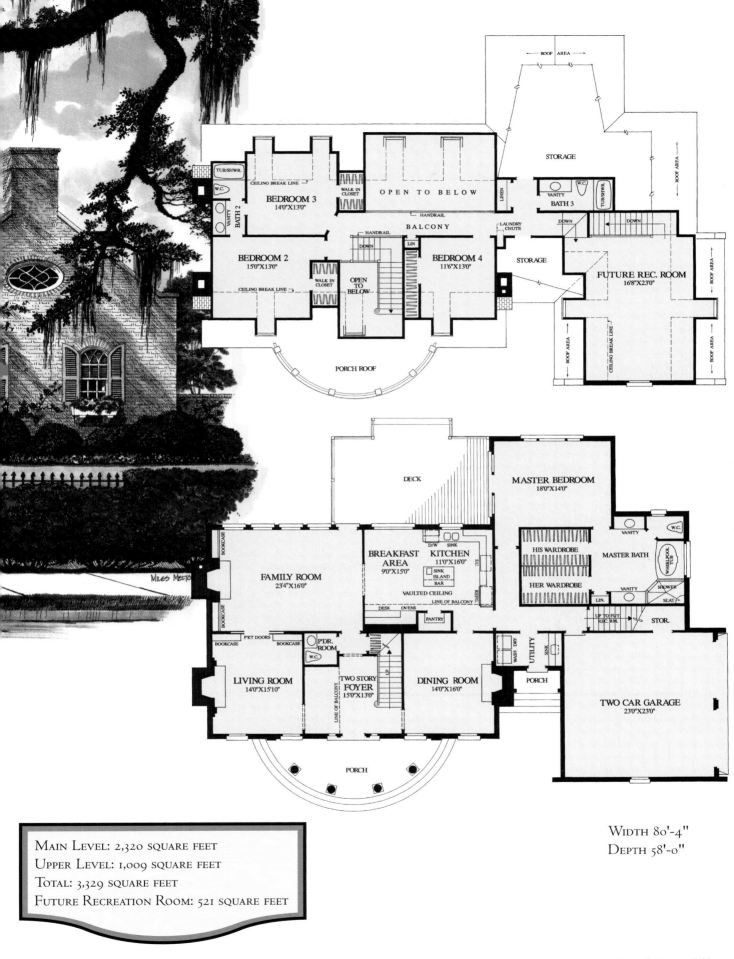

TUB/SHWR.

W.C.

BEDROOM 3
14'0"X13'0"

BATH 2

VANITY

CEILING BREAK LINE

WALK IN
CLOSET

OPEN TO BELOW

HANDRAIL

BALCONY

LINEN

VANITY

W.C.

BATH 3

TUB/SHWR.

STORAGE

ROOF AREA

ROOF AREA

DOWN

DOWN

LAUNDRY
CHUTE

BEDROOM 2
15'0"X13'0"

CEILING BREAK LINE

HANDRAIL

DOWN

WALK IN
CLOSET

OPEN
TO
BELOW

LIN.

BEDROOM 4
11'6"X13'0"

STORAGE

FUTURE REC. ROOM
16'8"X23'0"

ROOF AREA

ROOF AREA

CEILING BREAK LINE

ROOF AREA

PORCH ROOF

DECK

MASTER BEDROOM
18'0"X14'0"

VANITY

W.C.

BOOKCASE

FAMILY ROOM
23'4"X16'0"

BOOKCASE

BREAKFAST
AREA
9'0"X15'0"

KITCHEN
11'0"X16'0"

D/W SINK

SINK
ISLAND
BAR

VAULTED CEILING

LINE OF BALCONY

DESK   OVENS

HIS WARDROBE

HER WARDROBE

MASTER BATH

VANITY

WHIRLPOOL
TUB

LIN.

SHOWER

SEAT

MILES MELTON

BOOKCASE

BOOKCASE

P'KT DOORS

BOOKCASE

P'DR.
ROOM

W.C.

PANTRY

UP TO FUT.
REC. RM.

STOR.

WASH DRY

UTILITY

SINK

PORCH

LIVING ROOM
14'0"X15'10"

LINE OF BALCONY

TWO STORY
FOYER
15'0"X13'0"

UP

DINING ROOM
14'0"X16'0"

PORCH

TWO CAR GARAGE
23'0"X23'0"

PORCH

MAIN LEVEL: 2,320 SQUARE FEET

UPPER LEVEL: 1,009 SQUARE FEET

TOTAL: 3,329 SQUARE FEET

FUTURE RECREATION ROOM: 521 SQUARE FEET

WIDTH 80'-4"
DEPTH 58'-0"

Esprit de France 169

Mount Aire II

DESIGN HPT770077

Parasols, high-necked lace collars, white gloves and gold-tipped canes adorned lovely ladies from the past as they sipped their tea and visited amid the roses, hydrangeas, tulips and day lilies. The Mount Aire II, like many antebellum homes that capture the romance of the old South, graciously reflects the Greek Revival style of architecture. A home that is...simply Southern at its best!

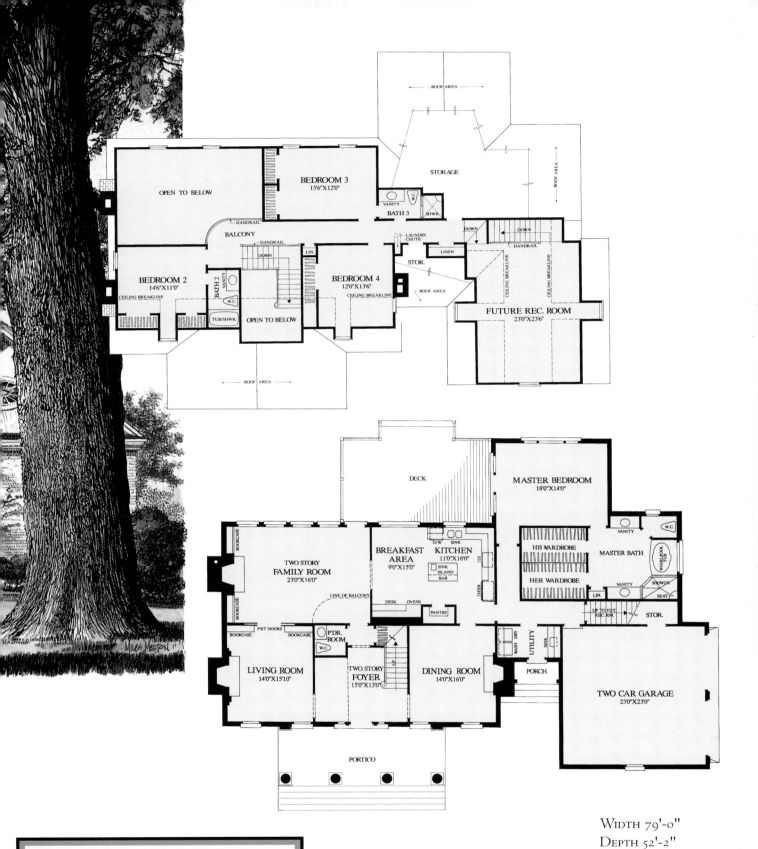

Upper Level:

OPEN TO BELOW

BEDROOM 3
15'6"X12'0"

STORAGE

ROOF AREA

ROOF AREA

HANDRAIL

BALCONY

BATH 3

VANITY W.C. SHWR.

HANDRAIL

BEDROOM 2
14'6"X11'0"

BATH 2

VANITY

W.C.

TUB/SHWR.

CEILING BREAKLINE

DOWN

LIN.

LAUNDRY CHUTE

STOR.

LINEN

DOWN

DOWN

HANDRAIL

CEILING BREAKLINE

CEILING BREAKLINE

OPEN TO BELOW

BEDROOM 4
12'0"X13'6"

CEILING BREAKLINE

ROOF AREA

FUTURE REC. ROOM
23'0"X23'6"

ROOF AREA

Main Level:

DECK

MASTER BEDROOM
18'0"X14'0"

BOOKCASE

TWO STORY
FAMILY ROOM
23'0"X16'0"

BOOKCASE

BREAKFAST AREA
9'0"X15'0"

KITCHEN
11'0"X16'0"

D/W SINK

SINK ISLAND BAR

DESK OVENS

PANTRY

REF.

HIS WARDROBE

HER WARDROBE

VANITY

W.C.

WHIRLPOOL BATH

MASTER BATH

LIN.

VANITY

SHOWER

SEAT

UP TO FUT. REC. RM.

STOR.

LINE OF BALCONY

BOOKCASE

BOOKCASE

P'KT DOORS

BOOKCASE

P'DR. ROOM

W.C.

LIVING ROOM
14'0"X15'10"

TWO STORY
FOYER
15'0"X13'0"

UP

DINING ROOM
14'0"X16'0"

WASH DRY

UTILITY

SINK

PORCH

TWO CAR GARAGE
23'0"X23'0"

PORTICO

WIDTH 79'-0"
DEPTH 52'-2"

MAIN LEVEL: 2,320 SQUARE FEET

UPPER LEVEL: 975 SQUARE FEET

TOTAL: 3,295 SQUARE FEET

FUTURE RECREATION ROOM: 540 SQUARE FEET

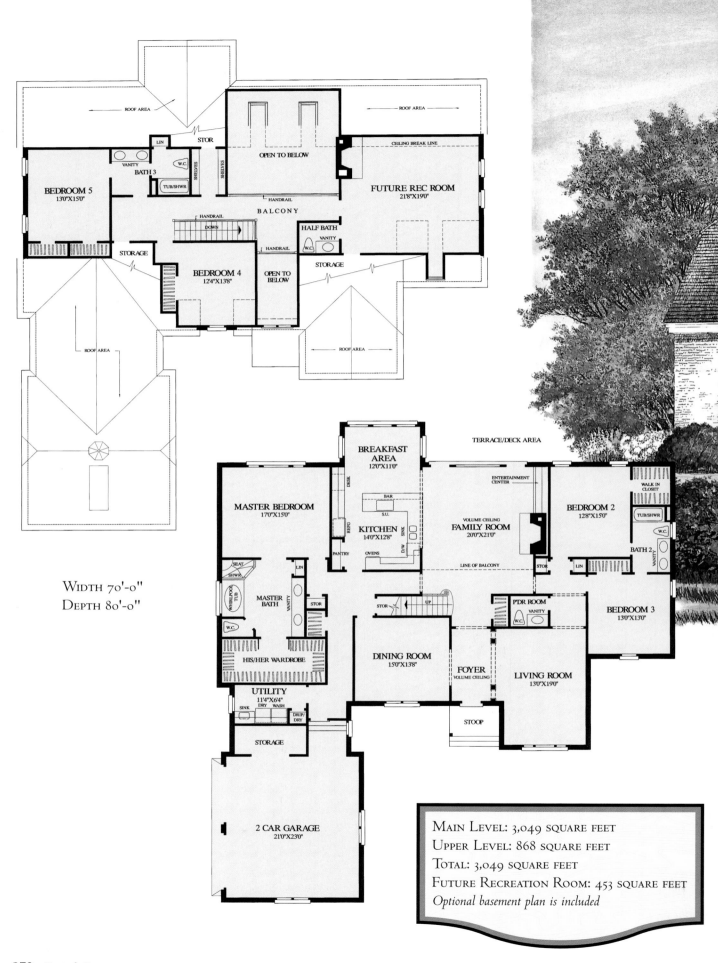

ROOF AREA

ROOF AREA

LIN STOR

BATH 3

VANITY

W.C.

TUB/SHWR

SHELVES

SHELVES

OPEN TO BELOW

CEILING BREAK LINE

FUTURE REC ROOM
21'8"X19'0"

BEDROOM 5
13'0"X15'0"

HANDRAIL

BALCONY

HANDRAIL
DOWN

HANDRAIL

HALF BATH

VANITY

W.C.

STORAGE

STORAGE

BEDROOM 4
12'4"X13'8"

OPEN TO
BELOW

ROOF AREA

ROOF AREA

ROOF AREA

WIDTH 70'-0"
DEPTH 80'-0"

TERRACE/DECK AREA

BREAKFAST
AREA
12'0"X11'0"

DESK

BAR

ENTERTAINMENT
CENTER

WALK IN
CLOSET

MASTER BEDROOM
17'0"X15'0"

REFG

S.U.

VOLUME CEILING
FAMILY ROOM
20'0"X21'0"

BEDROOM 2
12'8"X15'0"

TUB/SHWR

KITCHEN
14'0"X12'8"

SINK

D/W

W.C.

PANTRY

OVENS

LINE OF BALCONY

BATH 2

VANITY

SEAT

SHWR

LIN

STOR

STOR

UP

STOR

PDR ROOM

BEDROOM 3
13'0"X13'0"

WHIRLPOOL
TUB

MASTER
BATH

VANITY

W.C.

VANITY

LIN

W.C.

HIS/HER WARDROBE

DINING ROOM
15'0"X13'8"

FOYER
VOLUME CEILING

LIVING ROOM
13'0"X19'0"

UTILITY
11'4"X6'4"

DRY

WASH

STOOP

SINK

DRIP/
DRY

STORAGE

2 CAR GARAGE
21'0"X23'0"

MAIN LEVEL: 3,049 SQUARE FEET
UPPER LEVEL: 868 SQUARE FEET
TOTAL: 3,049 SQUARE FEET
FUTURE RECREATION ROOM: 453 SQUARE FEET
Optional basement plan is included

Les Serein

With hair flying and cheeks rosy, the lady of Les Serein pedaled her bicycle through the winding streets of town. Along her travels, greetings were exchanged with passing neighbors as they made their way–as they did every morning–to and from the bakery. In some places, some things never change, nor should they.

Romantic Retreats

Wild views of the wide-open spaces come to mind when considering your own private getaway–whether it's a seaboard cottage or a rustic mountain retreat. From Telluride to the Hamptons, the singular character of coastal and cliffside styles invites the enjoyment of sunsets, the study of stars.

With such diverse dialects as West Indies Conch and Cape Cod, Romantic Retreats brings out the best of relaxed resort vernaculars. Wraparound porches and wonderful bays, screen porches and rambling decks provide plenty of opportunities to connect with the great outdoors–even to dine in sunlight.

Serenity surrounds Eastshore Cottage (page 194), which provides an expansive front porch and access to the back property through the great room. A splendid morning bay brings in a sense of nature while plenty of windows all around offer wide views of the outdoors.

Currituck Cottage (page 200) is reminiscent of the raised houses of the Southern coastal plains. The added height, surrounding porch and long, low windows provide the home with views, shade and cooling breezes from all directions. With three levels, the design offers all of the ingredients for a charming year-round or vacation home.

These plans extend an invitation to enjoy your home as you enjoy your life–to the fullest. Evocative styles embrace the ultimate comforts of the 21st-century home, fully prepared to sink roots in any region.

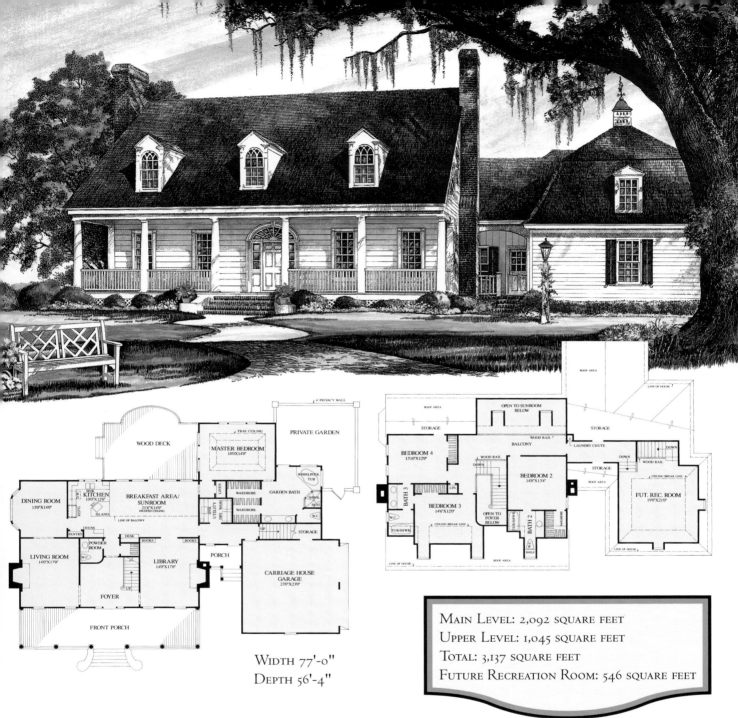

Main Level: 2,092 square feet
Upper Level: 1,045 square feet
Total: 3,137 square feet
Future Recreation Room: 546 square feet

Width 77'-0"
Depth 56'-4"

La Petite Natchez

Design HPT770086

It is often said that good things come in small packages—ask any connoisseur of fine jewelry! You made a request and we listened, thus from The Natchez sprang La Petit Natchez. Without sacrificing any of the rooms or amenities of the original, The Natchez was proportionately reduced and La Petite Natchez was born. This generation will create the history for La Petite. May it be a gracious time!

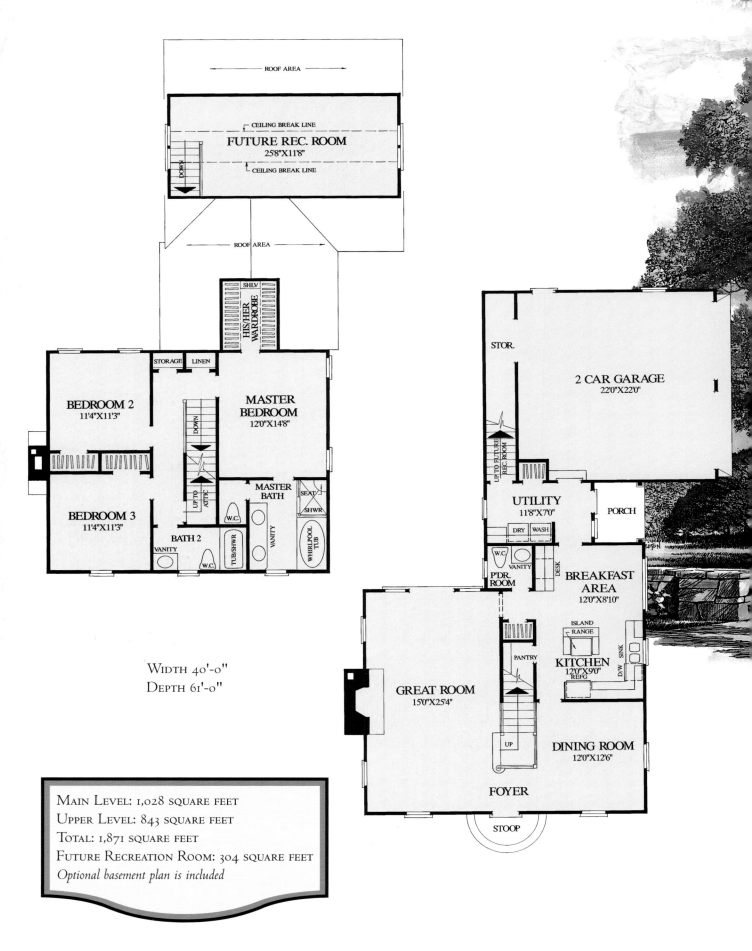

ROOF AREA

CEILING BREAK LINE

FUTURE REC. ROOM
25'8"X11'8"

CEILING BREAK LINE

DOWN

ROOF AREA

SHLV

HIS/HER WARDROBE

STORAGE LINEN

BEDROOM 2
11'4"X11'3"

MASTER BEDROOM
12'0"X14'8"

DOWN

BEDROOM 3
11'4"X11'3"

UP TO ATTIC

MASTER BATH

SEAT

SHWR

W.C.

VANITY

WHIRLPOOL TUB

BATH 2

VANITY

TUB/SHWR

W.C.

WIDTH 40'-0"
DEPTH 61'-0"

STOR.

2 CAR GARAGE
22'0"X22'0"

UP TO FUTURE REC. ROOM

UTILITY
11'8"X7'0"

PORCH

DRY WASH

W.C

P'DR. ROOM

VANITY

DESK

BREAKFAST AREA
12'0"X8'10"

ISLAND

RANGE

GREAT ROOM
15'0"X25'4"

PANTRY

SINK

KITCHEN
12'0"X9'0"

D/W

REFG

UP

DINING ROOM
12'0"X12'6"

FOYER

STOOP

MAIN LEVEL: 1,028 SQUARE FEET
UPPER LEVEL: 843 SQUARE FEET
TOTAL: 1,871 SQUARE FEET
FUTURE RECREATION ROOM: 304 SQUARE FEET
Optional basement plan is included

Kentucky Bluegrass

The wind blows gently across the billowing grasses. The colts and fillies frolic in the pastures. The gleaming white fences define the checkerboard spaces where this annual rite of spring progresses. From our breakfast nook window, we watch the seasons come and go in our Kentucky Bluegrass home.

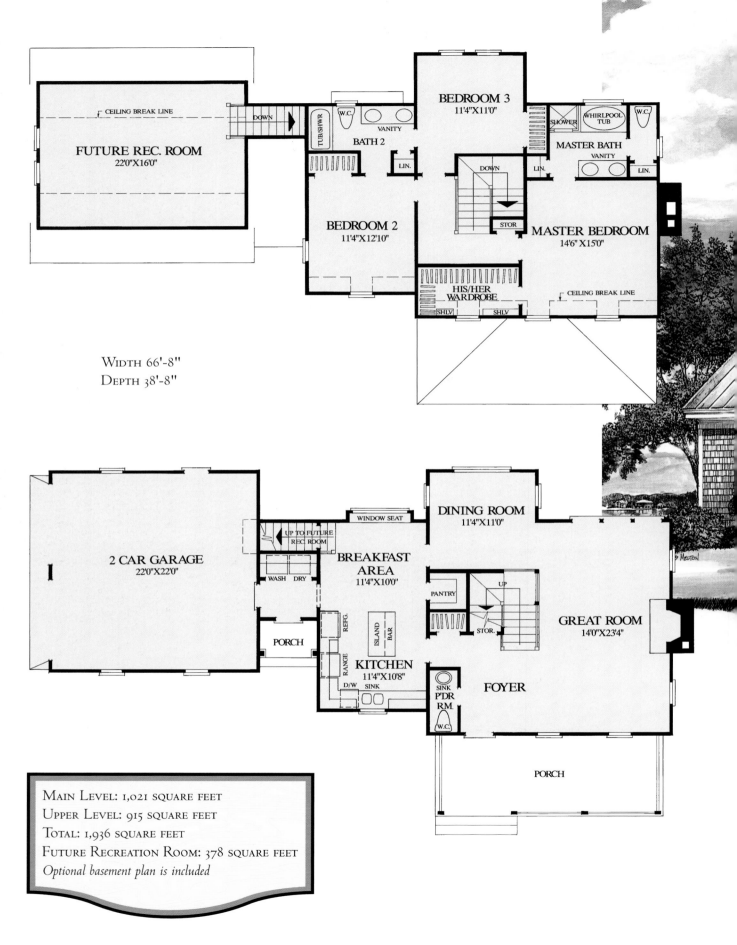

CEILING BREAK LINE

FUTURE REC. ROOM
22'0"X16'0"

DOWN

W.C

BATH 2

TUB/SHWR

VANITY

BEDROOM 3
11'4"X11'0"

SHOWER

WHIRLPOOL TUB

W.C.

MASTER BATH

VANITY

LIN.

DOWN

LIN.

STOR

MASTER BEDROOM
14'6" X15'0"

BEDROOM 2
11'4"X12'10"

HIS/HER WARDROBE

SHLV

SHLV

CEILING BREAK LINE

WIDTH 66'-8"
DEPTH 38'-8"

2 CAR GARAGE
22'0"X22'0"

UP TO FUTURE REC. ROOM

WINDOW SEAT

DINING ROOM
11'4"X11'0"

WASH   DRY

BREAKFAST AREA
11'4"X10'0"

PANTRY

UP

STOR.

GREAT ROOM
14'0"X23'4"

PORCH

REFG.

ISLAND   BAR

RANGE

KITCHEN
11'4"X10'8"

D/W   SINK

SINK

P'DR RM.

FOYER

W.C.

PORCH

MAIN LEVEL: 1,021 SQUARE FEET
UPPER LEVEL: 915 SQUARE FEET
TOTAL: 1,936 SQUARE FEET
FUTURE RECREATION ROOM: 378 SQUARE FEET
Optional basement plan is included

Ocracoke Cottage

DESIGN HPT770081

A little cottage on a small island off the coast of North Carolina hearkens back to the earliest of times. Many a yarn has been spun about pirates, fair maidens and such; but the truth of the matter is that families held together the fabric of Ocracoke Island then as they do now—gathering at dusk in their own Ocracoke Cottage.

Mount Pleasant

DESIGN HPT770082

A home on the water. Porches. Cool breezes and golden sunsets. White sails in the distance—gulls drifting overhead. Inner peace. Nothing is more satisfying and fulfilling than home, and home at Mount Pleasant is the stuff from which dreams are made.

MAIN LEVEL: 2,945 SQUARE FEET

UPPER LEVEL: 1,353 SQUARE FEET

TOTAL: 4,298 SQUARE FEET

FINISHED BASEMENT: 1,293 SQUARE FEET

WIDTH 61'-4"

DEPTH 72'-2"

Port Royal

DESIGN HPT770083

Every evening after supper, Uncle Henry wanders outdoors to the front porch. He has a ritual from which he never strays. As twilight settles in, he finishes his pipe and slowly unfolds his lanky frame from the creaky rocking chair. He is ready to rosin up his bow and strike the first lively chords of our favorite fiddle tunes. Many pleasant evenings are spent telling tales and making music at The Port Royal.

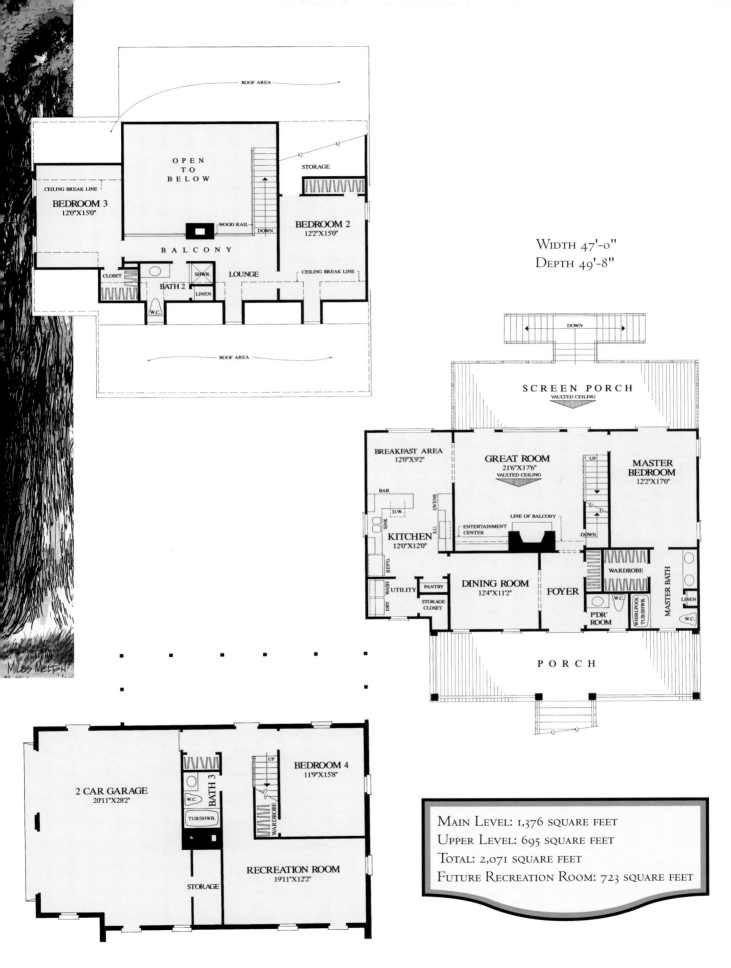

ROOF AREA

OPEN TO BELOW

STORAGE

CEILING BREAK LINE

BEDROOM 3
12'0"X15'0"

WOOD RAIL

DOWN

BEDROOM 2
12'2"X15'0"

BALCONY

CLOSET

SHWR.

LOUNGE

CEILING BREAK LINE

BATH 2

LINEN

W.C.

ROOF AREA

WIDTH 47'-0"
DEPTH 49'-8"

DOWN

SCREEN PORCH
VAULTED CEILING

BREAKFAST AREA
12'0"X9'2"

GREAT ROOM
21'6"X17'6"
VAULTED CEILING

UP

MASTER BEDROOM
12'2"X17'0"

BAR

D.W.

OVENS

KITCHEN
12'0"X12'0"

S.U.

ENTERTAINMENT CENTER

LINE OF BALCONY

DOWN

REFG.

WARDROBE

DRY WASH

UTILITY

PANTRY

DINING ROOM
12'4"X11'2"

FOYER

W.C.

LINEN

MASTER BATH

STORAGE CLOSET

P'DR' ROOM

WHIRLPOOL TUB/SHWR.

W.C.

PORCH

2 CAR GARAGE
20'11"X28'2"

W.C.

BATH 3

UP

BEDROOM 4
11'9"X15'8"

TUB/SHWR.

WARDROBE

RECREATION ROOM
19'11"X12'2"

STORAGE

MAIN LEVEL: 1,376 SQUARE FEET
UPPER LEVEL: 695 SQUARE FEET
TOTAL: 2,071 SQUARE FEET
FUTURE RECREATION ROOM: 723 SQUARE FEET

MILES MELLON

Colonial Cottage

An American tradition—that is what our Colonial Cottage is. No two are ever exactly alike, yet a similarity of classical details exists that strongly ties these cottages together. Try one on for size—reveal the inner you...you'll be glad you did.

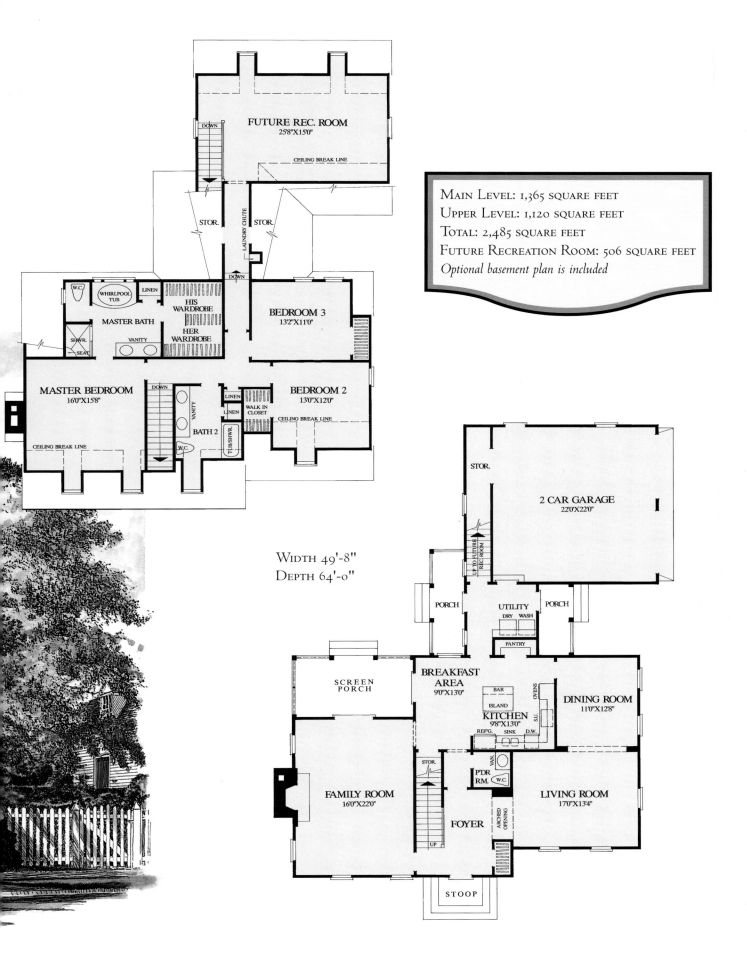

FUTURE REC. ROOM
25'8"X15'0"

DOWN

CEILING BREAK LINE

STOR.

LAUNDRY CHUTE

STOR.

DOWN

W.C.
WHIRLPOOL TUB
LINEN
HIS WARDROBE

MASTER BATH

HER WARDROBE

SHWR.
SEAT
VANITY

BEDROOM 3
13'2"X11'0"

MASTER BEDROOM
16'0"X15'8"

DOWN

VANITY

BATH 2

W.C.

LINEN
LINEN

WALK IN CLOSET

BEDROOM 2
13'0"X12'0"

CEILING BREAK LINE

TUB/SHWR.

CEILING BREAK LINE

MAIN LEVEL: 1,365 SQUARE FEET
UPPER LEVEL: 1,120 SQUARE FEET
TOTAL: 2,485 SQUARE FEET
FUTURE RECREATION ROOM: 506 SQUARE FEET
Optional basement plan is included

WIDTH 49'-8"
DEPTH 64'-0"

STOR.

2 CAR GARAGE
22'0"X22'0"

UP TO FUTURE REC ROOM

PORCH

UTILITY
DRY WASH

PORCH

PANTRY

SCREEN PORCH

BREAKFAST AREA
9'0"X13'0"

BAR
ISLAND
OVENS
S.U.

DINING ROOM
11'0"X12'8"

KITCHEN
9'8"X13'0"

REF'G. SINK D.W.

STOR.

VAN.

P'DR RM.
W.C.

FAMILY ROOM
16'0"X22'0"

UP

FOYER

ARCHED OPENING

LIVING ROOM
17'0"X13'4"

STOOP

Camellia Cottage II

DESIGN HPT770085

The struggle to return home. A young girl stands with a wicker basket over one arm while clutching her small dog in the other. She closes her eyes, clicks together the heels of her ruby-red slippers and utters repeatedly, "There's no place like home." Dorothy, and a multitude of others have touched our hearts and souls with their determination to reach their homes and families. Home. It's more than just a place to live. The Camellia Cottage II is dedicated to the wonderful characters, fictional and non-fictional, that believe home is an essential part of their beings.

ROOF AREA

STORAGE

BEDROOM 4
13'0"X14'0"

OPEN TO BELOW
CEILING BREAKLINE

BATH 4

TUB/SHWR.
W.C.
VANITY

BATH 3

TUB/SHWR.
W.C.
VANITY
VANITY

BALCONY

HANDRAIL

DOWN

OPEN
TO
BELOW

BEDROOM 3
12'5"X15'7"

BEDROOM 2
14'5"X13'0"

LAUNDRY CHUTE

STORAGE

STORAGE

DOWN

DOWN

HANDRAIL

CEILING BREAKLINE

FUTURE REC. ROOM
19'0"X 21'4"

WARDROBE

LINEN

SHELVES

CEILING BREAKLINE

TUB/SHWR.
VANITY
BATH 2
W.C.
WARDROBE
SHELVES

ROOF AREA

ROOF AREA

DECK AREA

MASTER BEDROOM
18'0"X14'0"

BOOKCASE

FAMILY ROOM
23'4" X16'0"

BREAKFAST AREA
9'0"X15'0"
VAULTED CEILING

KITCHEN
11'0"X16'0"

D/W SINK

SINK
ISLAND
BAR

REFG.

HIS WARDROBE

HER WARDROBE

VANITY

MASTER BATH

WHIRLPOOL TUB

W.C.

VANITY

SHOWER
SEAT

LIN.

BOOKCASE

DESK OVENS

LINE OF BALCONY

PANTRY

UP TO FUT.
REC. RM.

STOR.

BOOKCASE

P'KT DOORS

BOOKCASE

W.C.

PDR.
ROOM

TWO STORY
FOYER
15'0"X12'4"

LINE OF BALCONY

UP

LIVING ROOM
14'0"X15'10"

DINING ROOM
14'0"X16'0"

WASH DRY

UTILITY

SINK

PORCH

TWO CAR GARAGE
23'0"X23'0"

COVERED PORCH

WIDTH 81'-4"
DEPTH 58'-2"

MAIN LEVEL: 2,320 SQUARE FEET
UPPER LEVEL: 1,057 SQUARE FEET
TOTAL: 3,377 SQUARE FEET
FUTURE RECREATION ROOM: 608 SQUARE FEET

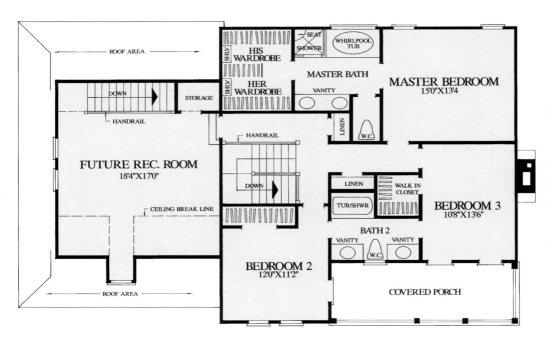

ROOF AREA

DOWN

HANDRAIL

STORAGE

SHLV
HIS WARDROBE

SHLV
HER WARDROBE

SEAT
SHOWER

WHIRLPOOL TUB

MASTER BATH

VANITY

LINEN

W.C.

MASTER BEDROOM
15'0"X13'4

FUTURE REC. ROOM
18'4"X17'0"

HANDRAIL

DOWN

CEILING BREAK LINE

LINEN

TUB/SHWR

WALK IN CLOSET

BEDROOM 3
10'8"X13'6"

BEDROOM 2
12'0"X11'2"

VANITY

W.C.

VANITY

BATH 2

ROOF AREA

COVERED PORCH

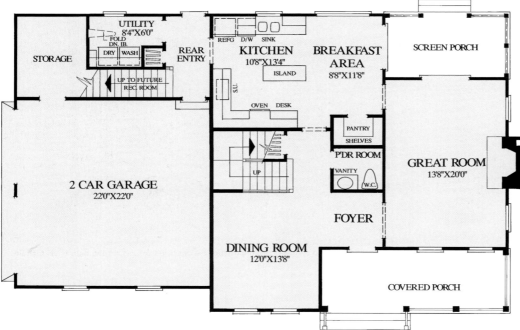

STORAGE

UTILITY
8'4"X6'0"
FOLD
DN. IB.

DRY   WASH

REAR ENTRY

UP TO FUTURE REC ROOM

2 CAR GARAGE
22'0"X22'0"

REFG   D/W   SINK

KITCHEN
10'8"X13'4"

ISLAND

S.U.

OVEN   DESK

UP

BREAKFAST AREA
8'8"X11'8"

SCREEN PORCH

PANTRY

SHELVES

P'DR ROOM

VANITY

W.C.

GREAT ROOM
13'8"X20'0"

FOYER

DINING ROOM
12'0"X13'8"

COVERED PORCH

WIDTH 56'-4"
DEPTH 35'-4"

Photo courtesy of Islands of Beaufort, Beaufort, S.C.

MAIN LEVEL: 1,075 SQUARE FEET
UPPER LEVEL: 994 SQUARE FEET
TOTAL: 2,069 SQUARE FEET
FUTURE RECREATION ROOM: 382 SQUARE FEET

This home, as shown in the photograph, may differ from the actual blueprints. For more detailed information, please check the floor plans carefully.

West Indies Cottage

DESIGN HPT770079

Blue waters of the Caribbean lap lazily against the dinghy. Bright colors of the rainbow attach themselves to the cluster of cottages lining the shore. Laughter trickles outward from the palm-strewn beaches. Music of the islands rises to meet us as we arrive at our romantic hideaway–the West Indies cottage.

This home, as shown in the photograph, may differ from the actual blueprints. For more detailed information, please check the floor plans carefully.

Hudson Valley

DESIGN HPT770087

Out on the trail, exhilarated by the pounding hooves beneath me and crisp morning air, I turn my mount towards home, a warm crackling fire and breakfast. As we draw near, smoke spirals from the chimney and my mouth waters in anticipation of sausages and eggs. The warmth, charm and texture of my beloved retreat greets me, as always. The best place I could ever hope to be–the Hudson Valley, my Dutch Colonial home.

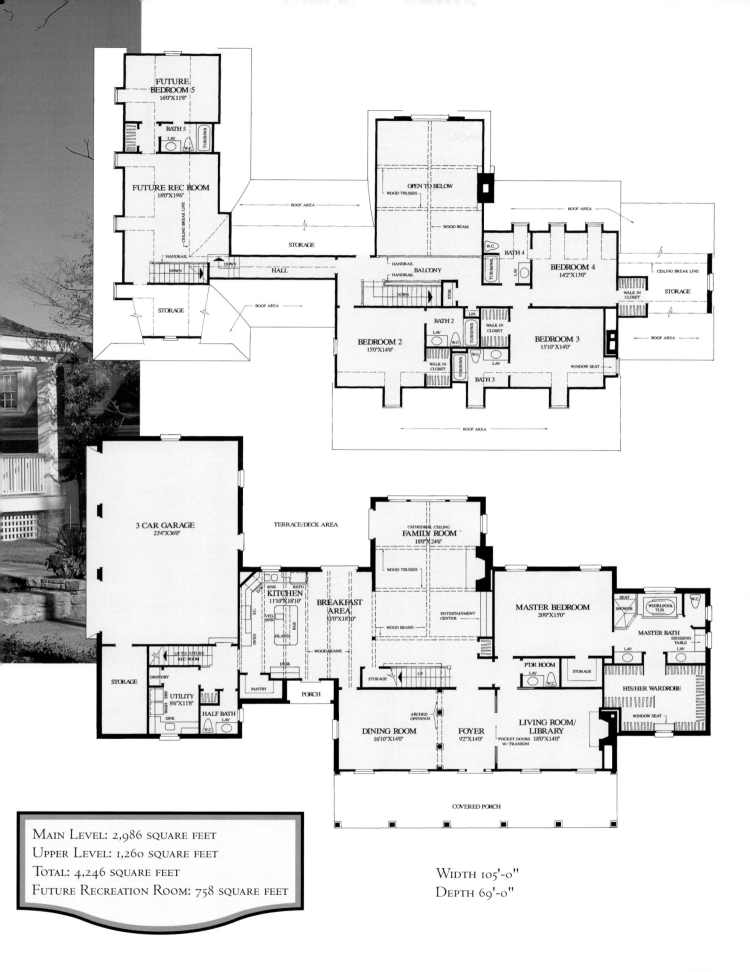

FUTURE
BEDROOM 5
16'0"X11'8"

BATH 5

LAV

W.C

TUB/SHWR

FUTURE REC ROOM
18'0"X19'6"

CEILING BREAK LINE

HANDRAIL

DOWN

HALL

STORAGE

ROOF AREA

STORAGE

DOWN

STORAGE

ROOF AREA

OPEN TO BELOW

WOOD TRUSSES

WOOD BEAM

ROOF AREA

HANDRAIL

BALCONY

HANDRAIL

DOWN

STOR.

W.C

TUB/SHWR

LAV

BATH 4

BEDROOM 4
14'2"X13'0"

CEILING BREAK LINE

STORAGE

WALK IN
CLOSET

BEDROOM 2
15'0"X14'0"

BATH 2

LAV

W.C

TUB/SHWR

LIN

WALK IN
CLOSET

BEDROOM 3
15'10"X14'0"

ROOF AREA

WALK IN
CLOSET

W.C

TUB/SHWR

LAV

BATH 3

WINDOW SEAT

ROOF AREA

3 CAR GARAGE
23'4"X36'0"

TERRACE/DECK AREA

CATHEDRAL CEILING
FAMILY ROOM™
18'0"X24'6"

WOOD TRUSSES

MASTER BEDROOM
20'0"X15'0"

SEAT

SHOWER

WHIRLPOOL
TUB

W.C

SINK

REFG

KITCHEN
11'10"X18'10"

VEG.
SINK

OVEN

TILE

BAR

ISLAND

BREAKFAST
AREA
11'0"X18'0"

WOOD BEAMS

ENTERTAINMENT
CENTER

WOOD BEAMS

MASTER BATH

DRESSING
TABLE

LAV

LAV

UP TO FUTURE
REC ROOM

DESK

STORAGE

DRIP/DRY

PANTRY

PORCH

STORAGE

WASH

DRY

UTILITY
8'6"X11'8"

SINK

HALF BATH

LAV

W.C

P'DR ROOM

LAV

W.C

STORAGE

HIS/HER WARDROBE

STORAGE

STORAGE

DINING ROOM
16'10"X14'0"

ARCHED
OPENINGS

UP

FOYER
9'2"X14'0"

LIVING ROOM/
LIBRARY
18'0"X14'0"

POCKET DOORS
W/ TRANSOM

WINDOW SEAT

COVERED PORCH

MAIN LEVEL: 2,986 SQUARE FEET
UPPER LEVEL: 1,260 SQUARE FEET
TOTAL: 4,246 SQUARE FEET
FUTURE RECREATION ROOM: 758 SQUARE FEET

WIDTH 105'-0"
DEPTH 69'-0"

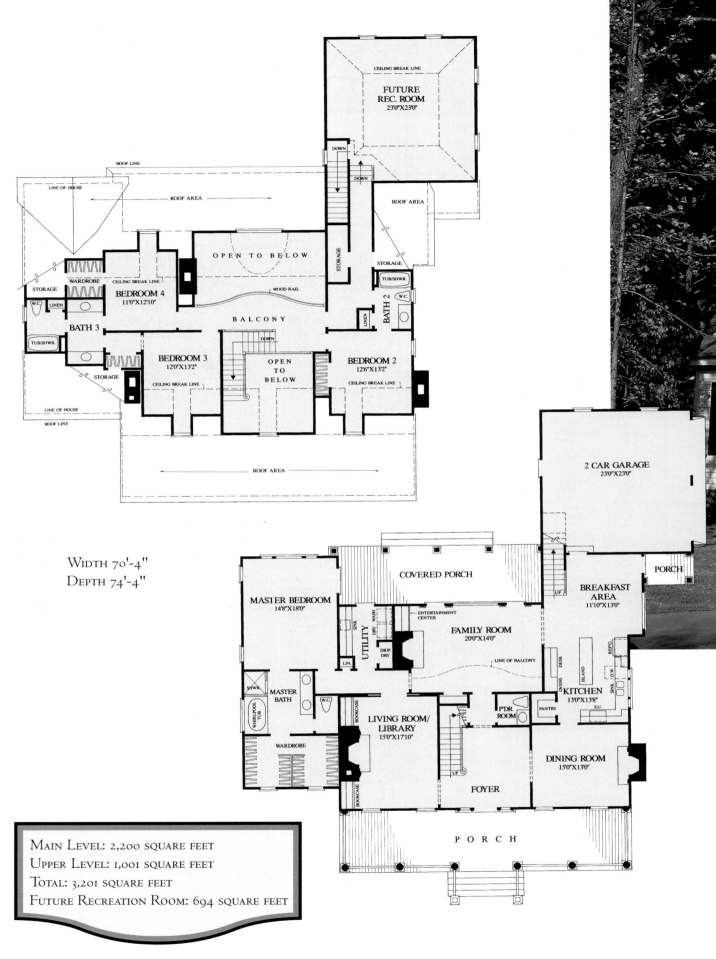

FUTURE
REC. ROOM
23'0"X23'0"

CEILING BREAK LINE

DOWN
DOWN

ROOF AREA

ROOF LINE
LINE OF HOUSE
ROOF AREA

OPEN TO BELOW

STORAGE
STORAGE

WOOD RAIL

WARDROBE
CEILING BREAK LINE

STORAGE

BEDROOM 4
11'0"X12'10"

W.C
LINEN

BATH 3

TUB/SHWR.

BALCONY

TUB/SHWR.
W.C

BATH 2

LINEN

STORAGE

BEDROOM 3
12'0"X13'2"

DOWN

OPEN
TO
BELOW

BEDROOM 2
12'6"X13'2"

CEILING BREAK LINE
CEILING BREAK LINE

LINE OF HOUSE
ROOF LINE

ROOF AREA

2 CAR GARAGE
23'0"X23'0"

WIDTH 70'-4"
DEPTH 74'-4"

PORCH

COVERED PORCH

BREAKFAST
AREA
11'10"X13'0"

MASTER BEDROOM
14'8"X18'0"

ENTERTAINMENT
CENTER

UTILITY
SINK
WASH
DRY

LIN.

DRIP
DRY

FAMILY ROOM
20'0"X14'0"

REFG.

DESK
ISLAND
OVENS

KITCHEN
13'0"X13'8"

SINK
D/W

LINE OF BALCONY

S.U.

SHWR

MASTER
BATH

WHIRLPOOL
TUB

W.C

BOOKCASE

LIVING ROOM/
LIBRARY
15'0"X17'10"

P'DR
ROOM

PANTRY

WARDROBE

UP

UP

DINING ROOM
15'0"X13'0"

BOOKCASE

FOYER

PORCH

MAIN LEVEL: 2,200 SQUARE FEET
UPPER LEVEL: 1,001 SQUARE FEET
TOTAL: 3,201 SQUARE FEET
FUTURE RECREATION ROOM: 694 SQUARE FEET

Melrose

DESIGN HPT770088

Porch swings, trailing wisteria vines, crocus that look like Easter eggs, buttercups and chirping birds—all senses are invaded with memories of our childhood. Visits to grandma's home included stories told, stories heard, and stories embellished upon. The best possible gift—here we were taught the lessons it had taken our grandparents a lifetime to learn. All this beauty, and a legacy too, was set in the old South—and in the Melrose.

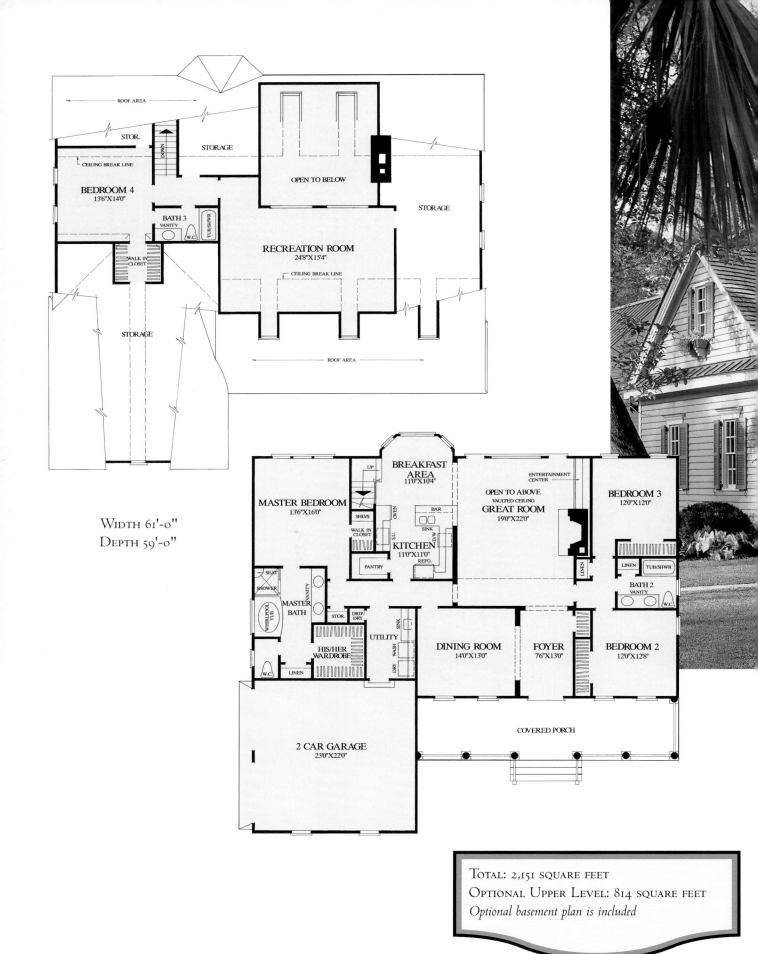

ROOF AREA

STOR.

STORAGE

CEILING BREAK LINE

DOWN

OPEN TO BELOW

STORAGE

BEDROOM 4
13'6"X14'0"

BATH 3
VANITY

W.C.

TUB/SHWR

WALK IN
CLOSET

RECREATION ROOM
24'8"X15'4"

CEILING BREAK LINE

STORAGE

ROOF AREA

WIDTH 61'-0"
DEPTH 59'-0"

UP

BREAKFAST
AREA
11'0"X10'4"

ENTERTAINMENT
CENTER

OPEN TO ABOVE
VAULTED CEILING
GREAT ROOM
19'0"X22'0"

BEDROOM 3
12'0"X12'0"

MASTER BEDROOM
13'6"X16'0"

SHLVS

OVEN

BAR

SINK

WALK IN
CLOSET

D.W.

KITCHEN
11'0"X11'0"

REFG.

LINEN

LINEN

TUB/SHWR

SEAT

SHOWER

WHIRLPOOL
TUB

MASTER
BATH

VANITY

PANTRY

STOR.

DRIP/
DRY

BATH 2
VANITY

W.C.

W.C.

HIS/HER
WARDROBE

LINEN

UTILITY

WASH

SINK

DRY

BEDROOM 2
12'0"X12'8"

LINEN

DINING ROOM
14'0"X13'0"

FOYER
7'6"X13'0"

COVERED PORCH

2 CAR GARAGE
23'0"X22'0"

TOTAL: 2,151 SQUARE FEET
OPTIONAL UPPER LEVEL: 814 SQUARE FEET
Optional basement plan is included

This home, as shown in the photograph, may differ from the actual blueprints. For more detailed information, please check the floor plans carefully.

Eastshore Cottage

Being of incisive line, thought, style and effect, the understated appeal of the Eastern Shore Cottage is reminiscent of a simpler life. Times when neighbor greeted neighbor, doors were left unlocked and a helping hand was near. We can have that again. Choose your neighborhood, plan your home—you've made a wise decision.

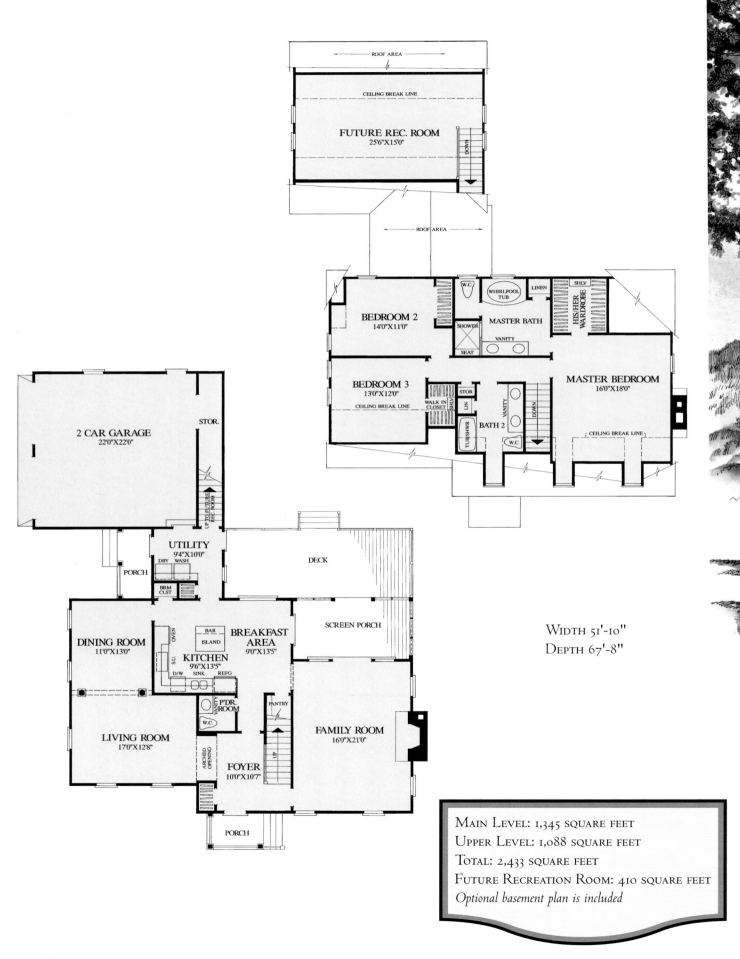

ROOF AREA

CEILING BREAK LINE

FUTURE REC. ROOM
25'6"X15'0"

DOWN

ROOF AREA

W.C.

WHIRLPOOL TUB

LINEN

SHLV

BEDROOM 2
14'0"X11'0"

MASTER BATH

SHOWER

HIS/HER WARDROBE

VANITY

SEAT

MASTER BEDROOM
16'0"X18'0"

BEDROOM 3
13'0"X12'0"

CEILING BREAK LINE

STOR

WALK IN CLOSET

SHLV

LIN

VANITY

DOWN

CEILING BREAK LINE

BATH 2

TUB/SHWR

W.C.

2 CAR GARAGE
22'0"X22'0"

STOR.

UP TO FUTURE REC. ROOM

UTILITY
9'4"X10'0"

DRY WASH

DECK

PORCH

BRM CLST

BREAKFAST AREA
9'0"X13'5"

OVEN

BAR

ISLAND

SCREEN PORCH

DINING ROOM
11'0"X13'0"

S.U.

KITCHEN
9'6"X13'5"

D/W SINK REFG

WIDTH 51'-10"
DEPTH 67'-8"

P'DR. ROOM

PANTRY

VANITY

W.C.

LIVING ROOM
17'0"X12'8"

FAMILY ROOM
16'0"X21'0"

ARCHED OPENING

UP

FOYER
10'0"X10'7"

PORCH

MAIN LEVEL: 1,345 SQUARE FEET
UPPER LEVEL: 1,088 SQUARE FEET
TOTAL: 2,433 SQUARE FEET
FUTURE RECREATION ROOM: 410 SQUARE FEET
Optional basement plan is included

Hollyhock Cottage

DESIGN HPT770090

After spending the day in New Bern, North Carolina, touring Tryon Palace and larger homes in the historic district, the most pleasant surprise was waiting just around the corner. We were captivated by the sight of the Hollyhock Cottage. The proportions were perfect, the size adorable, the simplicity engaging and the gardens ablaze in irregular charm and color. Feasting our eyes on this little cottage at the end of our stay was an unexpected and heartwarming delight.

Turnberry

Aunt Harriet lived in a home much like The Turnberry. She wore wide-brimmed, flowered hats and never went calling without first donning her white cotton gloves. But every day of her life was an adventure. While watching a well-known comedy, my cousin B.J. and I—between fits of laughter—agreed the leading lady fit Aunt Harriet right down to her familiar white gloves. As time marches on, this home's unique character will continue on and on—delightful, timeless. Like Aunt Harriet.

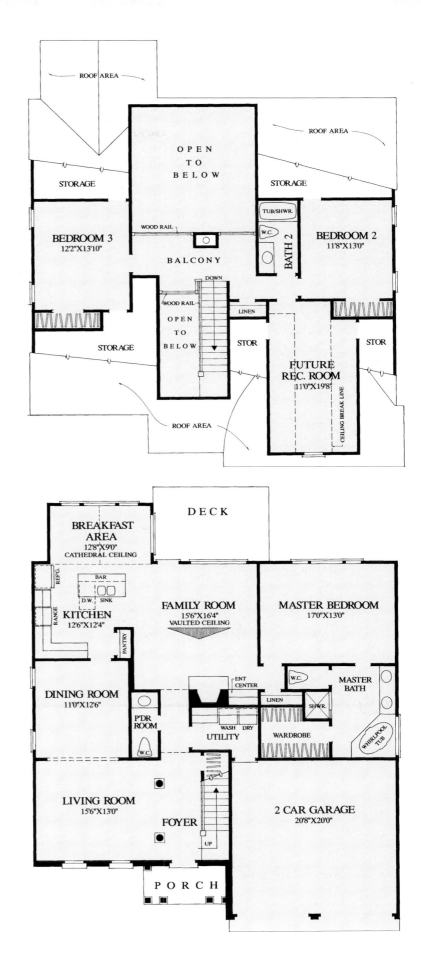

OPEN TO BELOW

ROOF AREA

ROOF AREA

STORAGE

STORAGE

BEDROOM 3
12'2"X13'10"

TUB/SHWR.

W.C.

BATH 2

BEDROOM 2
11'8"X13'0"

WOOD RAIL

BALCONY

STORAGE

DOWN

WOOD RAIL

OPEN TO BELOW

LINEN

STOR.

STOR

STOR

FUTURE REC. ROOM
11'0"X19'8"

CEILING BREAK LINE

ROOF AREA

DECK

BREAKFAST AREA
12'8"X9'0"
CATHEDRAL CEILING

BAR

D.W.   SINK

REFG.

RANGE

KITCHEN
12'6"X12'4"

PANTRY

FAMILY ROOM
15'6"X16'4"
VAULTED CEILING

MASTER BEDROOM
17'0"X13'0"

W.C.

MASTER BATH

SHWR.

WHIRLPOOL TUB

DINING ROOM
11'0"X12'6"

ENT CENTER

LINEN

P'DR ROOM

WASH   DRY

UTILITY

WARDROBE

W.C.

LIVING ROOM
15'6"X13'0"

FOYER

UP

2 CAR GARAGE
20'8"X20'0"

PORCH

WIDTH 46'-0"
DEPTH 54'-5"

MAIN LEVEL: 1,634 SQUARE FEET
UPPER LEVEL: 619 SQUARE FEET
TOTAL: 2,253 SQUARE FEET
FUTURE RECREATION ROOM: 229 SQUARE FEET

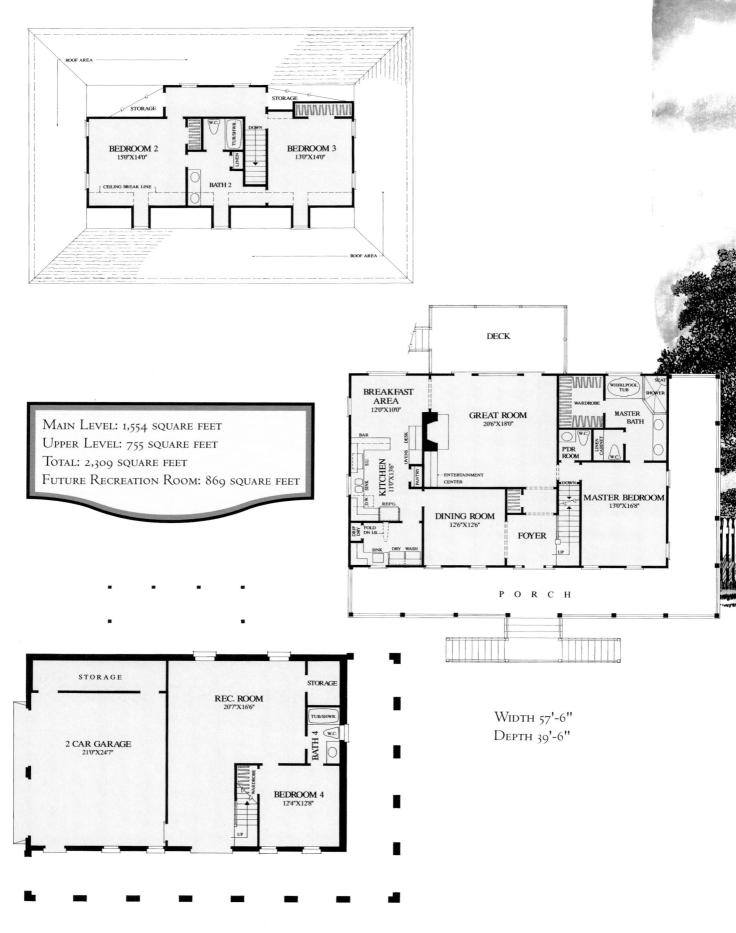

ROOF AREA

STORAGE

STORAGE

W.C.

TUB/SHWR.

DOWN

BEDROOM 2
15'0"X14'0"

LINEN

BEDROOM 3
13'0"X14'0"

CEILING BREAK LINE

BATH 2

ROOF AREA

DECK

BREAKFAST
AREA
12'0"X10'0"

BAR

S.U.

KITCHEN
11'0"X13'6"

SINK

D.W.

REF'G.

DRIP DRY

FOLD
DN I.B.

SINK   DRY WASH

OVENS

DESK

PANTRY

GREAT ROOM
20'6"X18'0"

ENTERTAINMENT
CENTER

DINING ROOM
12'6"X12'6"

FOYER

UP

DOWN

WARDROBE

P'DR
ROOM

W.C.

LINEN
CABINET

W.C.

WHIRLPOOL
TUB

SEAT

SHOWER

**MASTER
BATH**

MASTER BEDROOM
13'0"X16'8"

P O R C H

MAIN LEVEL: 1,554 SQUARE FEET

UPPER LEVEL: 755 SQUARE FEET

TOTAL: 2,309 SQUARE FEET

FUTURE RECREATION ROOM: 869 SQUARE FEET

STORAGE

STORAGE

REC. ROOM
20'7"X16'6"

TUB/SHWR.

W.C.

BATH 4

2 CAR GARAGE
21'0"X24'7"

WARDROBE

BEDROOM 4
12'4"X12'8"

UP

WIDTH 57'-6"
DEPTH 39'-6"

Currituck Cottage

DESIGN HPT770092

He was ten years old that first summer at the coast. When the tide was low he could walk all the way to the legendary rock, examining small sea creatures trapped in the tidepools. Other times he ran along the high bluffs, or dreamed of pirates and sailing ships. The coastal surroundings of his childhood had a profound effect on his career and he became one of the greatest artists of our time. Artistic demands have extended his travels, but he has never found a place he'd rather be. Currituck Cottage—a home he's comfortable in.

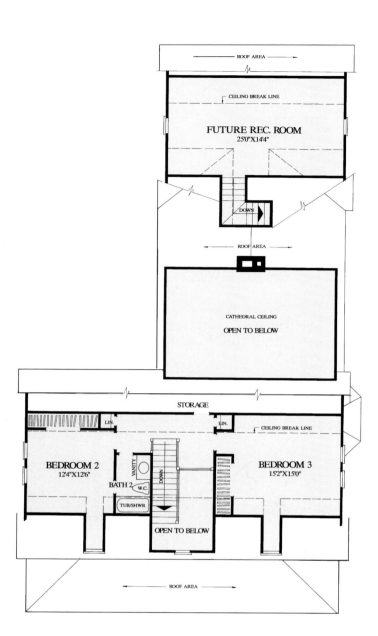

ROOF AREA

CEILING BREAK LINE

FUTURE REC. ROOM
25'0"X14'4"

DOWN

ROOF AREA

CATHEDRAL CEILING

OPEN TO BELOW

STORAGE

LIN.   LIN.   CEILING BREAK LINE

BEDROOM 2
12'4"X12'6"

VANITY

BATH 2   W.C.

DOWN

TUB/SHWR

BEDROOM 3
15'2"X15'0"

OPEN TO BELOW

ROOF AREA

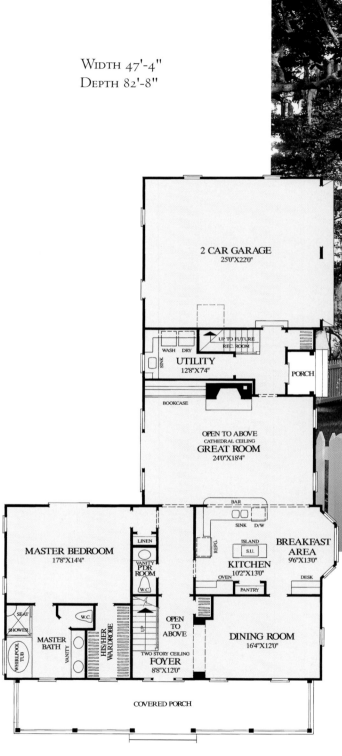

Width 47'-4"
Depth 82'-8"

2 CAR GARAGE
25'0"X22'0"

UP TO FUTURE
REC. ROOM

WASH DRY

SINK

UTILITY
12'8"X7'4"

PORCH

BOOKCASE

OPEN TO ABOVE
CATHEDRAL CEILING
GREAT ROOM
24'0"X18'4"

BAR

SINK   D/W

REFG.   ISLAND
S.U.

KITCHEN
10'2"X13'0"

BREAKFAST AREA
9'6"X13'0"

OVEN   DESK

PANTRY

LINEN

VANITY
PDR ROOM

W.C.

MASTER BEDROOM
17'8"X14'4"

SEAT

SHOWER

W.C.

WHIRLPOOL TUB

MASTER BATH

VANITY

HIS/HER WARDROBE

UP

OPEN TO ABOVE

TWO STORY CEILING
FOYER
8'8"X12'0"

DINING ROOM
16'4"X12'0"

COVERED PORCH

MAIN LEVEL: 1,819 SQUARE FEET
UPPER LEVEL: 638 SQUARE FEET
TOTAL: 2,457 SQUARE FEET
FUTURE RECREATION ROOM: 385 SQUARE FEET
Optional basement plan is included

This home, as shown in the photograph, may differ from the actual blueprints. For more detailed information, please check the floor plans carefully.

Gulf Coast Cottage

DESIGN HPT770093

Breathtaking sunsets. Sultry summer nights. The glow of the moon and starry skies— romance. Fireflies glowing in the dark, children laughing, playing in the park, the warmth of a hand holding mine, the tenderness of a first kiss—all the joys of a lifetime. Remembered from the porch of the Gulf Coast Cottage.

Edgewater

DESIGN HPT770094

On Sundays, when we were little, my parents would pile us all in the car and drive out to the Edgewater, Aunt Clara's house. We had cousins to play with, horses to ride, trees to climb and fields where we could run with the wind. We loved going to Aunt Clara's—and we loved Aunt Clara.

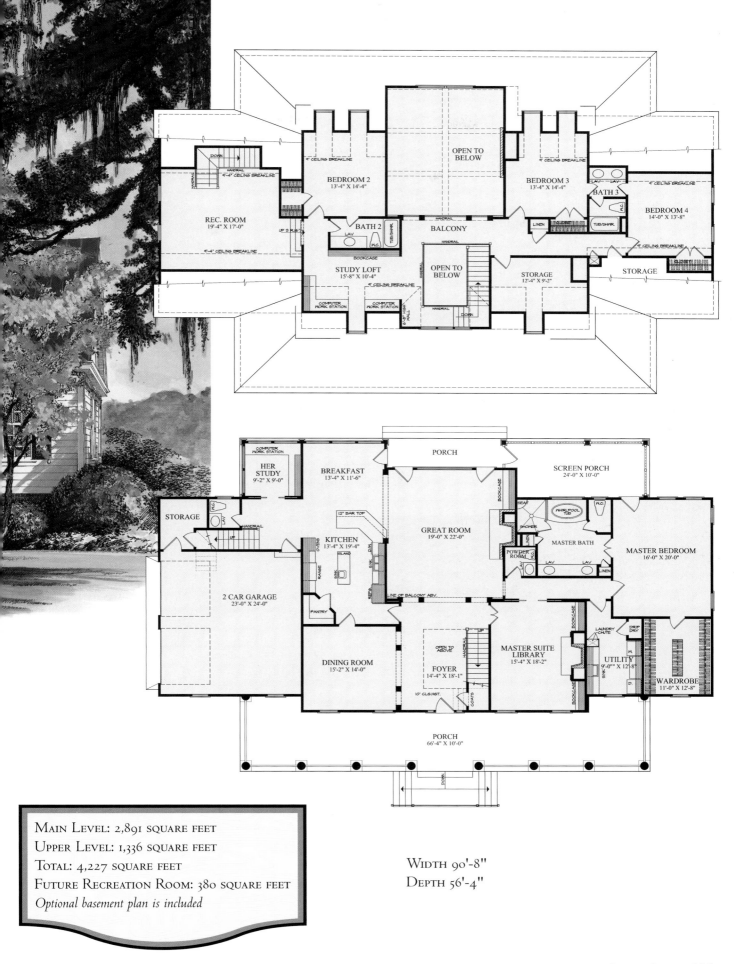

UPPER LEVEL

REC. ROOM
19'-4" X 17'-0"

BEDROOM 2
13'-4" X 14'-4"

OPEN TO BELOW

BEDROOM 3
13'-4" X 14'-4"

BATH 3

BEDROOM 4
14'-0" X 13'-8"

BATH 2

BALCONY

STUDY LOFT
15'-8" X 10'-4"

OPEN TO BELOW

STORAGE
12'-4" X 9'-2"

STORAGE

LINEN

COMPUTER WORK STATION

COMPUTER WORK STATION

MAIN LEVEL

HER STUDY
9'-2" X 9'-0"

BREAKFAST
13'-4" X 11'-6"

PORCH

SCREEN PORCH
24'-0" X 10'-0"

STORAGE

KITCHEN
13'-4" X 19'-4"

GREAT ROOM
19'-0" X 22'-0"

MASTER BATH

MASTER BEDROOM
16'-0" X 20'-0"

WHIRLPOOL TUB

2 CAR GARAGE
23'-0" X 24'-0"

POWDER ROOM

PANTRY

LINE OF BALCONY ABV.

DINING ROOM
15'-2" X 14'-0"

FOYER
14'-4" X 18'-1"

OPEN TO ABOVE

MASTER SUITE LIBRARY
15'-4" X 18'-2"

UTILITY
9'-0" X 12'-8"

WARDROBE
11'-0" X 12'-8"

LAUNDRY CHUTE

DRIP DRY

PORCH
66'-4" X 10'-0"

DOWN

MAIN LEVEL: 2,891 SQUARE FEET
UPPER LEVEL: 1,336 SQUARE FEET
TOTAL: 4,227 SQUARE FEET
FUTURE RECREATION ROOM: 380 SQUARE FEET
Optional basement plan is included

WIDTH 90'-8"
DEPTH 56'-4"

Carlyle

How special. How perfect. A moment to forever cherish when first we saw the Carlyle. Spiraling smilax, colorful hydrangeas, handsome English boxwoods–Southern plantings–for a wonderfully Southern Greek Revival home. The moment we first discovered The Carlyle was a moment to forever cherish. A classical combination for anytime, anywhere. One that will never grow old, because the really good things never do.

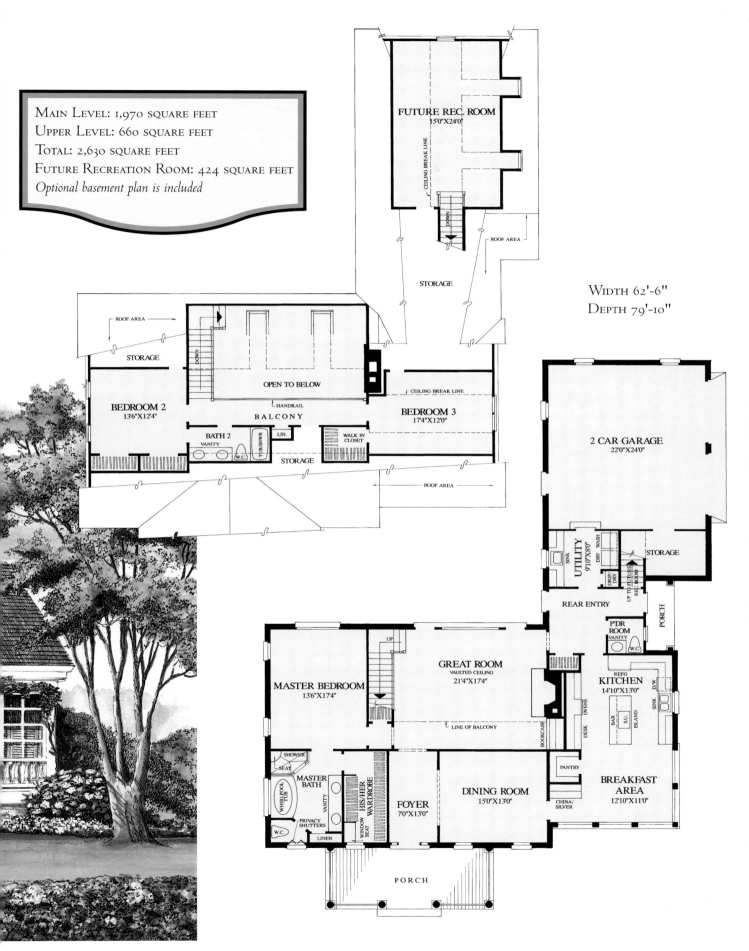

Main Level: 1,970 square feet

Upper Level: 660 square feet

Total: 2,630 square feet

Future Recreation Room: 424 square feet

Optional basement plan is included

FUTURE REC. ROOM
15'0"X24'0"

CEILING BREAK LINE

DOWN

STORAGE

ROOF AREA

WIDTH 62'-6"

DEPTH 79'-10"

ROOF AREA

STORAGE

DOWN

OPEN TO BELOW

CEILING BREAK LINE

BEDROOM 2
13'6"X12'4"

BALCONY

HANDRAIL

BEDROOM 3
17'4"X12'0"

BATH 2

VANITY

W.C.

LIN.

TUB/SHWR

WALK IN
CLOSET

STORAGE

ROOF AREA

2 CAR GARAGE
22'0"X24'0"

STORAGE

UTILITY
9'10"X8'0"

SINK   DRY   WASH

DRIP/
DRY

UP TO FUTURE
REC. ROOM

PORCH

REAR ENTRY

P'DR
ROOM
VANITY

W.C

MASTER BEDROOM
13'6"X17'4"

GREAT ROOM
VAULTED CEILING
21'4"X17'4"

UP

BOOKCASE

DESK   OVENS

KITCHEN
14'10"X13'0"

REFG

BAR   S.U.
ISLAND

SINK   D/W

LINE OF BALCONY

SHOWER

SEAT

MASTER
BATH

WHIRLPOOL
TUB

VANITY

HIS/HER
WARDROBE

FOYER
7'0"X13'0"

DINING ROOM
15'0"X13'0"

PANTRY

CHINA/
SILVER

BREAKFAST
AREA
12'10"X11'0"

WINDOW
SEAT

PRIVACY
SHUTTERS

W.C.

LINEN

PORCH

Belle Grove

An inviting home, the Belle Grove, bespeaks magnolias, dogwood blossoms, butterflies and the peaceful hospitality of the gracious South. Its inspiration came from Cottage Gardens. A noteworthy feature is the rare combination of the Natchez gallery recessed beneath an unbroken slope of gable roof with a triangular pediment. This home takes its cue from the gracious formality indigenous to the typical Mississippi River Delta Planters' Cottage.

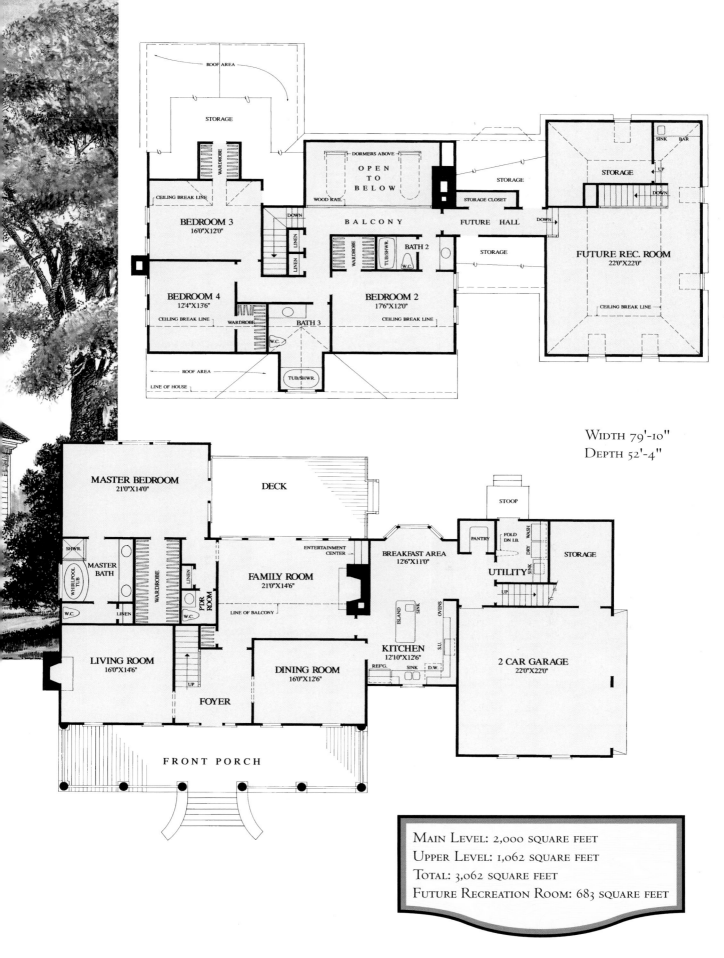

ROOF AREA

STORAGE

CEILING BREAK LINE

BEDROOM 3
16'0"X12'0"

BEDROOM 4
12'4"X13'6"

CEILING BREAK LINE

WARDROBE

WARDROBE

DOWN

LINEN LINEN

LINEN

W.C.

BATH 3

TUB/SHWR.

DORMERS ABOVE

OPEN
TO
BELOW

WOOD RAIL

BALCONY

WARDROBE

TUB/SHWR.

BATH 2

W.C.

BEDROOM 2
17'6"X12'0"

CEILING BREAK LINE

FUTURE HALL

STORAGE

STORAGE CLOSET

STORAGE

DOWN

SINK BAR

STORAGE

UP

DOWN

FUTURE REC. ROOM
22'0"X22'0"

CEILING BREAK LINE

ROOF AREA

LINE OF HOUSE

WIDTH 79'-10"
DEPTH 52'-4"

MASTER BEDROOM
21'0"X14'0"

DECK

STOOP

SHWR.

MASTER BATH

WHIRLPOOL TUB

W.C.

WARDROBE

LINEN

LINEN

PDR ROOM

W.C.

ENTERTAINMENT CENTER

FAMILY ROOM
21'0"X14'6"

LINE OF BALCONY

PANTRY

FOLD DN I.B.

WASH

DRY

SINK

UTILITY

UP

STORAGE

BREAKFAST AREA
12'6"X11'0"

ISLAND

SINK

OVENS

S.U.

2 CAR GARAGE
22'0"X22'0"

LIVING ROOM
16'0"X14'6"

UP

FOYER

DINING ROOM
16'0"X12'6"

KITCHEN
12'10"X12'6"

REF'G.

SINK

D.W.

FRONT PORCH

MAIN LEVEL: 2,000 SQUARE FEET
UPPER LEVEL: 1,062 SQUARE FEET
TOTAL: 3,062 SQUARE FEET
FUTURE RECREATION ROOM: 683 SQUARE FEET

Country Cottage

Every neighborhood has the perfect little Country Cottage just down the lane, all tucked into the perfect little yard. Simple, warmly detailed and much loved, everyone who passes feels that (should they enter) they would be greeted with a welcoming smile. All the children in the neighborhood know that "Mother Goose" lives there because a hug, a lap, and a nursery rhyme await them (along with milk and cookies) when they visit—which is often.

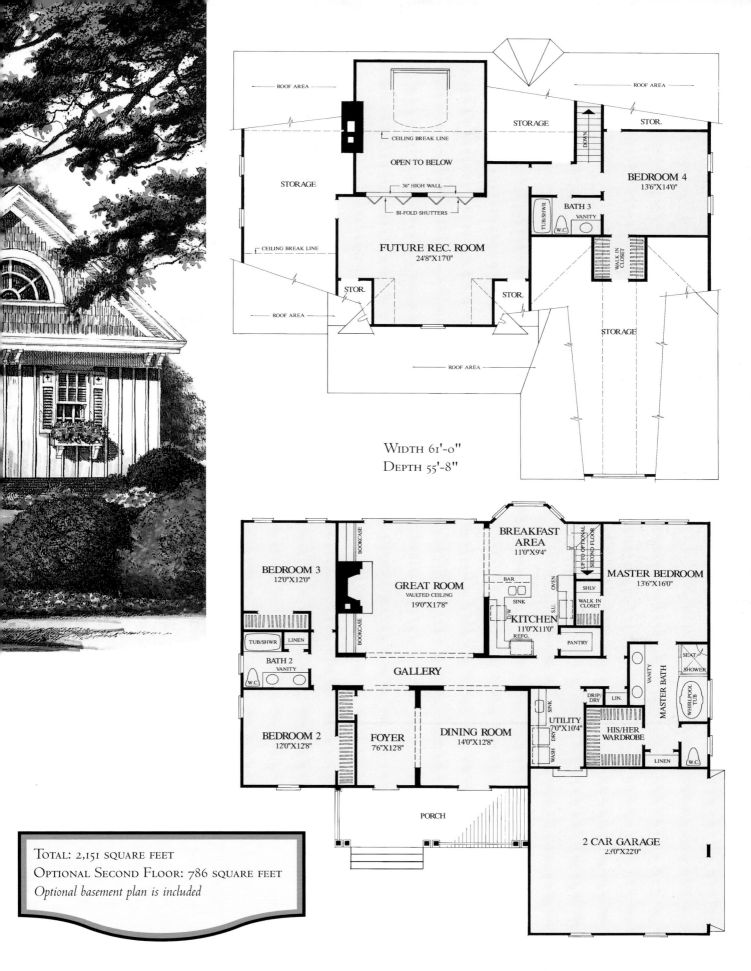

ROOF AREA

ROOF AREA

ROOF AREA

STORAGE

STOR.

CEILING BREAK LINE

OPEN TO BELOW

DOWN

STORAGE

STOR.

BEDROOM 4
13'6"X14'0"

STORAGE

36" HIGH WALL

BI-FOLD SHUTTERS

TUB/SHWR

BATH 3

VANITY

W.C

CEILING BREAK LINE

FUTURE REC. ROOM
24'8"X17'0"

WALK IN CLOSET

ROOF AREA

STOR.

STOR.

STORAGE

ROOF AREA

WIDTH 61'-0"

DEPTH 55'-8"

BEDROOM 3
12'0"X12'0"

BOOKCASE

BREAKFAST
AREA
11'0"X9'4"

UP TO OPTIONAL SECOND FLOOR

MASTER BEDROOM
13'6"X16'0"

GREAT ROOM
VAULTED CEILING
19'0"X17'8"

BAR

OVEN

SHLV

SINK

WALK IN
CLOSET

TUB/SHWR

LINEN

DW

S.U.

BATH 2

VANITY

BOOKCASE

KITCHEN
11'0"X11'0"

REFG.

PANTRY

SEAT

SHOWER

W.C

VANITY

MASTER BATH

GALLERY

WHIRLPOOL TUB

SINK

DRIP/DRY

LIN.

BEDROOM 2
12'0"X12'8"

FOYER
7'6"X12'8"

DINING ROOM
14'0"X12'8"

UTILITY
7'0"X10'4"

HIS/HER
WARDROBE

LINEN

WASH

DRY

LIN

W.C

PORCH

2 CAR GARAGE
23'0"X22'0"

TOTAL: 2,151 SQUARE FEET
OPTIONAL SECOND FLOOR: 786 SQUARE FEET
Optional basement plan is included

Cape Cod Cottage

DESIGN HPT770098

A little place where roses bloom. A little place where fires are cozy. A little place with picket fences. A little cottage with weathered blue shutters–Cape Cod Cottage...a little place that captures your heart.

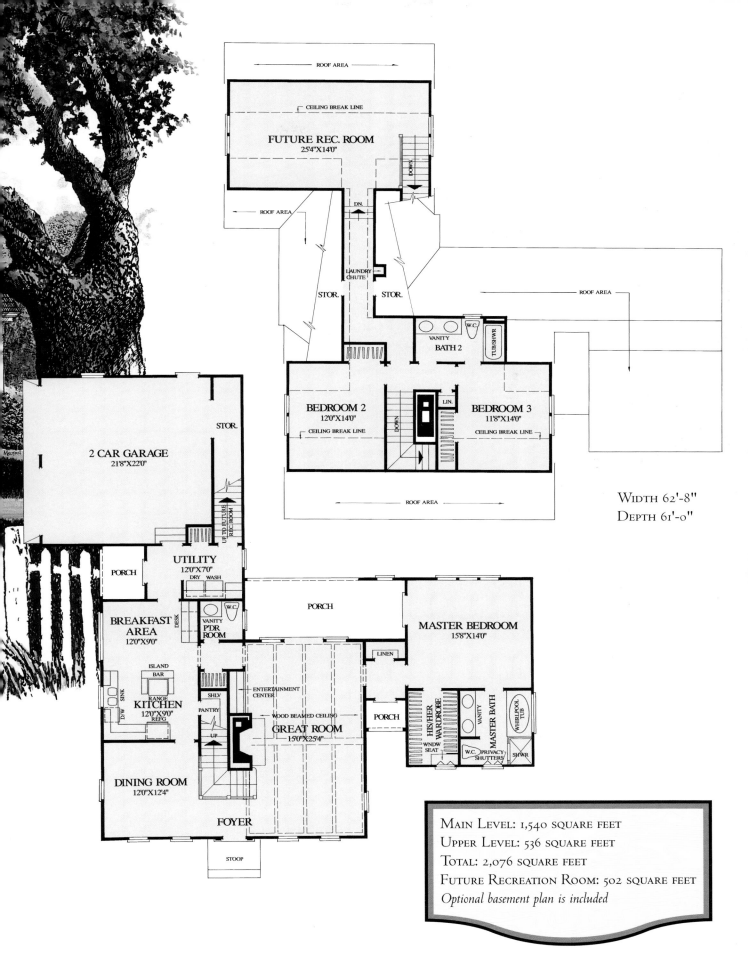

ROOF AREA

CEILING BREAK LINE

FUTURE REC. ROOM
25'4"X14'0"

DOWN

ROOF AREA

DN.

LAUNDRY
CHUTE

STOR.   STOR.

ROOF AREA

VANITY
W.C.
TUB/SHWR

BATH 2

LIN.

BEDROOM 2
12'0"X14'0"

DOWN

BEDROOM 3
11'8"X14'0"

CEILING BREAK LINE   CEILING BREAK LINE

ROOF AREA

WIDTH 62'-8"
DEPTH 61'-0"

2 CAR GARAGE
21'8"X22'0"

STOR.

PORCH

PORCH

MASTER BEDROOM
15'8"X14'0"

UTILITY
12'0"X7'0"

DRY WASH

DESK

VANITY
**PDR
ROOM**
W.C.

LINEN

**BREAKFAST
AREA**
12'0"X9'0"

ENTERTAINMENT
CENTER

PORCH

ISLAND
BAR

SHLV

HIS/HER
WARDROBE

VANITY

WHIRLPOOL
TUB

SINK
RANGE
KITCHEN
12'0"X9'0"
D/W   REFG

PANTRY

WOOD BEAMED CEILING

Master Bath

UP

GREAT ROOM
15'0"X25'4"

WNDW
SEAT
W.C.
PRIVACY
SHUTTERS
SHWR

DINING ROOM
12'0"X12'4"

FOYER

STOOP

MAIN LEVEL: 1,540 SQUARE FEET
UPPER LEVEL: 536 SQUARE FEET
TOTAL: 2,076 SQUARE FEET
FUTURE RECREATION ROOM: 502 SQUARE FEET
Optional basement plan is included

Telluride

DESIGN HPT770099

Rugged mountain peaks, lush green valleys, wide open spaces...and then there is Telluride. A charming Victorian village filled with delightful cottages on picturesque streets, rodeos beneath blazing blue skies, cherry cokes at the corner store and baby carriages galore—life goes on in Telluride.

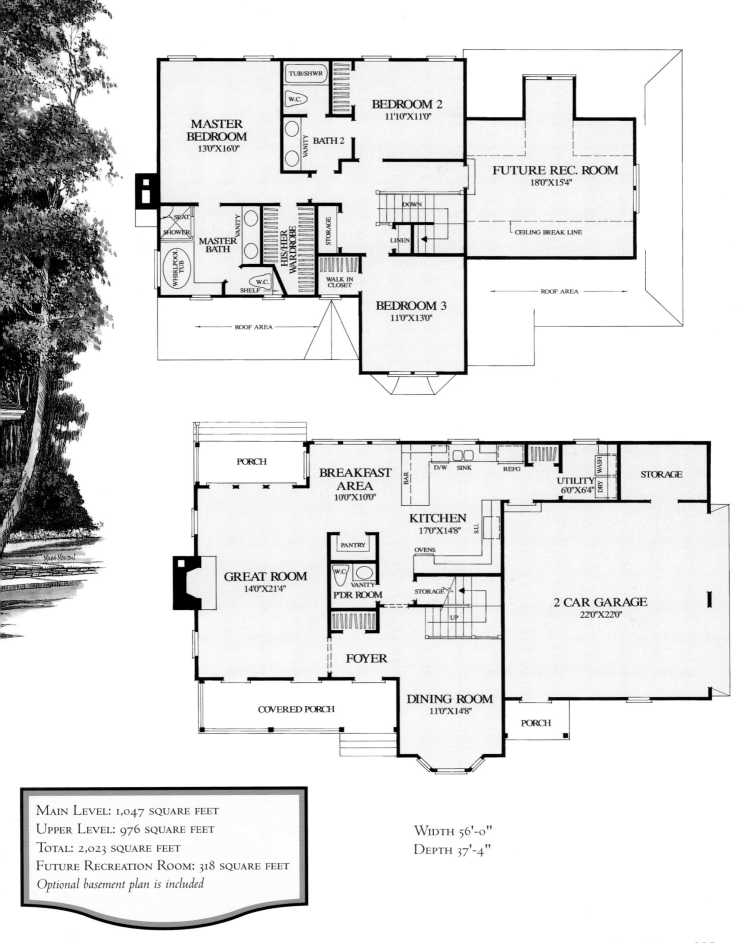

Upper Level

MASTER BEDROOM
13'0"X16'0"

TUB/SHWR

W.C.

VANITY

BATH 2

BEDROOM 2
11'10"X11'0"

FUTURE REC. ROOM
18'0"X15'4"

CEILING BREAK LINE

SEAT
SHOWER
MASTER BATH

VANITY

WHIRLPOOL TUB

HIS/HER WARDROBE

STORAGE

DOWN

LINEN

W.C.
SHELF

WALK IN CLOSET

BEDROOM 3
11'0"X13'0"

ROOF AREA

ROOF AREA

Main Level

PORCH

BREAKFAST AREA
10'0"X10'0"

BAR

D/W SINK REFG

UTILITY
6'0"X6'4"

WASH

DRY

STORAGE

GREAT ROOM
14'0"X21'4"

PANTRY

W.C. VANITY

P'DR ROOM

KITCHEN
17'0"X14'8"

S.U.

OVENS

STORAGE

UP

2 CAR GARAGE
22'0"X22'0"

FOYER

COVERED PORCH

DINING ROOM
11'0"X14'8"

PORCH

Miles Melton

MAIN LEVEL: 1,047 SQUARE FEET
UPPER LEVEL: 976 SQUARE FEET
TOTAL: 2,023 SQUARE FEET
FUTURE RECREATION ROOM: 318 SQUARE FEET
Optional basement plan is included

WIDTH 56'-0"
DEPTH 37'-4"

The Hamptons

DESIGN HPT770100

*S*hingle-style, traditional and modern—as diverse as these descriptions are, they are each appropriate for this uniquely handsome blending of both the old and the new in The Hamptons. The dramatic setting along the shore of Long Island is unrivaled in its beauty, solitude, serenity and, paradoxically, its immediate proximity to the city and all that it offers. The Hamptons—the best of all worlds, here for you.

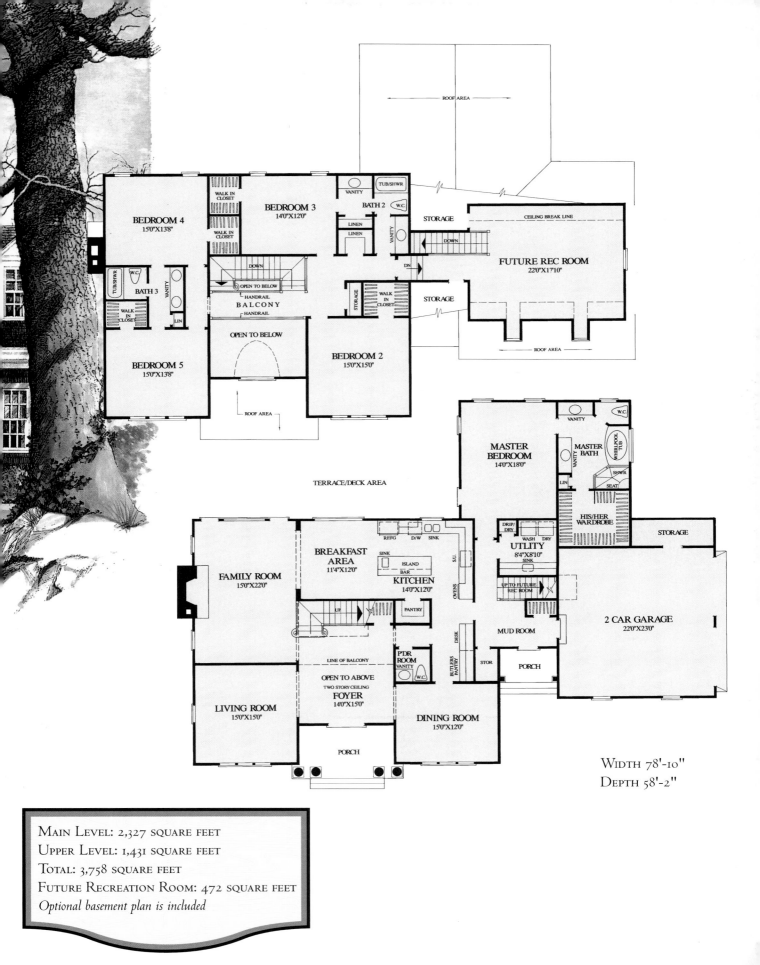

WALK IN CLOSET

BEDROOM 4
15'0"X13'8"

BEDROOM 3
14'0"X12'0"

WALK IN CLOSET

VANITY

BATH 2

W.C.

LINEN

LINEN

STORAGE

DOWN

CEILING BREAK LINE

FUTURE REC ROOM
22'0"X17'10"

TUB/SHWR

W.C.
BATH 3
VANITY

WALK IN CLOSET

LIN

OPEN TO BELOW

BALCONY

HANDRAIL

HANDRAIL

VANITY

STORAGE

WALK IN CLOSET

DN

STORAGE

BEDROOM 5
15'0"X13'8"

OPEN TO BELOW

BEDROOM 2
15'0"X15'0"

ROOF AREA

ROOF AREA

ROOF AREA

TERRACE/DECK AREA

MASTER BEDROOM
14'0"X18'0"

VANITY

VANITY

MASTER BATH

W.C.

TUB/WHIRLPOOL

SHWR

SEAT

LIN

HIS/HER WARDROBE

STORAGE

FAMILY ROOM
15'0"X22'0"

BREAKFAST AREA
11'4"X12'0"

REFG

D/W

SINK

SINK

ISLAND

BAR

KITCHEN
14'0"X12'0"

S.U.

OVENS

DRIP/DRY

WASH   DRY

UTILITY
8'4"X8'10"

SINK

UP TO FUTURE REC ROOM

STORAGE

2 CAR GARAGE
22'0"X23'0"

UP

PANTRY

LINE OF BALCONY

OPEN TO ABOVE
TWO STORY CEILING

FOYER
14'0"X15'0"

PDR ROOM
VANITY

W.C.

BUTLERS PANTRY

DESK

STOR

MUD ROOM

PORCH

LIVING ROOM
15'0"X15'0"

DINING ROOM
15'0"X12'0"

PORCH

WIDTH 78'-10"
DEPTH 58'-2"

MAIN LEVEL: 2,327 SQUARE FEET
UPPER LEVEL: 1,431 SQUARE FEET
TOTAL: 3,758 SQUARE FEET
FUTURE RECREATION ROOM: 472 SQUARE FEET
Optional basement plan is included

LET US SHOW YOU OUR HOME BLUEPRINT PACKAGE

BUILDING A HOME? PLANNING A HOME?

OUR BLUEPRINT PACKAGE HAS NEARLY EVERYTHING YOU NEED TO GET THE JOB DONE RIGHT,

whether you're working on your own or with help from an architect, designer, builder or subcontractors. Each Blueprint Package is the result of many hours of work by licensed architects or professional designers.

QUALITY

Hundreds of hours of painstaking effort have gone into the development of your blueprint plan. Each home has been quality-checked by professionals to insure accuracy and buildability.

VALUE

Because we sell in volume, you can buy professional quality blueprints at a fraction of their development cost. With our plans, your dream home design costs substantially less than the fees charged by architects.

SERVICE

Once you've chosen your favorite home plan, you'll receive fast, efficient service whether you choose to mail or fax your order to us or call us toll free at 1-800-521-6797. After you have received your order, call for customer service toll free 1-888-690-1116.

SATISFACTION

Over 50 years of service to satisfied home plan buyers provide us unparalleled experience and knowledge in producing quality blueprints.

ORDER TOLL FREE 1-800-521-6797

After you've looked over our Blueprint Package and Important Extras, call toll free on our Blueprint Hotline: 1-800-521-6797, for current pricing and availability prior to mailing the order form on page 223. We're ready and eager to serve you. After you have received your order, call for customer service toll free 1-888-690-1116.

Each set of blueprints is an interrelated collection of detail sheets which includes components such as floor plans, interior and exterior elevations, dimensions, cross-sections, diagrams and notations. These sheets show exactly how your house is to be built.

SETS MAY INCLUDE:

FRONTAL SHEET
This artist's sketch of the exterior of the house gives you an idea of how the house will look when built and landscaped. Large floor plans show all levels of the house and provide an overview of your new home's livability, as well as a handy reference for deciding on furniture placement.

FOUNDATION PLANS
This sheet shows the foundation layout including support walls, excavated and unexcavated areas, if any, and foundation notes. If slab construction rather than basement, the plan shows footings and details for a monolithic slab. This page, or another in the set, may include a sample plot plan for locating your house on a building site.

DETAILED FLOOR PLANS
These plans show the layout of each floor of the house. Rooms and interior spaces are carefully dimensioned and keys are given for cross-section details provided later in the plans. The positions of electrical outlets and switches are shown.

HOUSE CROSS-SECTIONS
Large-scale views show sections or cut-aways of the foundation, interior walls, exterior walls, floors, stairways and roof details. Additional cross-sections may show important changes in floor, ceiling or roof heights or the relationship of one level to another. Extremely valuable for construction, these sections show exactly how the various parts of the house fit together.

INTERIOR ELEVATIONS
Many of our drawings show the design and placement of kitchen and bathroom cabinets, laundry areas, fireplaces, bookcases and other built-ins. Little "extras," such as mantelpiece and wainscoting drawings, plus molding sections, provide details that give your home that custom touch.

EXTERIOR ELEVATIONS
These drawings show the front, rear and sides of your house and give necessary notes on exterior materials and finishes. Particular attention is given to cornice detail, brick and stone accents or other finish items that make your home unique.

CONSTRUCTION INFORMATION

IF YOU WANT TO KNOW MORE ABOUT TECHNIQUES— and deal more confidently with subcontractors — we offer these useful sheets. Each set is an excellent tool that will add to your understanding of these technical subjects. These helpful details provide general construction information and are not specific to any single plan.

PLUMBING

The Blueprint Package includes locations for all the plumbing fixtures, including sinks, lavatories, tubs, showers, toilets, laundry trays and water heaters. However, if you want to know more about the complete plumbing system, these Plumbing Details will prove very useful. Prepared to meet requirements of the National Plumbing Code, these fact-filled sheets give general information on pipe schedules, fittings, sump-pump details, water-softener hookups, septic system details and much more. Sheets also include a glossary of terms.

ELECTRICAL

The locations for every electrical switch, plug and outlet are shown in your Blueprint Package. However, these Electrical Details go further to take the mystery out of household electrical systems. Prepared to meet requirements of the National Electrical Code, these comprehensive drawings come packed with helpful information, including wire sizing, switch-installation schematics, cable-routing details, appliance wattage, doorbell hook-ups, typical service panel circuitry and much more. A glossary of terms is also included.

CONSTRUCTION

The Blueprint Package contains information an experienced builder needs to construct a particular house. However, it doesn't show all the ways that houses can be built, nor does it explain alternate construction methods. To help you understand how your house will be built—and offer additional techniques—this set of Construction Details depicts the materials and methods used to build foundations, fireplaces, walls, floors and roofs. Where appropriate, the drawings show acceptable alternatives.

MECHANICAL

These Mechanical Details contain fundamental principles and useful data that will help you make informed decisions and communicate with subcontractors about heating and cooling systems. Drawings contain instructions and samples that allow you to make simple load calculations, and preliminary sizing and costing analysis. Covered are the most commonly used systems from heat pumps to solar fuel systems. The package is filled with illustrations and diagrams to help you visualize components and how they relate to one another.

THE HANDS-ON HOME FURNITURE PLANNER

Effectively plan the space in your home using The **Hands-On Home Furniture Planner**. It's fun and easy—no more moving heavy pieces of furniture to see how the room will go together. And you can try different layouts, moving furniture at a whim.

The kit includes reusable peel and stick furniture templates that fit onto a 12" x 18" laminated layout board—space enough to layout every room in your home.

Also included in the package are a number of helpful planning tools. You'll receive:

✓ Helpful hints and solutions for difficult situations.
✓ Furniture planning basics to get you started.
✓ Furniture planning secrets that let you in on some of the tricks of professional designers.

The **Hands-On Home Furniture Planner** is the one tool that no new homeowner or home remodeler should be without. It's also a perfect housewarming gift!

SPECIFICATION OUTLINE

This valuable 16-page document is critical to building your house correctly. Designed to be filled in by you or your builder, this book lists 166 stages or items crucial to the building process. It provides a comprehensive review of the construction process and helps in choosing materials. When combined with the blueprints, a signed contract, and a schedule, it becomes a legal document and record for the building of your home.

To Order, Call Toll Free
1-800-521-6797

After you've looked over our Blueprint Package and Important Extras on these pages, call for current pricing and availability prior to mailing the order form. We're ready and eager to serve you. For any questions or claims on an order already received, call toll free for customer service 1-888-690-1116.

BLUEPRINT PRICE SCHEDULE

Prices guaranteed through December 31, 2003

TIERS	1-SET STUDY PACKAGE	4-SET BUILDING PACKAGE	8-SET BUILDING PACKAGE	1-SET REPRODUCIBLE*
A4	$575	$620	$660	$870
C1	$620	$665	$710	$935
C2	$670	$715	$760	$1000
C3	$715	$760	$805	$1075
C4	$765	$810	$855	$1150
L1	$870	$925	$975	$1300
L2	$945	$1000	$1050	$1420
L3	$1050	$1105	$1155	$1575
L4	$1155	$1210	$1260	$1735
SP1	$1155	-	$1365	-
SP2	$1155	-	$1515	-
SQ1				.35/sq. ft.

* Requires a fax number

OPTIONS FOR PLANS IN TIERS A4-SP2

Additional Identical Blueprints
in same order for "A1–L4" price plans ....$50 per set
Reverse Blueprints (mirror image)
with 4- or 8-set order for "A1–L4" plans ....$50 fee per order
Specification Outlines ....$10 each
Materials Lists for "A1–C3" plans ....$60 each
Materials Lists for "C4–L4" plans ....$70 each

REPRODUCIBLE VELLUMS

Reproducible vellums are granted with a non-exclusive license to do the following:
• Modify the drawings for use in the construction of a single home
• Make up to twelve (12) copies of the plans for use in the construction of a single HOME PLANNERS, LLC Construct one and only one home based on the plans, either in the original form or as modified by you

Limitations on use of the plans. You may NOT do any of the following with the reproducible vellum:
• Use the plans in either their original form or as modified to construct more than one home.
• Permit others to use or copy the plans
• Make more than twelve (12) copies of the plans (if additional plans are needed, you must first obtain written permission)
• Sell, lend or otherwise transfer the plans to another

TO ORDER, Call toll free 1-800-521-6797 for current pricing and availability prior to mailing the order form. FAX: 1-800-224-6699 or 520-544-3086.

IMPORTANT NOTES

• SQ one-set building package includes one set of reproducible vellum construction drawings plus one set of study blueprints.
• The 1-set study package is marked "not for construction."
• Prices for 4- or 8-set Building Packages honored only at time of original order.
• Additional identical blueprints may be purchased within 60 days of original order.

Purchase Policy: Accurate construction-cost estimates should come from your builder after review of the blueprints. Your purchase includes a license to use the plans to construct one single-family residence. Blueprints may NOT be reproduced, modified or used to create derivative works. Additional sets of the same plan may be ordered within a 60-day period at $50 each, plus shipping and tax, if applicable. After 60 days, re-orders are treated as new orders.

Title: You have purchased a license to use the plans. The title to and intellectual property rights in the plans shall remain with William E. Poole Designs, Inc. Use of the plans in a manner inconsistent with this agreement is a violation of U.S. copyright laws. These designs are protected under the terms of United States Copyright Law and may not be copied or reproduced in any way. We authorize the use of your chosen design as an aid in the construction of one single family home only. You may not use this design to build a second or multiple dwellings without purchasing another blueprint or blueprints or paying additional design fees.

Modifications and warranties. Any modifications made to the vellums by parties other than William E. Poole Designs, Inc. voids any warranties express or implied including the warranties of fitness for a particular purpose and merchantability. William E. Poole Designs, Inc. is a residential design firm. Our house plans are not intended to eliminate the use of local architects or engineers. We recommend that an architect or engineer in your area review your plans before actual construction begins.

11" x 17" FULL-COLOR RENDERING
24" x 36" BLACK & WHITE RENDERING

Full-color and Black-and-White renderings suitable for framing are available for all of the plans in this portfolio. For prices and additional information, please see page 223 or call Toll Free 1-800-521-6797.

BEFORE FILLING OUT THE ORDER FORM, PLEASE CALL US ON OUR TOLL-FREE BLUEPRINT HOTLINE 1-800-521-6797. YOU MAY WANT TO LEARN MORE ABOUT OUR SERVICES AND PRODUCTS. HERE'S SOME INFORMATION YOU WILL FIND HELPFUL.

OUR EXCHANGE POLICY

With the exception of reproducible plan orders, we will exchange your entire first order for an equal or greater number of blueprints within our plan collection within 90 days of the original order. The entire content of your original order must be returned before an exchange will be processed. Please call our customer service department for your return authorization number and shipping instructions. If the returned blueprints look used, redlined or copied, we will not honor your exchange. Fees for exchanging your blueprints are as follows: 20% of the amount of the original order...plus the difference in cost if exchanging for a design in a higher price bracket or less the difference in cost if exchanging for a design in a lower price bracket. **(Reproducible blueprints are not exchangeable or refundable.)** Please call for current postage and handling prices. Shipping and handling charges are not refundable.

ABOUT REPRODUCIBLES

When purchasing a reproducible you may be required to furnish a fax number. The designer will fax documents that you must sign and return to them before shipping will take place.

ABOUT REVERSE BLUEPRINTS

Although lettering and dimensions will appear backward, reverses will be a useful aid if you decide to flop the plan. See Price Schedule and Plans Index for pricing.

REVISING, MODIFYING AND CUSTOMIZING PLANS

Like many homeowners who buy these plans, you and your builder, architect or engineer may want to make changes to them. We recommend purchase of a reproducible plan for any changes made by your builder, licensed architect or engineer. As set forth below, we cannot assume any responsibility for blueprints which have been changed, whether by you, your builder or by professionals selected by you or referred to you by us, because such individuals are outside our supervision and control.

ARCHITECTURAL AND ENGINEERING SEALS

Some cities and states are now requiring that a licensed architect or engineer review and "seal" a blueprint, or officially approve it, prior to construction due to concerns over energy costs, safety and other factors. Prior to application for a building permit or the start of actual construction, we strongly advise that you consult your local building official who can tell you if such a review is required.

ABOUT THE DESIGNS

Each plan was designed to meet the requirements of a nationally recognized model building code in effect at the time and place the plan was drawn. Because national building codes change from time to time, plans may not comply with any such code

at the time they are sold to a customer. In addition, building officials may not accept these plans as final construction documents of record as the plans may need to be modified and additional drawings and details added to suit local conditions and requirements. We strongly advise that purchasers consult a licensed architect or engineer, and their local building official, before starting any construction related to these plans.

LOCAL BUILDING CODES AND ZONING REQUIREMENTS

At the time of creation, our plans are drawn to specifications published by the Building Officials and Code Administrators (BOCA) International, Inc.; the Southern Building Code Congress (SBCCI) International, Inc.; the International Conference of Building Officials (ICBO); or the Council of American Building Officials (CABO). Our plans are designed to meet or exceed national building standards. Because of the great differences in geography and climate throughout the United States and Canada, each state, county and municipality has its own building codes, zone requirements, ordinances and building regulations. Your plan may need to be modified to comply with local requirements regarding snow loads, energy codes, soil and seismic conditions and a wide range of other matters. In addition, you may need to obtain permits or inspections from local governments before and in the course of construction. Prior to using blueprints ordered from us, we strongly advise that you consult a licensed architect or engineer—and speak with your local building official—before applying for any permit or beginning construction. We authorize the use of our blueprints on the express condition that you strictly comply with all local building codes, zoning requirements and other applicable laws, regulations, ordinances and requirements. Notice: Plans for homes to be built in Nevada must be re-drawn by a Nevada-registered professional. Consult your building official for more information on this subject.

TOLL FREE
1-800-521-6797

REGULAR OFFICE HOURS:
8:00 a.m.-9:00 p.m. EST, Monday-Friday

If we receive your order by 3:00 p.m. EST, Monday-Friday, we'll process it and ship within **two business days**. When ordering by phone, please have your credit card or check information ready. We'll also ask you for the Order Form Key Number at the bottom of the order form.

By FAX: Copy the Order Form on the next page and send it on our FAX line: 1-800-224-6699 or 520-544-3086.

Canadian Customers
Order Toll Free 1-877-223-6389

DISCLAIMER

The designers we work with have put substantial care and effort into the creation of their blueprints. However, because they cannot provide on-site consultation, supervision and control over actual construction, and because of the great variance in local building requirements, building practices and soil, seismic, weather and other conditions, WE CANNOT MAKE ANY WARRANTY, EXPRESS OR IMPLIED, WITH RESPECT TO THE CONTENT OR USE OF THE BLUEPRINTS, INCLUDING BUT NOT LIMITED TO ANY WARRANTY OF MERCHANTABILITY OR OF FITNESS FOR A PARTICULAR PURPOSE. **ITEMS, PRICES, TERMS AND CONDITIONS ARE SUBJECT TO CHANGE WITHOUT NOTICE. REPRODUCIBLE PLAN ORDERS MAY REQUIRE A CUSTOMER'S SIGNED RELEASE BEFORE SHIPPING.**

TERMS AND CONDITIONS

These designs are protected under the terms of United States Copyright Law and may not be copied or reproduced in any way, by any means, unless you have purchased Reproducibles which clearly indicate your right to copy or reproduce. We authorize the use of your chosen design as an aid in the construction of one single family home only. You may not use this design to build a second or multiple dwellings without purchasing another blueprint or blueprints or paying additional design fees.

HOW MANY BLUEPRINTS DO YOU NEED?

Although a standard building package may satisfy many states, cities and counties, some plans may require certain changes. For your convenience, we have developed a Reproducible plan which allows a local professional to modify and make up to 10 copies of your revised plan. As our plans are all copyright protected, with your purchase of the Reproducible, we will supply you with a Copyright release letter. The number of copies you may need: 1 for owner; 3 for builder; 2 for local building department and 1-3 sets for your mortgage lender.

ORDER TOLL FREE!

**For information about
any of our services
or to order call
1-800-521-6797**

**Browse our website:
www.eplans.com**

**BLUEPRINTS ARE
NOT REFUNDABLE
EXCHANGES ONLY**

**For Customer Service,
call toll free
1-888-690-1116.**

HOME PLANNERS, LLC wholly owned by Hanley-Wood, LLC

3275 WEST INA ROAD, SUITE 110 • TUCSON, ARIZONA • 85741

THE BASIC BLUEPRINT PACKAGE

Rush me the following (please refer to the Plans Index and Price Schedule in this section):

___Set(s) of reproducibles*, plan number(s) _____ $_____

    indicate foundation type _____ surcharge (if applicable): $_____

___Set(s) of blueprints, plan number(s) _____ indicate foundation type _____ $_____

    indicate foundation type _____ surcharge (if applicable): $_____

___Additional identical blueprints (standard or reverse) in same order @ $50 per set $_____

___Reverse blueprints @ $50 fee per order. $_____

IMPORTANT EXTRAS

Rush me the following:

___11"x17" Four Color Rendering @ $125 each

    for plans _____ $_____

___24"x 36" Black and White Rendering @ $85 each

    for plans _____ $_____

___Specification Outlines @ $10 each $_____

___Detail Sets @ $14.95 each; any two $22.95; any three $29.95; all four for $39.95 (save $19.85) $_____

___❑ Plumbing ❑ Electrical ❑ Construction ❑ Mechanical

___Home Furniture Planner @ $15.95 each $_____

POSTAGE AND HANDLING *SIGNATURE IS REQUIRED FOR ALL DELIVERIES.*	1–3 sets	4+ sets
DELIVERY No CODs (Requires street address—No P.O. Boxes) •Regular Service (Allow 7–10 business days delivery) •Priority (Allow 4–5 business days delivery) •Express (Allow 3 business days delivery)	 ❑ $20.00 ❑ $25.00 ❑ $35.00	 ❑ $25.00 ❑ $35.00 ❑ $45.00
OVERSEAS DELIVERY	fax, phone or mail for quote	

Note: All delivery times are from date Blueprint Package is shipped.

POSTAGE (From box above) $_____

SUBTOTAL $_____

SALES TAX (AZ & MI residents, please add appropriate state and local sales tax.) $_____

TOTAL (Subtotal and tax) $_____

YOUR ADDRESS (please print legibly)

Name _____

Street _____

City _____ State _____ Zip _____

Daytime telephone number (required) (_____) _____

* Fax number (required for reproducible orders) _____

TeleCheck® Checks By Phone℠ available

FOR CREDIT CARD ORDERS ONLY

Credit card number _____ Exp. Date: (M/Y) _____

Check one ❑ Visa ❑ MasterCard ❑ American Express

Order Form Key

HPT77

Signature (required) _____

Please check appropriate box: ❑ Licensed Builder-Contractor ❑ Homeowner

ORDER TOLL FREE!
1-800-521-6797

BY FAX: Copy the order form above and send it on
our FAXLINE: 1-800-224-6699 OR 520-544-3086

Make the Place you Live the Place you Love®

The chinese characters on the scroll: 景曜祥雲昭瑞應

To view floor plans, see page 22.

Photo by Maura McEvoy

William E. Poole™